CONTENTS :
1 v.
CD-ROM (1)

ORTON / LIBRARY OF CONGRESS VISUAL SOURCEBOOKS IN ARCHITECTURE, DESIGN AND ENGINEERING

ROBERT J. KAPSCH

W. W. Norton & Company, New York and London | In association with the Library of Congress

CANALS

To Perry

For information about permission to reproduce
selections from this book, write to Permissions,
W. W. Norton & Company, Inc., 500 Fifth Avenue,
New York, NY 10110

Manufacturing by Courier Westford
Book design by Kristina Kachele Design LLC
Production manager: Leeann Graham

*Norton/Library of Congress Visual Sourcebooks
in Architecture, Design and Engineering*

Library of Congress
Cataloging-in-Publication Data

Kapsch, Robert J.
Canals / Robert J. Kapsch.
p. cm. – (Norton/Library of Congress visual
sourcebooks in architecture, design and
engineering)
Includes bibliographical references and index.
ISBN 0-393-73088-3
1. Canals—United States—History. 2. Inland
navigation—United States—History. I. Title. II.
Series.

HE395 .A3K36 2004
386'.4'0973—dc22

2004043393

ISBN 0-393-73088-3

W. W. Norton & Company, Inc., 500 Fifth Avenue,
New York, N.Y. 10110
www.wwnorton.com
W. W. Norton & Company Ltd., Castle House,
75/76 Wells St., London W1T 3QT

0 9 8 7 6 5 4 3 2 1

The Norton/Library of Congress Visual
Sourcebooks in Architecture, Design
and Engineering series is a project of the
Center for Architecture, Design and
Engineering in the Library of Congress,
established through a bequest from the
distinguished American architect Paul
Rudolph. The Center's mission is not
only to support the preservation of the
Library's enormously rich collections in
these subject areas, but also to increase the
public knowledge of and access to them.
Paul Rudolph hoped that others would
join him in supporting these efforts. The
Library of Congress is therefore pleased
to accept contributions to the Center for
Architecture, Design and Engineering
Fund or to the Paul Rudolph Trust to
further this progress, and to support
additional projects such as this one.

For further information on the Center
for American Architecture, Design and
Engineering, you may visit its website:
http://www.loc.gov/rr/print/adecen
ter/adecent.html

The Center for Architecture, Design and Engineering and the Publishing Office of the Library of Congress are pleased to join with W. W. Norton & Company to publish the pioneering series of the Norton/Library of Congress Visual Sourcebooks in Architecture, Design and Engineering.

Based on the unparalleled collections of the Library of Congress, this series of handsomely illustrated books is drawn from the collections of the nation's oldest federal cultural institution and the largest library in the world, with more than 128 million items on approximately 530 miles of bookshelves. The collections include more than 29 million books, 2.5 million recordings, 12 million photographs, 4.8 million maps, and 57 million manuscripts.

The subjects of architecture, design, and engineering are threaded throughout the rich fabric of this vast archive, and the books in this new series will serve not only to introduce researchers to the illustrations selected by their authors, but also to build pathways to adjacent and related materials, and even entire archives—to millions of photographs, drawings, prints, views, maps, rare publications, and written information in the general and special collections of the Library of Congress, much of it unavailable elsewhere.

Each volume will serve as an entry to the collections, providing a treasury of select visual material, much of it in the public domain, for students; scholars; teachers; researchers; historians of art, architecture, design, and technology; and practicing architects, engineers, and designers of all kinds.

A CD-ROM accompanying each volume contains high-quality, downloadable, and uncropped versions of all the illustrations. It offers a direct link to the Library's online, searchable catalogs and image files, including the hundreds of thousands of high-resolution photographs, measured drawings, and data files in the Historic American Buildings Survey, Historic American Engineering Record, and, eventually, the recently inaugurated Historic American Landscape Survey. The Library's website has rapidly become one of the most popular and valuable locations on the Internet, experiencing over three billion hits a year and serving audiences ranging from school children to the most advanced scholars throughout the world, with a potential usefulness that has only begun to be explored.

Among the subjects to be covered in this series are building types, building materials and details, historical periods and movements, landscape architecture and garden design, interior and ornamental design and furnishings, and industrial design. *Canals* is an excellent exemplar of the possibilities and goals on which the series is based.

C. FORD PEATROSS

5

HOW TO USE THIS BOOK

The introduction to this book provides a masterly overview of the development and types of inland waterway routes that have served to define the very nature and growth of the United States and its people. It is a view that is new and fresh and inspired by the depth and quality of the resources of the Library of Congress, and it substantially expands our knowledge of the subject. The balance of the book, containing 555 images, which can be found on the CD at the back of the book, is organized into four sections. Figure-number prefixes designate the section.

Short captions give the essential identifying information: subject, location, date, creator(s) of the image, and Library of Congress call number, which can be used to find the image online. Note that a link to the Library of Congress website may be found on the CD.

ABBREVIATIONS USED IN CAPTIONS

DPCC
Detroit Publishing Company Collection

G & M
Geography and Map Division

HABS
Historic American Buildings Survey

HAER
Historic American Engineering Record

LC
Library of Congress

MRC
Microform Reading Room

MSS
Manuscript Division

P & P
Prints and Photographs Division

RBSCD
Rare Book & Special Collection Division

CONTENTS

AMERICAN CANALS

By the end of the American Revolution it was obvious to the inhabitants of the young country that they needed improved access to the interior of the continent. Most Americans had settled along the eastern edge of North America, where communication by coastal boats was cheap and easy. But the new lands and their immense resources were to the west, above the fall line and across the Appalachian Mountains, beyond the reach of the tidewater vessels.

At a time when land was a primary measure of fortune, the resources of the extensive Northwest Territories, and later the Louisiana Purchase, could not be counted as wealth, but only potential wealth. Their value would be realized only if the products of these new lands could be transported eastward to the coastal cities, where they could be consumed by the growing population in those cities or shipped overseas. But roads or navigable water routes around the falls and through the mountains were lacking.

The need to ship agricultural produce and raw materials was only one reason to develop access to the lands beyond the falls and across the Appalachians. Reliable communication would facilitate the settlement of these areas by immigrants arriving in the coastal cities. Improved communications with the inland would tie the hinterland politically to the settled regions along the coast. Militarily, reliable routes would facilitate the movement of troops and supplies. England dominated the world's oceans; inland routes would lessen the young nation's vulnerability to the British navy's disruption of tidewater commerce.

On a local level, development of improved inland communication was vital for bringing regular shipments of farm produce to market. Merchants of the coastal towns also needed timber, iron, lime, and building stone from upriver, above the falls, as well as goods from beyond the mountains.

9

IN-001

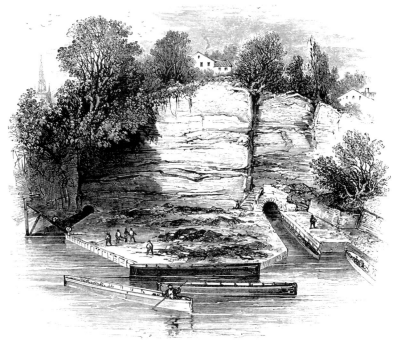

IN-002

Improved roads were an obvious means to improve communications, but an existing and extensive system of American rivers partially penetrated into the hinterland and could, it was thought, be effectively used. At a time when animals were the primary source of motive power, a boat drawn by horses or mules could haul vastly larger cargoes than a wagon hitched to the same animals. The difference in cost between land and water transportation was estimated to favor water hauling by ten to one or more.[1] Not only was water transportation substantially less expensive, but it could produce excess water to power factories and mills, increasing the economic benefit to the owners.

Perhaps the strongest argument for using water rather than land for long-distance transportation was that water had already proved best in England, the mother country. In 1760 Francis Egerton, the third Duke of Bridgewater (IN-001 and IN-002) began construction on the first of two canals to facilitate the shipment of coal from his mines in Worsley seven miles east, to the industrial city of Manchester, and to move goods produced in Manchester overseas via the canal and transshipment at the seaport of Liverpool. These canals, designed by engineer James Brindley, were immensely successful financial and commercial ventures.[2] The price of coal delivered to Manchester dropped significantly. The quantity delivered increased significantly. The canals were instrumental in the development of Manchester as an exporting city. And the tolls generated on them brought a good income. Fascinated by the duke's success, both Englishmen and American colonists flocked to his canals to study and, if possible, to replicate them.[3] George Washington and his fellow planters sent John Ballendine, a colonial ironmaster and entrepreneur, to bring back knowledge of how to build similar canals in order to open the Potomac and James Rivers to navigation (IN-003). Americans

this page
IN-001. Francis Egerton, third Duke of Bridgewater, from Samuel Smiles, *Lives of Engineers* (1861). LC-TA 139.S64.

IN-002. Worsley Basin, England, the terminus of the Duke of Bridgewater's first canal, which extended into the coal mines so canal boats could be loaded underground and coal economically hauled to Manchester. From Samuel Smiles, *Lives of Engineers* (1861). LC-TA 139.S64.

opposite
IN-003. Canal routes to the west along the Potomac and James Rivers, ca. 1773. A group of Virginia planters sent John Ballendine, a colonial ironmaster and entrepreneur, to study English canals. This map of potential canal routes to the west along the Potomac and James Rivers was prepared to encourage investors, but Ballendine did not secure financing. G & M, G3880 1773 .B Vault.

IN-004. Languedoc Canal, France (opened 1681), showing the operation of two lift locks, with lock gates, balance beams, and gate valves for raising (or lowering) boats. The illustrations from Diderot's *Encyclopedié* were influential in teaching Englishmen and Americans how canals worked. From Denis Diderot, *A Pictorial Encyclopedia of Trades and Industry* (1993 reprint of 1751 work), LC-T9.E472513.

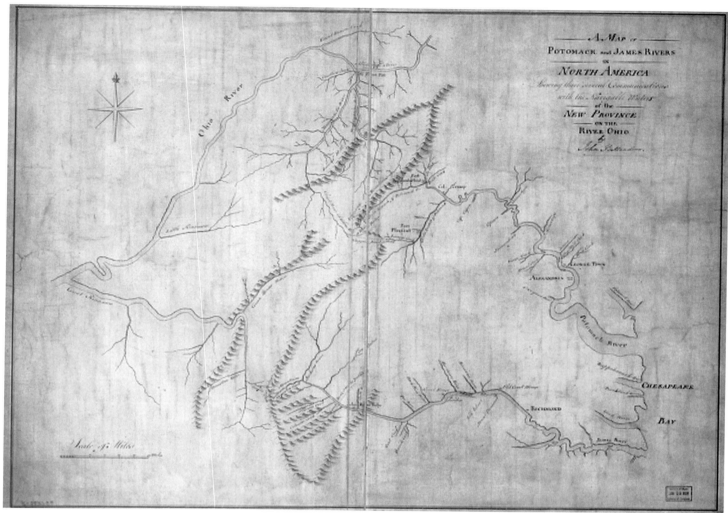

IN-003

IN-004

IN-005

IN-005. Languedoc Canal. The *Encyclopedia Britannica* unabashedly copied the drawings from Diderot's delineation of the Languedoc Canal in his *Encyclopedié*, although the image is reversed. From *Encyclopedia Britannica*, First Edition (1771). LC-AE5 .E396, v.2.

who could not visit studied the drawings of canals published in encyclopedias such as Diderot's *Pictorial Encyclopedia of Trades and Industry* (IN-004 and IN 005) . The Duke of Bridgewater's canals engendered canal mania in England. The wave would sweep the United States decades later, when the success of the duke's canals was reproduced by that of the Erie Canal.

IN-006

IN-007

IN-006. Lewis and Miller Flat Boat Yard, Kanawha Falls, Virginia (now West Virginia), ca. 1856, from Edward Beyer, *Album of Virginia* (1858). RBSCD, F227.B48.

IN-007. View on the Susquehanna River at Liverpool, Pennsylvania, W. H. Bartlett, delineator. From Nathaniel Parker Willis, *American Scenery* (1840). RBSCD, E165.W73.

TYPES OF CANAL

When rivers as nature made them were used for transportation, downstream navigation was usually limited to springtime, when they flowed full. Upstream navigation was difficult or impossible. The earliest water transportation systems constructed in the United States were not true canals but rather river navigation improvement projects (IN-006 and IN-007). One of the first was that of the Potomac Canal Company, formed shortly after the Revolutionary War by George Washington, to make the Potomac River navigable. In 1785, as the first president of the company, Washington developed a plan to build bypasses equipped with locks, so boats could be raised or lowered around the 76-foot-high Great Falls (IN-008) and 37-foot-high Little Falls, the principal obstructions on the river. Elsewhere, the boats traveled the river; the company improved the riverbed, removing boulders and other obstacles, digging channels in the river, and constructing low walls to raise the level of the water.[4] The Great Falls bypass opened in 1802. Similar construction on the James River was authorized at the same time as the Potomac River navigation, and a bypass canal around the falls of the James River opened in 1795.[5]

FV

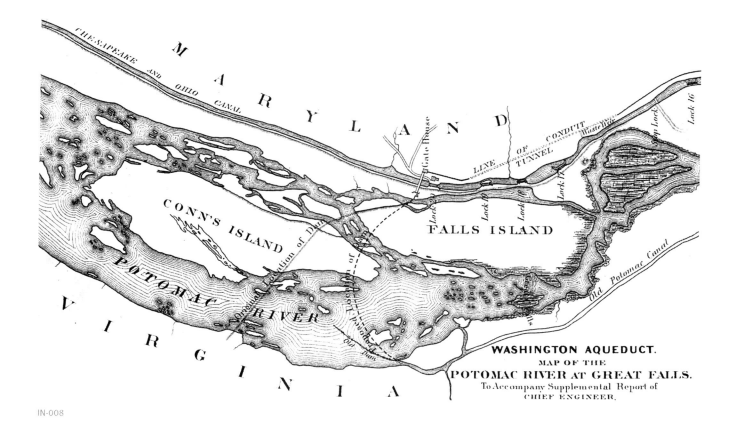

Map labels: CHESAPEAKE AND OHIO CANAL · MARYLAND · CONN'S ISLAND · FALLS ISLAND · POTOMAC RIVER · VIRGINIA · Old Potomac Canal · LINE OF CONDUIT · TUNNEL · Gate House · Waste Weir · Stop Lock · Lock 17 · Lock 16 · Old Plan

WASHINGTON AQUEDUCT.
MAP OF THE
POTOMAC RIVER AT GREAT FALLS.
To Accompany Supplemental Report of
CHIEF ENGINEER.

IN-008

IN-008. Potomac Canal on the Virginia side of the river, and the Chesapeake and Ohio Canal on the Maryland side of the river, around Great Falls, Maryland/Virginia. February 1864. G & M, G3842.W3 svar .M3.

Other attempts to improve navigation included a bypass canal around Conewago Falls, northeast of York, Pennsylvania, on the Susquehanna River, where work under the leadership of Philadelphia financier Robert Morris began in 1793 and was completed in 1797. Chief engineer of the canal was James Brindley, nephew of the James Brindley who built the Duke of Bridgewater's canals. The younger Brindley had come from the Manchester region with other "mechanics" almost twenty years earlier to work with John Ballendine on the Potomac and James River navigations. The Conewago Canal was less than a mile long and had three locks: two lift locks to raise or lower boats at the 19-foot drop in the Susquehanna, and a guard lock, which prevented unwanted water from entering the canal, particularly in times of flood. One of the first canals in America, the Conewago could be navigated by a canal boat going upriver in thirty-seven minutes, compared with a day's work for thirty to forty men on shore pulling the boat.[6]

Overall, however, river improvement efforts of the late eighteenth century like the Potomac and Conewago canals proved less than satisfactory. Despite the bypass canals, seasonal variations in river flow, both flood and drought, and winter ice still limited the use of rivers to a few months of the year. Improvements made in the riverbed tended to increase the velocity of river flow, hazardous for boats headed downstream. Hauling or poling boats back upriver against the current remained a problem without towing

IN-009

IN-010

paths. It was difficult to collect tolls: most people thought that river navigation should be free. Only with difficulty did Francis Thomas, owner of the Conewago Canal, get the Pennsylvania legislature to authorize tolls, and then boat captains used a sturdy new type of vessel, the Susquehanna River ark, to run the rapids, circumventing the canal and the toll. On the Potomac Canal, toll collection could be enforced at Great Falls in order to pass through the locks, but in the river navigation stretches, boat operators simply avoided the collectors.

The lock-and-pond scheme was a second type of river navigation improvement. Here the river was divided into a number of mill ponds made by constructing dams along its course. Boats traversed these relatively quiet ponds, moving through the dams by means of either a lift lock or a flash lock, in which boards or other impediments to river flow were removed and the boat proceeded through the dam on a rush of released water (IN-009–IN-011).

Lock-and-pond navigation was of limited use, however, because the ponds usually had an irregular shoreline, making it difficult or impossible to use animals to tow the vessel. Frequently the goal of river captains to release water through the dams conflicted with the dam owners' desire to impound

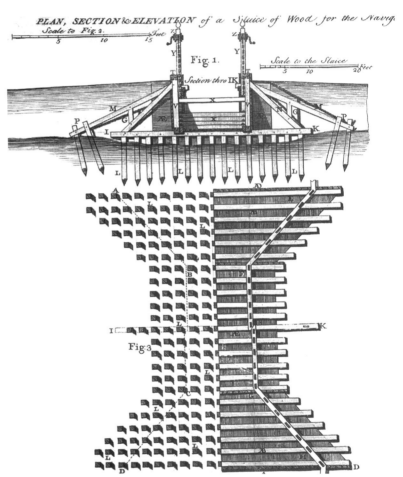
IN-011

IN-009. Bypass canal (right) around the dam (far left) on the Schuylkill River for Fairmount Water Works (center), Philadelphia, Pennsylvania, one of the earliest municipal water supply systems in the United States. The dam also provided lock-and-pond navigation: impounded water behind the dam allowed navigation up the Schuylkill River. W. H. Bartlett, delineator. From Nathaniel Parker Willis, *American Scenery* (1840). RBSCD, E165.W73.

IN-010. Another view of the bypass canal around the dam at the Fairmount Water Works, Philadelphia, Pennsylvania. James Fuller Queen, artist, ca. 1856. P & P, LC-USZC4-6723.

IN-011. Section and plan of a wooden sluice, from Charles Vallancey, *A Treatise on Inland Navigation* (1763). RBSCD, TC744.V17, detail.

this page

IN-012. View of Northumberland, on the Susquehanna River, Northumberland, Pennsylvania. River navigation (right) is adjacent to the stillwater canal (left). In the distance are Northumberland and the bridges across the West Branch (left) and North Branch (right) of the Susquehanna River. W. H. Bartlett, delineator. From Nathaniel Parker Willis, *American Scenery* (1840). RBSCD, E165.W73.

IN-013. Erie Canal, New York. Photograph of a painting, 1825. P & P, LC-USZ62-1025.

IN-012

IN-013

water for mill operations. Dams were expensive to build, and in large rivers the volume of water to be contained made dams hard to build and impoundment impractical.

The stillwater canal—the system used by James Brindley for the Duke of Bridgewater—was the third and most fully developed form of canal (IN-012 and IN-013). A long ditch, called the prism, was dug, usually parallel to an existing river, with a towpath alongside (IN-024). Low dams built at intervals along the river route diverted river water into the canal. The water in the prism was kept level for as long a stretch as possible. Because most canals traverse a descending river valley, eventually any given section had to make a transition to a lower level, a transition that was usually made by a lift lock, which raised or lowered the canal boat from one level to the other. It consisted of a rectangular chamber with gates at either end (IN-004 and IN-005). The chamber was filled or drained to raise or lower the boats within.

A variant of the stillwater canal was the summit level canal. Instead of paralleling an existing river, the summit level canal connected one river valley to another, the highest elevation between the two being called the summit. Summit level canals were more difficult to engineer because of the need to provide adequate water at the summit, particularly during the dry summer and autumn months. Some summit level canals were provided with steam-powered pumps to bring water to the summit level (see 2-133 and 2-134).

The Santee Canal, connecting the Santee and Cooper Rivers in South Carolina to provide a route for shipping goods, particularly cotton, from inland South Carolina to Charleston, was the first summit level canal built in the United States. Proposed before the Revolutionary War, it was authorized in 1786, begun in 1793, and completed in 1800. Despite problems supplying adequate water at the summit, the canal functioned for fifty years.[7]

The Middlesex Canal, authorized in 1794 and completed in 1803, was also a summit level canal. It connected the Merrimack River, in Massachusetts, with Boston Harbor, a distance of 27½ miles (see 1-002–1-005). It operated until 1853.[8]

The Susquehanna Canal (also called the Conowingo Canal or the Port Deposit Canal), an early stillwater canal, was authorized in 1783 and completed in 1801. It extended 7 miles on the eastern edge of the Susquehanna River from the Pennsylvania/Maryland state line to the Chesapeake Bay. James Brindley and, later, Christian Hauducoeur were the chief engineers. Above the state line, Benjamin Henry Latrobe was hired to make improvements in the navigation of the Susquehanna River.[9] This combined river navigation and stillwater canal was never successful and was finally abandoned in 1840 with the opening of the Susquehanna and Tidewater Canal.

Other early canals included a series of navigation projects across New York State, along the Mohawk River, Wood Creek and other rivers by the Western Inland Lock Navigation Company; the Dismal Swamp Canal in Virginia; the South Hadley Falls Canal on the Connecticut River in Massachusetts; the Bellows Falls Canal along the Connecticut River in Vermont; and others. Generally these projects were small and did not prove profitable. By the start of the War of 1812, no substantial canal in the United States had met with real success.

THE ERIE CANAL

Lack of success did not dampen the ardor of canal enthusiasts, however, particularly in New York State. In 1808 the State of New York passed its first law authorizing the construction of a canal linking the Hudson River to Lake Erie. A small amount was appropriated for surveys and James Geddes was hired as engineer. In 1810 and 1811 commissions were authorized to study the project, and DeWitt Clinton, who had held office as state senator, United States senator, and mayor of New York City, was appointed to both. Clinton became the primary proponent for the trans–New York canal, and the commissions he served on issued a series of reports urging public action. In 1816, the New York State Legislature approved construction of the Erie Canal. Clinton was named a commissioner to oversee the planning, design, and construction of what came to be called "Clinton's ditch." It was to be 350 miles long, 40 feet wide at the water level, 28 feet wide at the bottom, and 4 feet deep, and to cost $5 million. A second canal, to link Lake Champlain with the Hudson River, was to cost an additional million dollars.[10]

To build the canal, the commissioners turned to the highly respected canal engineer William Weston, who came from England to work on the Schuylkill and Susquehanna navigation projects and remained to work on most of the other canals then under design and construction, among them the James River Canal, the Potomac Canal, the Middlesex

ENTRANCE TO THE ERIE CANAL AT TROY.

IN-014

At Little Falls.

IN-015

Canal, and the various projects of the Western Inland Lock Navigation Company in upstate New York. Weston had returned to England in 1801, however, and declined the job when it was offered.[11] In his place, the commissioners appointed his former assistant at the Western Inland Lock Navigation Company, Judge Benjamin Wright. Wright, originally from Wethersfield, Connecticut, had served as a county judge in upstate New York. The Erie Canal, a project of unprecedented scale, would be the first major American canal engineered by an American.

Construction on the Erie Canal began on July 4, 1817, and was completed on October

IN-016

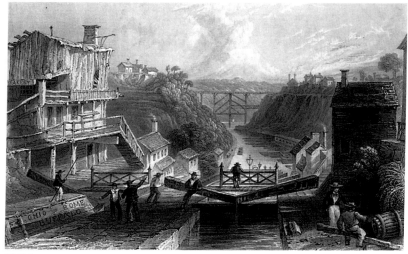

IN-017

CANAL Packet Boat **GEO. WASHINGTON.**
The Packet Boat George Washington will commence her daily trips to Crommelin and Seneca to-morrow morning, leaving the temporary lock above Georgetown at ¼ past 7 o'clock, to return the same evening. The proprietors will spare no effort on their part to render satisfaction to all who patronize their boat. They are provided with good teams, and every arrangement is made in their boat and bar for the comfort of the public.

Parties wishing to make an excursion to either of the above places, by giving short notice, will be accommodated in best style. Those who have not already enjoyed the delight, which the scenery of the contiguous country, and the great work itself, (the Chesapeake and Ohio Canal) afford, will now have the opportunity of gratifying themselves.

Fare to Crommelin   37½ cents.
   " to Seneca   50 cents.
         Same returning.

P. S. In a few days the proprietors hope to get their Boat into Georgetown, when they will, until further notice, leave the Market House, at the hour above named, and return to the same spot.

SAMUEL CUNNINGHAM,
THOS. NOWLAN.

Georgetown, July 12—tf

IN-018

26, 1825. The Champlain Canal, undertaken at the same time, was completed in 1823 (see 1-036–1-039).[12] DeWitt Clinton, now governor of New York State, and other functionaries made a celebratory trip from Lake Erie to the Hudson River, and a series of galas were held throughout New York to celebrate the linking of the waters of the Great Lakes and the Atlantic Ocean.

On completion, the Erie Canal was 363 miles long (it was to be rebuilt and enlarged a decade later). Its eighty-four masonry locks, 15 feet wide and 90 feet long, overcame a fall in elevation of 642 feet and a rise in elevation of 56 feet from Lake Erie to the Hudson (IN-014–IN-017).

The Erie Canal was an immense success. Unlike the Potomac and James River navigations, it didn't have to cross the Appalachian Mountains to reach the West. Geography provided that the Erie Canal would exploit a route that was already behind the Appalachian Mountains. Commercially, the canal connected the lands of the west to the Port of New York, through the continuous passage of canal boats. Financially, it brought vast revenue to the State of New York. Because of the Erie Canal, New York City would rise to ascendancy among American cities. And the canal sparked a new industry, tourist travel, via packet boats, to locations such as Niagara Falls.

Canal mania now seized the United States (IN-019–IN-022). The Erie Canal stimulated the development of the Pennsylvania State Canals; in Maryland and northern Virginia it revitalized George Washington's old dream of developing a transportation corridor to the new territories

THE JAMES RIVER AND KANAWHA CANAL, RICHMOND, VIRGINIA.—[Sketched by J. R. Hamilton.]

IN-019

IN-020

IN-021

IN-019. Loading of a packet boat on the James River and Kanawha Canal at Richmond, Virginia. J. R. Hamilton, delineator. From *Harper's*, 1865. LC, Harper's: AP2 .H32, 1865.

IN-020. Miami and Erie Canal basin, Cincinnati, Ohio, ca. 1894, from William Cullen Bryant (ed.), *Picturesque America, or, The Land We Live In* (1894). LC-E168 .P5893.

IN-022

IN-021. Aqueduct over the Passaic River, Morris Canal, New Jersey, ca. 1894, from William Cullen Bryant (ed.), *Picturesque America, or, The Land We Live In* (1894). LC-E168 .P5893.

IN-022. Mauch Chunk (now Jim Thorpe) and Mt. Pisgah, Pennsylvania. Coal brought down from the mines to the Lehigh Canal was shipped to Easton, Pennsylvania, then to Philadelphia via the Delaware Canal along the Delaware River, or to New York via the Morris Canal across the north of New Jersey or the Delaware and Raritan Canal across the middle of New Jersey. From William Cullen Bryant (ed.), *Picturesque America, or, The Land We Live In* (1894). LC-E168 .P5893.

of the Ohio Valley through the Potomac River Valley with the new Chesapeake and Ohio Canal Company. In lower Virginia it triggered renewed interest in the James River as a corridor to the Ohio valley. Canals were developed on a very large scale from the Northeast to the South, and into the Midwest. Within ten years after the completion of the Erie Canal, the country had over 2,600 miles of completed canals.

Constructing these canals required an army to plan, design, and supervise. The Erie Canal was the training ground for American canal engineers. It provided the nation with a cadre of Americans ready and available to build other canals. Engineers such as Benjamin Wright (who became chief engineer of the Chesapeake and Ohio Canal, and worked on the Delaware and Hudson Canal, the Blackstone Canal, and others), Nathan Roberts (the Chesapeake and Delaware Canal, the Chesapeake and Ohio Canal, the Pennsylvania Canal, and others), James Geddes (the Chesapeake and Ohio Canal and various proposed canals in Maine, Pennsylvania, and elsewhere), Canvass White (chief engineer of the Union Canal, Lehigh Canal, and Delaware and Raritan Canal), John Jervis (chief engineer of the Delaware and Hudson Canal and the Chenango Canal and the Croton Aqueduct for the New York City water supply), and others went on to distinguished careers on other canal projects and, eventually, other engineering projects.[13] The construction of the Erie Canal marked the beginning of American civil engineering.

The Erie Canal was also the laboratory for developing methods for engineering, administering, and managing large canal construction projects. Earlier canal projects were small and met their labor needs by using laborers, indentured servants, or (in the South) slaves. These workers were supervised by a company employee, usually an overseer. Neither overseer nor workers had incentive to complete the work, one of the stable sources of employment in early America. Construction was slow and costs high. Benjamin Wright introduced the system of contracting work by the unit cost. Contractors received a contract on, typically, a half-mile of canal to be excavated, based on the engineers' estimate of how many cubic yards of material had to be excavated in that section, and a unit price for that work. The contractor then had an economic motive

CANALS OF THE UNITED STATES AS OF JANUARY 1835 [14]

	Length in Miles		Length in Miles
Cumberland and Oxford, Maine	20.50	West Philadelphia, Pennsylvania	.08
New Hampshire Canals	10.08	Chesapeake and Delaware, Delaware	13.62
Vermont Canals, estimated	1.00	Chesapeake and Ohio, Maryland	110.50
Middlesex, Massachusetts	27.00	Port Deposit, Maryland	10.00
Pawtucket, Massachusetts	1.50	Great and Little Falls, Maryland	3.20
Blackstone, Massachusetts and Rhode Island	45.00	Washington City Branch, District of Columbia	1.20
Hampshire and Hampden, Massachusetts	20.00	Dismal Swamp, Virginia and North Carolina	23.00
South Hadley Canal, Massachusetts	2.00	James and Jackson River, Virginia	37.50
Montague Canal, Massachusetts	3.00	North-West, North Carolina	6.00
Farmington, Connecticut	58.00	Weldon, North Carolina	12.00
Enfield, Connecticut	5.50	Club Foot and Marlow, North Carolina	1.50
New York State Canals	539.00	Santee, South Carolina	22.00
Delaware and Hudson, New York and Pennsylvania	108.00	Winyaw, South Carolina	7.50
		Saluda, South Carolina	6.25
Chittenango, New York	1.50	Catawba, Wateree, and others, South Carolina	16.00
Morris, New Jersey	90.00	Savannah and Ogeechee, Georgia	16.00
Delaware and Raritan, New Jersey	65.00	Carondolet, Louisiana	1.50
Salem, New Jersey	4.00	Lake Veret, Louisiana	8.00
Washington, New Jersey	1.00	Louisville, Kentucky	2.00
Pennsylvania State Canals	601.71	Ohio and Erie, and branches, Ohio	334.00
Union and Feeder, Pennsylvania	106.00	Miami, and branch, Ohio	66.00
Schuylkill Navigation, Pennsylvania	108.00	Lancaster Lateral Canal, Ohio	9.00
Lehigh, Pennsylvania	46.75	Wabash and Erie, Indiana	15.00
Conestoga, Pennsylvania	18.00		
Codorus, Pennsylvania	11.00	TOTAL	2,617.89
Conewago, Pennsylvania	2.50		

for closely superintending his men and urging them to greater productivity. Many canal contractors became rich, and the canal companies benefited by having established costs.

Building the Erie Canal required many men, more than casual laborers, indentured servants, or slaves could supply. Instead, labor contractors hired immigrants off boats arriving from Ireland, housed them in shanty workers' huts, fed them, and put them to work. (The Irish also built England's canals, where they came by the name "navvies," short for navigations—i.e., inland navigations, or canals.) The canal companies employed other nationalities, but they tended to be skilled workers—Scottish masons for aqueducts and bridges, Welsh miners for tunnel construction. It was the Irish who cleared the line of the canal, pulled the stumps, excavated or blasted the dirt or rock, shaped the prism, and lined it with clay. The pattern established on the Erie Canal continued in the construction of the numerous canals to follow.

Most canals were financed by public expense. At $10,000 to $20,000 or more per canal mile (when a working man earned a dollar per day or less), an enormous amount of money was expended on canal construction between 1825 and 1835, the high point of the canal-building era. It was also the high point of graft, corruption, and fraud, with bribery of state legislators, collusion between those establishing the value of land to be paid to land owners by the canal company (usually by neighbors and adjacent land owners organized into legal panels called "inquisitions"), and construction fraud. Many canals were constructed to satisfy greed, with no economic justification for their existence or continuance. Other canals were built in a shoddy manner and would have to be rebuilt in years to come. And everywhere there were enormous escalating costs. The panic of 1837 hit the eastern and midwestern states, particularly Pennsylvania, Maryland, Indiana, Illinois, and Michigan. Pennsylvania owed $34 million and defaulted on the interest on its debt in 1840. Special taxes were levied, and canals were sold. Most limped through this economic crisis but the mania cooled.[15]

CANAL ENGINEERING, CONSTRUCTION, AND OPERATION

Stillwater canals like the Erie required considerable planning and design by engineers before work could begin. Once work did begin, large number of construction workers needed to be organized and supervised (IN-023 and IN-024).

Stillwater canals included a variety of structures, but the two elements basic to them are the level and the lift lock.

The canal level consisted of the prism, so-called because the water in the ditch, if viewed as a volume, with its flat top and bottom and sloping sides, is prism-shaped. Prisms were small, typically ranging in width from 40 to 70 feet at the top, 28 to 58 feet at the bottom, and 4 to 7 feet in depth. The slightly sloped bottom provided a minimal

IN-023

IN-024

opposite

IN-023. Rendering showing the construction of a typical, albeit imaginary, section of the Chesapeake and Ohio Canal, Maryland. Donald Demers, artist. From U.S. Department of the Interior, *Chesapeake and Ohio Canal: A Guide to Chesapeake and Ohio Canal National Historical Park, Handbook 142* (1989). LC-F187. C47 C47.

Crews work to clear the line of construction previously identified by survey parties (2), followed by teams of horses that pull up the tree stumps (3). Below are the workers' huts. Excavation of the canal prism is accomplished by horse-pulled graders (4) and hand labor (5). Workers build the side-walls of the canal prism, probably of dry laid masonry (6). A stockpile of cut stone supplies construction on the masonry lock (8). Workmen are constructing an aqueduct (10) while a crib dam is under construction (11); to its left is a temporary cofferdam, a structure to divert the river water from the construction site. A guard lock (12) and culvert (13) are under construction. Tracks have been laid for hauling stone across the river (bottom left) to the aqueduct (14). A waste weir is being constructed (16). Compare with the completed canal, IN-024.

IN-024. Rendering showing the completed Chesapeake and Ohio Canal, Maryland. The drawing shows a stop gate (lower left), locks and lockhouses (lower middle), dam (middle), waste weir (immediately below dam), towpath, feeder lock (usually used with a feeder canal, but in this case the canal is immediately adjacent to the river), drydock, aqueduct, and tunnel (all upper right). Donald Demers, artist. From U.S. Department of the Interior, *Chesapeake and Ohio Canal: A Guide to Chesapeake and Ohio Canal National Historical Park, Handbook 142* (1989). LC-F187 .C47 C47.

this page

IN-025. The canal boy. On stillwater canals, motive power was provided by horse or mule. Loads of a hundred tons or more could be hauled at 3 to 4 miles per hour. Woodcut by H & C Koevoets. P & P, LC-USZ62-40065.

IN-025

current. Some levels were very long—one on the Erie Canal stretched a little over 69 miles, without an intervening lock, from Syracuse to Frankfort, New York. Boat operators preferred long, straight levels, since canal boats, typically about 90 feet long, could not negotiate tight curves.

On one side of the prism was the berm, a small horizontal shelf intended to provide stability for the earth slope adjacent to the ditch (IN-026). Along the other side of the prism was the towpath, typically about 8 feet wide, for the tow animals, mules or horses. A pair could pull a canal boat along a level at approximately 3 to 4 miles per hour. (Attempts to move through the canals at the higher speeds of steam-propelled canal boats, introduced early in the nineteenth century, were unsuccessful because the wake of these boats undermined the sloping banks of the prism.) Long tow ropes kept the team of animals well ahead of the canal boat so the rope was as nearly parallel to the line of the forward direction of the boat as possible to maximize the hauling power of the animals and minimize the adjustment necessary at the tiller.

Water was held in the prism by puddling—a process by which liquid clay was applied to the bottom and sides, typically in layers 6 inches thick, to a depth of 2 to 3 feet. Pounded to drive out excess water by canal workers (IN-027), the clay was then covered with dry soil to ensure that it did not dry out. Puddling provided an impervious liner for the canal prism. Its use was attributed to James Brindley; it is said that as he lay dying, some canal engineers told him that their canal would not hold water. Brindley told them to puddle it; when they responded that they had already done so, Brindley said, "Then puddle it again—and again."

Connecting one level and the next were one or more lift locks for raising and

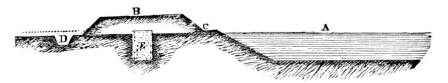

Fig. 236—Cross section of a canal in level cutting.
A, water-way.
B, tow-paths.
C, berms.
D, side-drains.
E, puddling of clay or sand.

IN-026

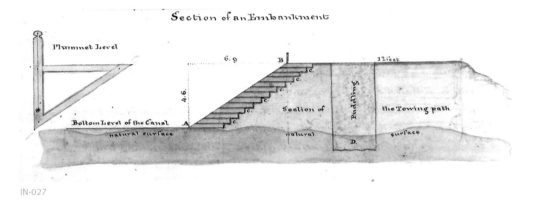

IN-027

this page

IN-026. Section of a canal in a level cutting: the waterway (A), the towpath (B), the shelf or berm (C), side drains or ditches on the side of the canal to draw water away from the canal (D), and impervious tamped clay puddling (E). From D. H. Mahan, *A Treatise of Civil Engineering* (1873). LC-TA 145. M3.

IN-027. Section of an embankment, illustration from the first American manuscript on canal construction. From Isaac Roberdeau, *Mathematics and Treatise on Canals* (1796). MSS, MMC 1649.

opposite

IN-028. Plan of a typical canal lock, showing the upper and lower gates with their corresponding miter gates and balance beams, masonry retaining walls, wood flooring, and the counterforts on either side of the masonry retaining walls, which provided extra strength against the water pressure within the lock. From D. H. Mahan, *A Treatise of Civil Engineering* (1873). LC-TA 145. M3.

IN-029. Typical section of a masonry arch showing the chamber walls (A), the chamber (B), and the inverted arch foundation used in lock construction to distribute the weight of the masonry lock over a wide surface area. From D. H. Mahan, *A Treatise of Civil Engineering* (1873). LC-TA 145. M3.

IN-030. Drawings from Diderot's *Encyclopedié* of how a canal lock works. At top, the canal boat enters the lock and the lower lock gates close behind it. The valve (E) closes and the lock fills with water. The boat is lifted to the higher water level (middle). The upper lock gates then open and the canal boat proceeds to the upper canal level. The bottom drawing shows the lock in plan view, including the miter gates and balance beams used to open and close the gates. From Denis Diderot, *A Pictorial Encyclopedia of Trades and Industry* (1993 reprint of 1751 work). LC-T9.E472513.

IN-031. Elevation, plan, and sections of a typical lock, Erie Canal, New York. Orlando Poe, delineator, 1855 or 1856. P & P, LC-USZC4-4567.

lowering boats, typically a height of 8 feet, but sometimes as high as 18 feet. A lift lock was a chamber 15 to 18 feet wide and 70 to 110 feet long—adequate to accommodate one canal boat (IN-030 and IN-031). Lift locks were wood, masonry, or composite: wood locks were generally used by early canal builders because of the abundance and low cost of wood, but they did not last long, perhaps a maximum of twenty years. Masonry locks were more durable but also expensive (IN-028 and IN-029). Composite locks, typically constructed of dry laid masonry within a wooden framework (see 2-012 and 2-060), lay somewhere between all-wooden and all-masonry locks in cost and durability.

On each end of the lock chamber was a pair of swing gates, usually made of wood (IN-032, IN-035–IN-038). The gates opened by means of balance beams mounted on top, to allow the boat to pass into the chamber. A quoin post, usually mounted on an iron pin (IN-040) and secured to the lock wall by an anchor-and-collar device, served as the hinge or gate post (IN-039 and IN-041). A miter sill on the floor of the chamber provided the structure needed to support the gates at their lower extremity. These wood members were constructed with iron-braced mortise-and-tenon joints (IN-036).

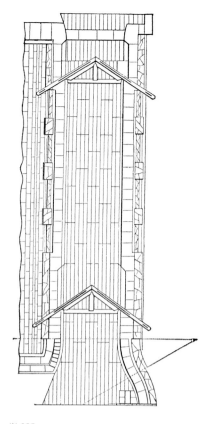

IN-028

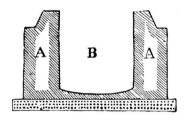

IN-029

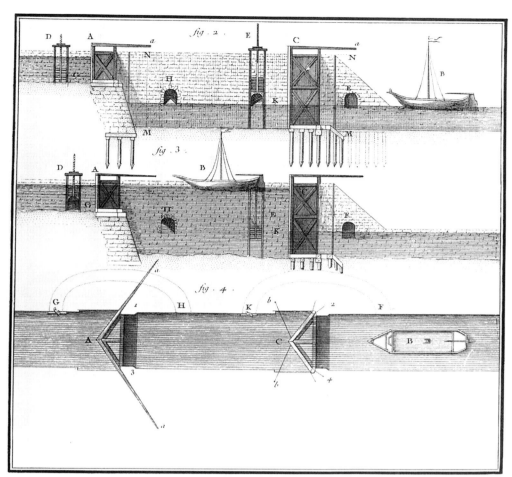

fig. 2.

fig. 3.

fig. 4.

IN-030

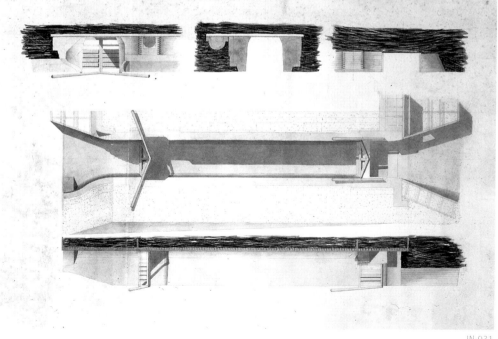

IN-031

IN-032

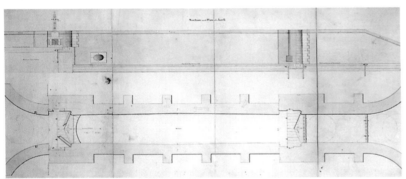

IN-033

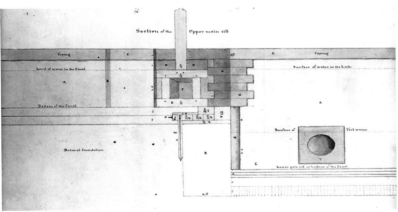

IN-034

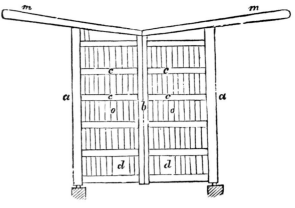

IN-035

IN-032. Lock gate. From bottom to top: cross framing, sheathing, T-shaped iron plates, miter posts (where the gates come together), and balance beams. The quoin post is adjacent to the masonry lock walls and secured at the top to the masonry by an iron anchor or anchor strap. Champlain and Hudson Canal, Saratoga, New York. Jack E. Boucher, photographer, November, 1959. P & P, HABS, NY,46-SAR,2-3.

IN-033. Section and plan of a typical masonry canal lift lock with counterforts on either side of the masonry retaining walls (compare IN-031). From Isaac Roberdeau, *Mathematics and Treatise on Canals* (1796). MSS, MMC 1649.

IN-034. Section of the upper main sill, illustrating the intake valve located upstream of the upper gate locks (middle) and the entrance opening within the lock chamber (right). When the slide valve is pulled up, water from the upper canal rushes into the intake valve, through a pipe in the masonry wall and into the lock chamber through the entrance opening. When the water in the lock chamber reaches the level of the water upstream, the upper lock gates are opened and the boat proceeds into the lock. From Isaac Roberdeau, *Mathematics and Treatise on Canals* (1796). MSS, MMC 1649.

IN-035. The component parts of a pair of lock gates in a closed position: quoin posts (a), which serve as the gates' hinges; miter posts (b), where the gates come together; cross framing (c), giving the gates strength; valves (d), allowing water to enter the lock chamber; planking or sheathing (o), applied to the gate structure; and balance beams (m), mounted on top of the gates and used to open and close the gates. From D. H. Mahan, *A Treatise of Civil Engineering* (1873). LC-TA 145. M3.

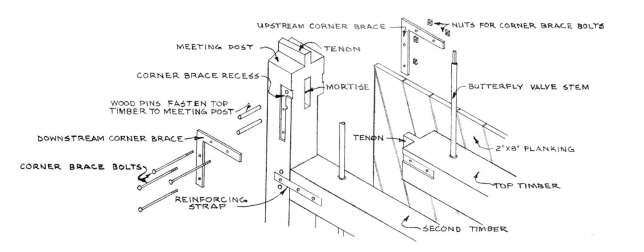

Labels in IN-036 drawing:
UPSTREAM CORNER BRACE — NUTS FOR CORNER BRACE BOLTS
MEETING POST — TENON
CORNER BRACE RECESS — MORTISE
WOOD PINS FASTEN TOP TIMBER TO MEETING POST
DOWNSTREAM CORNER BRACE — TENON — BUTTERFLY VALVE STEM
CORNER BRACE BOLTS — 2"X8" PLANKING
REINFORCING STRAP — TOP TIMBER — SECOND TIMBER

IN-036

IN-036. Axonometric drawing of a typical lock detail: mortise-and-tenon connections are used to mount the cross framing to the meeting post (miter post). The connection is reinforced with L- and I-shaped iron plates. The gate sheathing is diagonal to provide extra rigidity so the gate does not rack or otherwise distort in operation. The circular rods shown control butterfly gates at the bottom of the lock gate that when open emptied the lock. Chesapeake and Ohio Canal, Maryland. C. H. Lavers, Jr., delineator. P & P, HABS MD-767, sheet no. 1, detail.

IN-037. Elevation of a typical lock gate. The balance beam is shown in dotted lines atop the gate. These canal gates are massive—almost 20 feet high—and constructed of 10-inch-square wooden members. The quoin post is a foot in diameter. The planking itself is made up of 2- by 8-inch members. These dimensions were necessary to resist over a thousand pounds of water pressure per square foot exerted on the base of the gate when the lock was full. Chesapeake and Ohio Canal, Maryland. C. H. Lavers, Jr., delineator. P & P, HABS MD-767, sheet no. 1, detail.

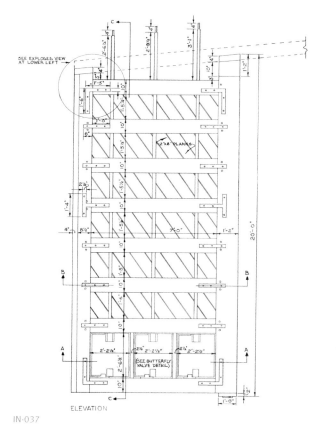

IN-037

IN-038. Elevation of a typical lock gate. Here the quoin post, the hinge of the gate, is called the heel post and the balance beam is called the gate sweep. Ohio and Erie Canal. Alan J. Rutherford, delineator, 1987. P & P, HAER OH-60, sheet no. 2, detail.

IN-038

IN-039

IN-039. Anchor-and-collar device securing the top of the quoin post to the top of the masonry lock wall, Lock 44, Chesapeake and Ohio Canal, Williamsport, Maryland. Jack E. Boucher, photographer, December 1960. P & P, HABS, MD,22-WILPO.V,4-3.

IN-040. Detail of the pivot at the bottom of the quoin post, typical lock gate, Chesapeake and Ohio Canal, Harper's Ferry Vic., Maryland. C. H. Lavers, Jr., delineator. P & P, HABS MD-767, sheet no. 1, detail.

IN-041. Plan and elevations of anchor and collar device to secure the top of the quoin post or heel post to the top of the masonry lock, designed to allow the quoin post to be taken down for maintenance or replacement, Lock 35, Chesapeake and Ohio Canal, Harper's Ferry Vic., Maryland. C. H. Lavers, Jr., delineator. P & P, HABS MD-773, sheet no. 2, detail.

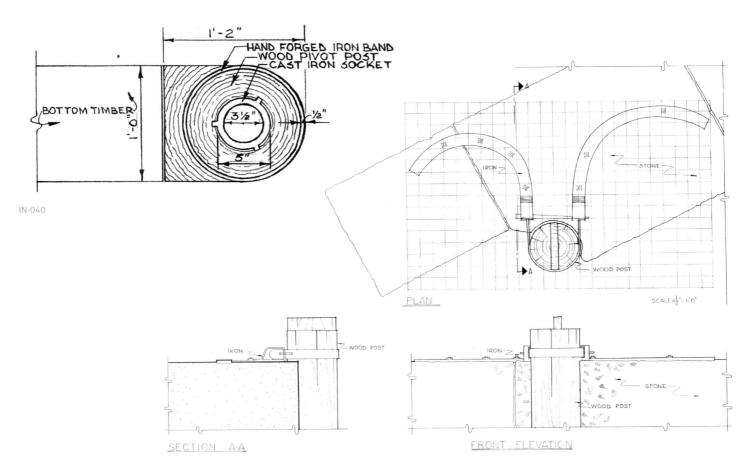

IN-040

IN-041

IN-042. Miter sill, Lock 55, Chesapeake and Ohio Canal, Hancock Vic., Maryland. Since the lock gates are no longer present, the miter sill can readily be seen. Jack E. Boucher, photographer, 1959–60. P & P, HABS, MD,22-HAN.V,5-3.

IN-043. Plan of a miter sill: framed miter sill (a, b, c), quoin posts (d), and the miter posts (e) that meet to form the seal between the two gates. The bottom of the gates closed tight against the sill, while the angle of the sill forced the quoin posts into their masonry pockets, for a watertight seal on both sides of the gates. From D. H. Mahan, *A Treatise of Civil Engineering* (1873). LC-TA 145. M3.

IN-042

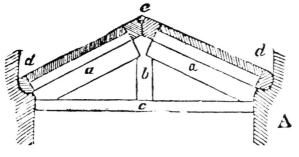

IN-043

For boats going downstream, the gates were closed and the lock filled with water from the upper level; then the upstream gates opened and the boat entered the lock. The upstream gates then closed, the lock was drained by means of valves—either in the downstream gates, the sides of the chamber, or both—and the canal boat was lowered to the level of the water in the downstream level, a process that typically took about ten minutes. The lower gates then swung open and the canal boat proceeded on the lower level. This sequence was reversed for boats going upstream (IN-030).

When more than one lift lock was used in sequence, a staircase of locks was created. Probably the most impressive staircase of locks built was that on the Erie Canal at Lockport (IN-016 and IN-017). These were double locks, meaning that one canal boat could ascend while another descended.

The lift lock was the most common but not the only device for lifting (or lowering) a canal boat from one level to another. Some canals, such as the Pennsylvania Canal (see 1-042), the Morris Canal (see 3-002–3-009), and the Chesapeake and Ohio Canal (see 4-023–4-024), used inclined planes for the same purpose. The canal boat was hauled onto a cradle mounted on rails that were secured to an earthen inclined plane. The cradle with its canal boat was pulled to the top of the incline by cables or ropes, usually of iron, steel, or hemp or a combination of these, by a steam engine (at the Pennsylvania Canal) or by a hydraulically powered turbine (at the Morris Canal). Usually these inclined planes were

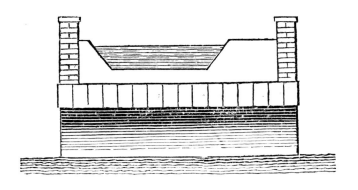

IN-044

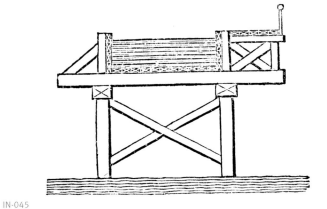

IN-045

counterbalanced—that is, as one cradle was raised, an adjacent one, or a counterweight, was lowered. At the top of the inclined plane the boat was dislodged from the cradle and floated onto the new level. Canal boats on the Morris Canal were hinged so the boat could bend over the hump at the top of the inclined plane and into the water at the higher level. At the Chesapeake and Ohio Canal, to provide access to the canal from the Potomac River near Washington, the canal boat was guided into a tank of water and fastened. Hydraulic turbines, and later steam engines, at the top of the inclined plane hauled up both canal boat and the tank of water. This took more power but avoided the sagging, or deformation, of the canal boat's hull when it sat, without water, in a cradle.

All canals lost water throughout their length. Lift locks were a major source of loss. Opening a lock might typically result in the loss from one level to the next of 13,000 cubic feet, or about 100,000 gallons, of water. Evaporation was another source of loss. Inevitably, leakage occurred: locks were rarely completely water-tight. Puddling could be breached by muskrats digging through the clay liner; some companies placed a bounty on the animals. Rainfall added some water, but runoff from the streams and creeks that intersected the canal usually resulted in no addition because these waterways were usually routed under the canal in culverts (or canals were carried over them in aqueducts) to avoid sediment buildup in the prism as well as possible damage from flooding.

To compensate for water loss, diversion dams on the river, at intervals along the length of the canal, channeled water into the prism. These dams were usually short, typically 4 to 5 feet in height, and usually made of timber logs laid in rectangles to make cribs and filled with rock (IN-049–IN-051). Some dams were constructed of rock and brush; a few were masonry. The dam impounded river water, which was admitted to the canal through a diversion, or feeder, canal, a small canal from the dam impoundment to the canal proper. The diversion canal was usually equipped with a guard lock to admit river craft into the canal as well as regulate the amount of water entering the canal proper.

IN-044. Section of a typical masonry aqueduct, from bottom to top: river to be crossed (rippled horizontal lines), masonry arch (horizontal lines), ring stones (white rectangles), infill material, usually loose masonry with a hydraulic cement binder (blank white space), canal prism (dashed horizontal lines), and the parapet walls on either side. From James Renwick, *Elements of Mechanics* (1832). LC-QC125 .R43.

IN-045. Section, wooden aqueduct. Few have survived. From James Renwick, *Elements of Mechanics* (1832). LC-QC125 .R43.

IN-046. Elevation of upstream face, Conococheague Aqueduct, Chesapeake and Ohio Canal, Williamsport, Maryland. The upstream parapet wall is almost completely missing, exposing the infill material above the ring stones to further erosion and eventual aqueduct collapse. The upstream face of this aqueduct, like those on most Chesapeake and Ohio Canal aqueducts, has separated from the main structure because of water pressure within the prism accelerated by the impact of canal boat 73 on April 20, 1920. The wall collapsed, washing the boat into the Conococheague Creek below. Jack E. Boucher, photographer, 1959–60. P & P, HABS, MD,22-WILPO.V,2-3.

IN-047. Elevation of upstream face, showing the exposed rubble fill and remedial actions taken to stabilize the arch structure following the 1920 collapse, including shotcrete, a liquid form of concrete sprayed on the exposed rubble and the steel channels to bind the arch together. Conococheague Aqueduct, Chesapeake and Ohio Canal, Williamsport, Maryland. Dana Lockett, delineator, 1997. P & P, HAER MD-123, sheet no. 1, detail.

IN-048. Axonometric drawing of the Conococheague Aqueduct, Chesapeake and Ohio Canal, Williamsport, Maryland. After failure of the upstream wall, the wall was rebuilt in wood, as shown here. Dana Lockett, delineator, 1997. P & P, HAER MD-123, sheet no. 4.

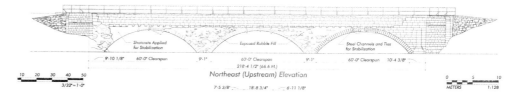

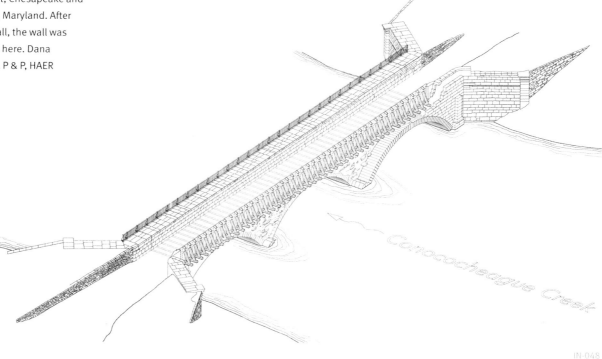

IN-049

IN-049. Hokendauqua Dam, Lehigh Canal, Lehigh River, Northampton County, Pennsylvania. Floods have torn off some of the dam's sheathing and have demolished some of the cribs. Jet T. Lowe, photographer, 1979. P & P, HAER, PA,48-CATSN,1A-1.

IN-050. Section of a canal crib dam. The interior (downstream) crib (A) is adjacent to the puddling and sheet piles (C) that serve to limit seepage through the dam. The exterior (upstream) crib (B) is somewhat larger than the interior crib. From D. H. Mahan, *A Treatise of Civil Engineering* (1873). LC-TA 145 .M3.

IN-051. Elevation and section of the dam constructed in the Schuylkill River at Fairmount Water Works, Philadelphia, Pennsylvania, ca. 1820. The upstream face of the crib dam is partially sheathed: the upstream cribbing contains smaller stones and is backed by larger stones downstream. From David Stevenson, *Sketch of the Civil Engineering of North America* (1838). LC-TA22 .S84.

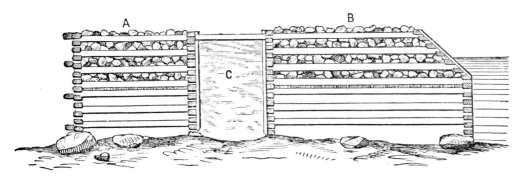

IN-050

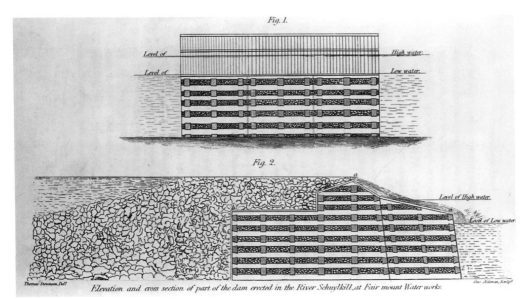

IN-051

The guard lock also prevented floodwater from entering the canal. Weirs, small dams that spilled excess water over their crest back into the river, were a safety valve to ensure that water did not overflow locks and erode their foundation.

Tunnels were sometimes driven under hills or mountains to avoid a more circuitous route—for example, on the Chesapeake and Ohio Canal, where construction of the Paw Paw Tunnel avoided a more circuitous route of some six miles (see 2-124–2-126; 4-126–4-129), or because the canal couldn't be built otherwise.

Besides aqueducts, culverts, and dams, canals also required bridges. In urban areas crossings were unavoidable; in rural areas the canal companies typically did everything they could to avoid the expense and delay to canal traffic that a bridge involved. They attempted to buy the land between the canal and the river to block the need for farmers' access. They installed ferries, as on the Chesapeake and Ohio Canal, to transport farmers' wagons across. But they could not avoid the need for bridges entirely. Masonry arch bridges were most common (see 2-112–2-114). These could not be too tall because they were expensive to build and because gradual approaches to a bridge were required for animal-drawn traffic: it was the masonry arch bridge that gave birth to the canal boat call, "Low bridge, everybody down." Other types of bridges, notably the lift bridge and the swing bridge, were also used (see 2-116–2-123 for examples).

Along the canals were lockhouses, typically two-story houses for the lockkeeper and his family (see 2-047–2-063). Since the lockkeeper had to open locks to canal traffic day and night, lockhouses were almost always sited near the lock. The Erie Canal provided the model for lockhouses built elsewhere, though later local and regional building types influenced their form. Lockhouses have tended to survive, even when the canal has not.

CANAL BOATS

One element of canal travel has not survived—the boats. When river navigation dominated commerce, trips were usually one way; the river vessel was broken up for wood at its destination. With the advent of stillwater canals, canal boats became longer lived

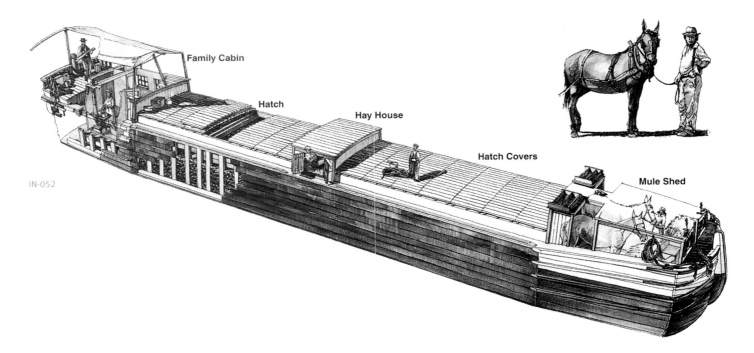

IN-052

and more standardized (see IN-019 and IN-052). During the construction of the Chesapeake and Ohio Canal, company president Charles Mercer asked chief engineer Benjamin Wright what boats for the new canal might look like. Wright answered that the size of the locks would determine their design:

> The Locks on the Ches & Ohio Canal are 100 feet by 15 in the Chamber. Consequently a Boat with its extreme length from Stem to Stern, 90 feet will pass thro these Locks and if we say 14½ feet for the extreme width leaving 6 inches play, it is ample . . . A Boat of this form drawing 5 feet Water would displace water equal to 78 x 14 x 5 = 5460 Cubic feet equal to 341300 lbs or 152 Tons & 820 lbs — Now if we suppose the Boat to weigh when empty 22 Tons 820 lbs we shall then have 130 Tons of Lading . . .[16]

Canal boats that plied the Union, Delaware, and Morris canals were smaller because the locks were smaller or because inclined planes obviated lifting a 152-ton boat. But canals boats of the size Wright specified became the standard for most American canals and thus could pass from one canal to another. Packet boats, which carried passengers, mail, and some cargo, were about the same size (IN-019). Although canal boats were more durable than the river craft built for only one downriver trip, they still had short lives, perhaps twenty to thirty years.

Life on a canal boat might have looked idyllic. Travel through ever-changing scenery was pleasant. Little physical exertion was usually required. The boatman and his family traveled together as a crew, along with their animals (IN-053). Winter, when the canal

IN-053

froze or was drained, was a time off. Perhaps it is this slow-paced lifestyle that makes the canal era so appealing to contemporary Americans.

DECLINE OF THE CANAL ERA

The canal that was to be the supreme example of canal technology and efficiency was the Chesapeake and Ohio Canal. It was to be bigger and better than any canal yet built. It was seen as the national canal of the United States, one that would capture the dreams of George Washington and connect the Chesapeake Bay with the Ohio Territory. But on July 4, 1828, as President John Quincy Adams thrust the first spade into the ground at Little Falls, Maryland, to celebrate the beginning of its construction, a group of men gathered in Baltimore to lay the cornerstone of the transportation system that would link Baltimore with the west—the Baltimore and Ohio Railroad. Because of the high ridge separating Baltimore from the Potomac valley, the merchants of Baltimore could not use a canal to connect them with the western lands. Instead they turned to the railroad.

Competition between the new canal and the new railroad was to be severe. There was only a narrow shelf of land through the mountain passes of the Potomac valley through which both had to pass. For the next several years that competition was played out in the courts of Maryland. The Chesapeake and Ohio Canal won the legal case and was awarded the right to use the narrow passes of the Potomac River. The Baltimore and Ohio Railroad was forced to build a bridge over the Potomac River (see 4-076–4-077) and continue their

IN-054

this page
IN-054. Chesapeake and Ohio Canal boat
and Baltimore and Ohio Railroad train,
Harper's Ferry Vic., West Virginia. From U.S.
Department of the Interior, *Chesapeake and
Ohio Canal: A Guide to Chesapeake and
Ohio Canal National Historical Park,
Handbook 142* (1989). LC-F187 .C47 C47.

opposite
IN-055. Lock 11, New York Barge Canal. John
Collier, photographer, October 1941. P & P,
LC-USF34-081526-E.

IN-056. New York Barge Canal lock, New
York. John Collier, photographer, October
1941. P & P, LC-USF34-081533-E.

IN-057. Remains of outlet of Lock 5,
Potomac Canal, Great Falls, Virginia.
Excavated almost totally from solid rock by
slaves under the supervision of Leonard
Harbaugh, Lock 5 had a drop of 18 feet,
probably the deepest in America at the time
(1802). Theodor Horydczak, photographer,
1943. P & P, HAER, VA,30-GREFA,1C-3.

IN-058. Boy on a balance beam of a disused
lock, Chesapeake and Ohio Canal,
Georgetown, Washington, D.C. P & P, LC-
USZ62-82960.

route on that side of the river. But, by the end of the 1830s, it was clear that the Baltimore and Ohio Railroad would reach the western lands first. It also became clear that the railroad would be the future of American transportation (IN-054). The topography that prevented the construction of a canal to Baltimore provided no obstacle to the railroad. At the peak of canal enthusiasm, the seeds had thus been sown for its successor.

Nevertheless, canals continued to be built across the United States for several decades, particularly in Ohio, Indiana, and Illinois. By the onset of the Civil War in 1861, however, railroads, and to a lesser extent toll roads, were putting canals out of business. A few canals struggled along, many in railroad ownership, into the twentieth century. The Chesapeake and Ohio Canal continued in operation until put out of business by a flood in 1924.

Not all canals succumbed to railroad competition. Canals that could afford to enlarge the width, depth, and length of their locks to accommodate larger boats and barges were able to lower operating costs and effectively compete with the railroads. The Erie Canal transformed itself, first into a larger stillwater canal, and then into a much larger barge canal (IN-055 and IN-056). Those canals associated with the western rivers, like the Louisville and Portland Canal, were enlarged to accommodate the larger river boats traveling the Ohio River. Strategically placed canals like the Chesapeake and Delaware Canal were enlarged for an intracoastal waterway system.

Most of the stillwater canals constructed in the early nineteenth century, however, could not negotiate the change from narrow canal boats to large barges, because of either lack of capital or lack of adequate water. Most of these canals were abandoned by the end of the nineteenth century.

Once a canal was abandoned, its components met varying fates. Generally, features of canals in urban areas were obliterated from the landscape. The waterways were filled in for other land uses, and cut stone from them was mined for other building purposes.

IN-055

IN-056

Today physical remains of canals that ran through urban areas, such as the Morris Canal in northeastern New Jersey, are difficult to find. Canals in rural areas fared better. Locks and prisms frequently survived well into the twentieth century (IN-057–IN-061).

IN-057

IN-058

IN-059

IN-059. Ruins of Black Oak Lock, Santee Canal, Lake Moultrie Vic., South Carolina, ca. 1930s. P & P, HABS, SC-8-_____,1-1.

IN-060. Ruins of lockhouse, Black Oak Swamp, Santee Canal, Lake Moultrie Vic., South Carolina, ca. 1930s. P & P, HABS, SC-8-_____,1-2.

IN-061. Ruins of Lock 37, Union Canal, Bernville Vic., Pennsylvania, ca. 1976. P & P, HAER, PA,6-BERN.V,7-15.

IN-060

IN-061

IN-062. Canoeing through the Little Falls Aqueduct across the Passaic River, Morris Canal, New Jersey. P & P, HAER, NJ,21-PHIL,1-113.

IN-063. Canal boat, *The Georgetown*, used for tours in Georgetown, Washington, D.C., along the Chesapeake and Ohio Canal. From U.S. Department of the Interior, *Chesapeake and Ohio Canal: A Guide to Chesapeake and Ohio Canal National Historical Park, Handbook 142* (1989). LC-F187. C47 C47.

REBIRTH

Since World War II, and particularly since just before the turn of the twenty-first century, there has been great interest in saving what remains of early American canals, and in exploring canal history and folklore. In some cases this interest is related to recreational boating opportunities. The New York Barge Canal, the latest enlarged version of the Erie Canal, provides the opportunity to sail through much of the country, from New York City to Chicago. The Chesapeake and Delaware Canal, enlarged from the original stillwater canal, provides an important link in the intracoastal waterway system that allows northern boat owners to travel to Florida on protected waters. But unwatered canals and canal remnants are important as well. Old canal sites have become local, state, and national parks that provide scenic recreational areas with historical interest

IN-064

IN-064. James River and Kanawha Canal with the James River and Richmond, Virginia, in the background. Engraved by W. J. Bennett from a painting by G. Cooke, ca. 1834. P & P, LC-USZC4-4539.

(IN-062 and IN-063). Increasingly, the physical remnants of canals are being organized into Heritage Corridors where the early canal is regarded as inseparable from the history of the region: the Ohio and Erie Canal National Heritage Corridor, the Schuylkill River Heritage Corridor, the Blackstone River Valley Canal National Heritage Corridor, the Erie Canal Heritage Corridor, the Illinois and Michigan Heritage Corridor, the Delaware and the Lehigh Canal National Heritage Corridor, and others. Within these corridors, surviving elements of early canals are being stabilized, preserved, restored, and interpreted for the public through a partnership of all levels of government and the interested public.

American canals are enjoying a renaissance. No longer significant means of transportation, they are places for recreation, enjoyment, and appreciation of the past. It is difficult to find a surviving section of an early American canal that has not been made into a park or heritage area. This interest says that there is something about canals that greatly appeals to Americans of the twenty-first century. Perhaps it is a view of life when travel was leisurely or when technology was understandable: canal remnants of what was state-of-the-art in transportation provide insight into another time, when cargo and passengers were delivered at 4 miles per hour by mild-mannered mules (IN-064).

NOTES

1. In a letter to Secretary of Treasury Albert Gallatin, Robert Fulton wrote that for the cost of transporting one ton of goods 300 miles on the best roads, "it could be boated *three thousand five hundred miles*, and draw resources from the centre of this vast continent." U.S. Treasury, *Report of the Secretary of the Treasury, on the Subject of Public Roads and Canals* (1808. Reprint. New York: Augustus M. Kelley, Publishers, 1968), 114.

2. A. W. Skempton, et al., *A Biographical Dictionary of Civil Engineers in Great Britain and Ireland* (London: Thomas Telford for The Institution of Civil Engineers, 2002), 75–80.

3. Samuel Smiles, *Lives of the Engineers* (London: John Murray, 1861), vol. I.

4. Robert J. Kapsch, "The Potomac Canal: A Construction History," *Canal History and Technology Proceedings, Volume XXI* (Easton, Pa.: National Canal Museum, 2002), 143–235.

5. Wayland Fuller Dunaway, *History of the James River and Kanawha Company* (1922. Reprint. New York: AMS Press, 1969), 29.

6. Conewago Canal Company, *Account of the Conewago-Canal, on the river Susquehanna* (Philadelphia: Whitehall-Press, 1798), 4–5.

7. F. A. Porcher, *The History of the Santee Canal* (1875. Reprint. Monck's Corner, S.C.: Berkeley County Tricentennial Committee, 1970), 10–16; 18.

8. Christopher Roberts, *The Middlesex Canal 1793–1860* (Cambridge: Harvard University Press, 1938), 160.

9. Edward C. Carter II, editor-in-chief, *The Engineering Drawings of Benjamin Henry Latrobe* (New Haven: Yale University Press, 1980), 76.

10. Franz Anton Ritter von Gerstner, *Early American Railroads* (Stanford, Calif.: Stanford University Press, 1997 reprint of 1842–1843 work, *Die innern Communicationen*), 50.

11. A. W. Skempton, et al., *A Biographical Dictionary of Civil Engineers in Great Britain and Ireland* (London: Thomas Telford for The Institution of Civil Engineers, 2002), 773.

12. Franz Anton Ritter von Gerstner, *Early American Railroads* (Stanford, Calif.: Stanford University Press, 1997 reprint of 1842–1843 work, *Die innern Communicationen*), 56.

13. Committee on History and Heritage of American Civil Engineering, *A Biographical Dictionary of American Civil Engineers* (New York: American Society of Civil Engineers, 1972), 49, 69–71, 126–27; *Volume II* (New York: American Society of Civil Engineers, 1991), 97.

14. *Mitchell's Compendium of the Internal Improvements of the United States* (1835. Reprint. Sheperdstown, W.V.: American Canal and Transportation Center, ca. 1970), 9. Although mostly correct, this table does contain some minor errors. The Great and Little Falls, Maryland, canals, for example, had been abandoned by 1835 due to the construction of the Chesapeake and Ohio Canal.

15. Alvin F. Harlow, *Old Towpaths* (New York: D. Appleton & Co., 1926), 132–34; 270–73.

16. Letter, Benjamin Wright to Charles Mercer, February 3, 1839, Chesapeake and Ohio Canal Company, Record Group 79, National Archives.

CANALS ACROSS AMERICA

NEW ENGLAND
Massachusetts, Rhode Island, Connecticut, Maine

The canals of New England were built to bring farm products to the cities and seaports on the coast and to harness the abundant water power of the region. The three most prominent farm-to-market canals were the Middlesex, the Blackstone, and the Farmington (1-001). The Middlesex Canal was one of the earliest canals constructed in the United States (1789–1808) and one of the first to be planned and supervised by an American, Loammi Baldwin (1-002–1-005; see also 2-052 and 2-112). The Blackstone Canal (1-006 and 1-007; see also 2-008) was one of the canals developed in the aftermath of the opening of the Erie Canal in 1825. The Farmington Canal in Connecticut, and its connecting canal in Massachusetts—the Hampshire and Hampden (1-008 and 1-009)—also belong to the era of canal development that swept the country then. The early Pawtucket Canal (1797) near Lowell, Massachusetts, was later modified and extended to develop the extensive power system for Lowell textile factories (1-010). Other, smaller canals served local needs—for example, the Cumberland and Oxford in Maine, which brought timber to Portland.

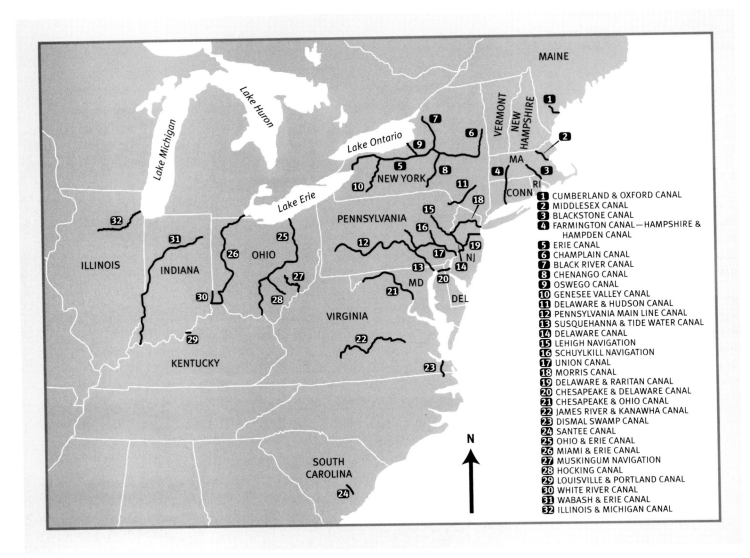

1. CUMBERLAND & OXFORD CANAL
2. MIDDLESEX CANAL
3. BLACKSTONE CANAL
4. FARMINGTON CANAL—HAMPSHIRE & HAMPDEN CANAL
5. ERIE CANAL
6. CHAMPLAIN CANAL
7. BLACK RIVER CANAL
8. CHENANGO CANAL
9. OSWEGO CANAL
10. GENESEE VALLEY CANAL
11. DELAWARE & HUDSON CANAL
12. PENNSYLVANIA MAIN LINE CANAL
13. SUSQUEHANNA & TIDE WATER CANAL
14. DELAWARE CANAL
15. LEHIGH NAVIGATION
16. SCHUYLKILL NAVIGATION
17. UNION CANAL
18. MORRIS CANAL
19. DELAWARE & RARITAN CANAL
20. CHESAPEAKE & DELAWARE CANAL
21. CHESAPEAKE & OHIO CANAL
22. JAMES RIVER & KANAWHA CANAL
23. DISMAL SWAMP CANAL
24. SANTEE CANAL
25. OHIO & ERIE CANAL
26. MIAMI & ERIE CANAL
27. MUSKINGUM NAVIGATION
28. HOCKING CANAL
29. LOUISVILLE & PORTLAND CANAL
30. WHITE RIVER CANAL
31. WABASH & ERIE CANAL
32. ILLINOIS & MICHIGAN CANAL

1-001

1-001. Map of the principal canal and water navigations of the United States as planned or constructed ca. 1835.

1-002. Middlesex Canal, North Billerica, Massachusetts. Arthur C. Haskell, photographer, ca. 1930s. P & P, HABS, MASS,9-____,2-1.

An early New England canal, the company was incorporated in 1789 and the canal completed in 1808. It operated from 1809 until 1852. It was a small canal with a prism 30 feet wide at the surface, 20 feet wide at the bottom, and 3 feet deep.

1-003. Pier and abutments, Maple Meadow Brook Aqueduct, Middlesex Canal, Wilmington, Massachusetts. Arthur C. Haskell, photographer, ca. 1930s. P & P, HABS, MASS,9-____,6-1.

Loammi Baldwin planned and built eight aqueducts for the Middlesex Canal. The masonry piers and abutments seen here supported a wooden trough, long since deteriorated, that carried the canal and towpath over the stream.

1-002

1-003

1-004

1-004. Canal office, Middlesex Canal, Middlesex Village, Lowell, Massachusetts. Arthur C. Haskell, photographer, ca. 1930s. P & P, HABS, MASS,9-____,9-1.

1-005. Pier and abutments, Shawsheen Aqueduct, Middlesex Canal, Wilmington-Billerica, Massachusetts. Arthur C. Haskell, photographer, ca. 1930s. P & P, HABS, MASS,9-____,7-1.

The largest of the eight aqueducts on the Middlesex Canal, the Shawsheen Aqueduct was 188 feet long and 30–35 feet above the Shawsheen River. As at the Maple Meadow Brook Aqueduct, a wooden trough supported by masonry piers and abutments carried the canal prism and towpath.

1-005

1-006. Blackstone Canal at the rear of Charles Street, Providence, Rhode Island. Jack E. Boucher, photographer, 1971. P & P, HAER, RI,4-PROV,173-4.

1-007. Lock 24, Blackstone Canal, Millville, Massachusetts. Martin Stupich, photographer, September 1987. P & P, HAER, MASS, 14-MIL,V,2-5.

The route for the Blackstone Canal was surveyed by Benjamin Wright, chief engineer of the Erie Canal. Work began in 1825 and the canal opened in 1828. Forty-eight locks were constructed on the Blackstone Canal, the lock chambers measuring 10 feet wide and 80 feet long, to overcome a total elevation difference between Providence and Worcester of 450 feet. The canal was abandoned in 1846.

1-006

1-007

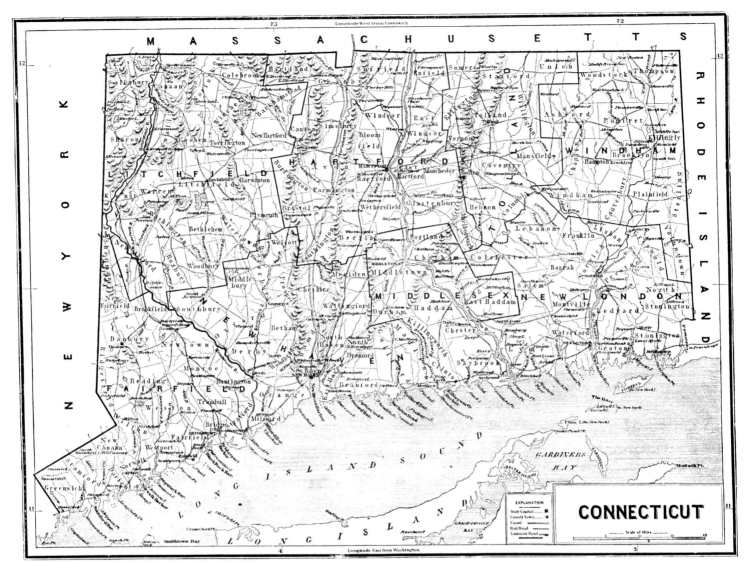

1-008

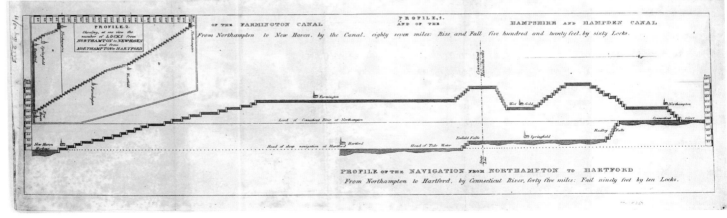

1-009

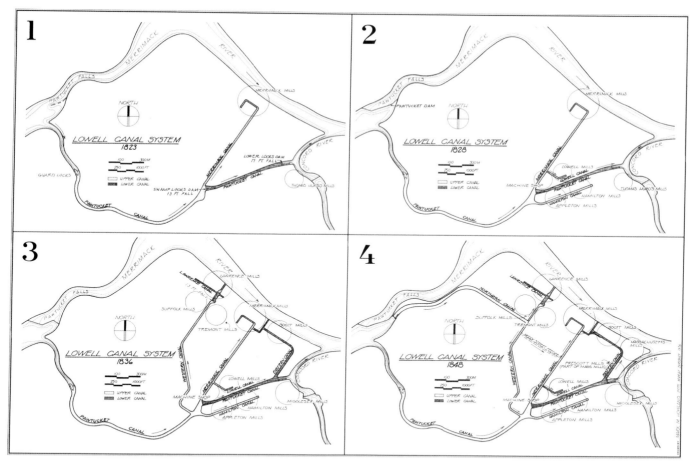

1-010

opposite

1-008. Map of Connecticut, showing the Farmington Canal adjacent to the Connecticut River. From Morse and Breese, *Maps for an Emerging Nation*, ca. 1842. G & M, neg. no. 998.

Begun in 1825, the Farmington Canal was completed by 1828 and operational through 1848.

1-009. Profile of the navigation from Northampton, Massachusetts, to New Haven, Connecticut, 1835. LC-TC624 .C8P7.

Canal engineers used profiles to show the changes in elevation requiring locks, exaggerating the vertical distance in the drawing in relationship to the horizontal distance. This early profile shows the changes in elevation of the Farmington Canal from New Haven to the Connecticut–Massachusetts state line and the Hampshire and Hampden Canal from the state line to Northampton, Massachusetts. Sixty locks were required to accommodate the 520-foot rise/fall in elevation in the 87 miles between New Haven and Northampton.

this page

1-010. Evolution of the canal system at Lowell, Massachusetts. Mark M. Howland, Margy Chrisney, delineators, 1975–76. P & P, HAER MA-1, sheet no. 2.

The Pawtucket Canal was a very early New England canal. Originally constructed in 1797, its one-and-a-half-mile channel connected the Merrimack River to the Concord River (1). It was converted and extended into several canals to power the machinery of the mills at Lowell (2, 3, 4).

New York, Pennsylvania, New Jersey

Following the end of the War of 1812, state-promoted canals in New York and Pennsylvania dominated canal construction in the middle Atlantic States. The goal was to open navigation from the coastal cities across the Appalachian Mountains to the Midwest. New York had the advantage of the Hudson River, which provided water access through the Appalachian chain. With the completion of the Erie Canal in 1825, New York State set about developing a statewide canal network to provide feeder lines to the main stem of the Erie.

A single canal could not be constructed across the state of Pennsylvania. Rather, a system of canals and railroads was constructed to link Philadelphia to Pittsburgh (1-042), which became known as the Pennsylvania Main Line (1-044–1-047; see also 2-108 and 2-109). As in New York State, Pennsylvania developed feeder canals to the Main Line, such as up the North Branch of the Susquehanna (1-048–1-051; see also IN-012) and up the West Branch of the Susquehanna (1-052 and 1-053; see also 2-015 and 2-050), the Delaware Canal, and others. Private companies also built canals: the Delaware and Hudson hauled coal from northeast Pennsylvania across lower New York to the Hudson River (1-040 and 1-041; see also 2-012, 2-028, 2-037, 2-038, 2-043, 2-064, 2-066, and 2-088–2-095); the Schuylkill River navigation (1-054) began at the Fairmount Water Works in Philadelphia (see IN-009 and IN-010); the Union Canal connected the Schuylkill River with the Susquehanna (1-055–1-061; see also IN-061); the Lehigh River navigation loaded coal in Mauch Chunk (see IN-022) and transported it to Easton on the Delaware River (1-063–1-068; see also IN-049; 2-053, 2-054, 2-127, 2-128); the small Wiconisco Canal brought coal to the Susquehanna River (1-062); and the Conewago Canal in York Haven, the first canal to be built in Pennsylvania, opened the Susquehanna to river commerce by providing a route around Conewago Falls.

New Jersey's canals were privately owned (1-069), bringing coal from the coal fields of northeast Pennsylvania to the New York City market via the Morris Canal (see IN-021 and IN-062 and section 3) and the Delaware and Raritan Canal (1-070 and 1-071; see also 2-018, 2-029, 2-035, 2-058–2-061, 2-107, 2-118, 2-122).

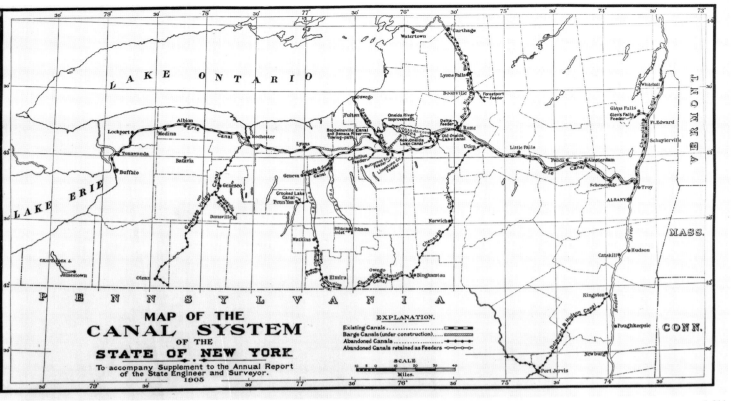

1-011. Map of the Canal System of the State of New York, from Noble E. Whitford, *History of the Canal System of the State of New York (1905)*. LC Suppl. TC624 .N7 A1.

The Erie Canal stretched 363 miles from Albany to Buffalo. New York State constructed an extensive network of feeder canals to convey commerce to the Erie. The Champlain Canal provided access from Whitehall on Lake Champlain to Troy, New York, and then to Albany, a distance of 63 miles. The Black River Canal extended 35 miles north from Rome, New York, to the High Falls on the Black River and an additional 42 miles of river improvement from High Falls to Carthage, New York. The Chenango Canal began at the Erie Canal near Utica, New York, and ran 97 miles south to Birmingham, New York, on the Susquehanna River. Later it was extended to the New York/Pennsylvania border by the Chenango Extension Canal. The Oswego Canal, some 38 miles long (almost half being river navigation), connected Lake Ontario, at Oswego, New York, with the Erie Canal, near Syracuse, New York. The Chemung Canal flowed southward 23 miles from the headwaters of Seneca Lake to Elmira, New York, on the Chemung River. An additional 13 miles of navigable water on the Chemung River brought the total length of this waterway to 36 miles. The Cayoga and Seneca Canal ran 23 miles from Geneva on Seneca Lake to Montezuma on the Erie Canal, consisting of one-half canal and one-half river navigation. The Crooked Lake Canal connected Crooked Lake, near Penn Yan, New York, to the outlet at Seneca Lakes, a distance of 8 miles. And the Genesee Valley Canal extended 120 miles southward from Rochester, on the Erie Canal, to Olean, in the southern part of New York.

Privately owned canals were also constructed in New York State. The Delaware and Hudson Canal, for example, carried coal from Pennsylvania to the Hudson River—82 miles of the canal were in New York and 26 miles in Pennsylvania. Other states admired not just the Erie Canal but also the overall canal system developed by the State of New York.

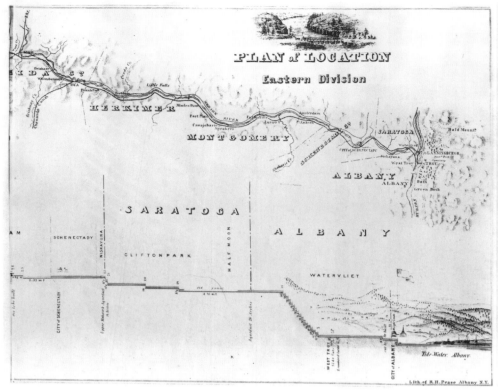

1-012

1-013

1-014

this page

1-012. Plan and profile of the Eastern Division, Erie Canal. H. C. Seymour, senior engineer; J.P. Goodsell, resident engineer; C. A. Olmsted, division engineer; David Vaughan, draftsman; R. H. Pease, lithographer, 1851. P & P, HAER, NY,1-COHO,5A-11.

1-013. Entrance to the Erie Canal from the Hudson River, from *Frank Leslie's Illustrated Newspaper*, November 22, 1856. MRC, Leslie's: Microfilm 02282.

1-014. Erie Canal at Little Falls, New York. William Henry Jackson, photographer, ca. 1880–97. P & P, DPCC, LC-D418-7626.

opposite

1-015. Erie Canal at Little Falls, New York. W. H. Bartlett, delineator. From Nathaniel Parker Willis, *American Scenery* (1840). RBSCD, E165. W73.

1-016. Erie Canal near Little Falls, New York. W. H. Bartlett, delineator. From Nathaniel Parker Willis, *American Scenery* (1840). RBSCD, E165. W73.

1-015

1-016

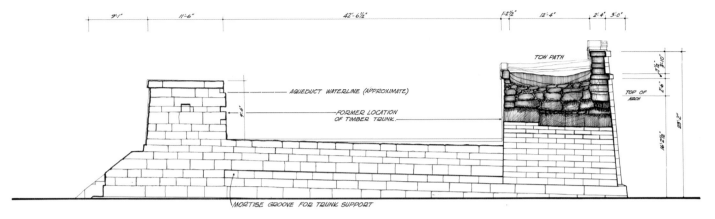

AQUEDUCT WATERLINE (APPROXIMATE)

FORMER LOCATION
OF TIMBER TRUNK.

TOW PATH

TOP OF
ARCH

MORTISE GROOVE FOR TRUNK SUPPORT

SECTION LOOKING AT PIER 9

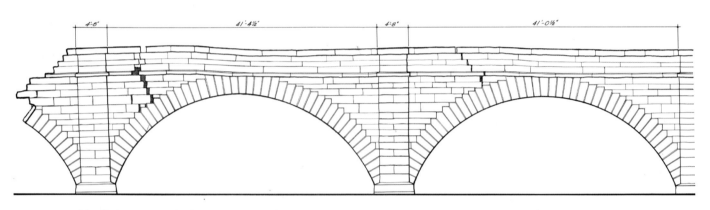

VOUSSOIRS: SMOOTH FACED DIMENSION STONE
REMAINING STRUCTURE: ROUGH POINTED DIMENSION STONE.

PARTIAL WEST ELEVATION LOOKING AT PIERS 8 & 9

1-017

1-017. Section of Pier 9 and elevation of
Piers 8 and 9, Schoharie Aqueduct, Erie
Canal, Fort Hunter Vic., New York. David
Bouse, delineator, 1969. P & P, HAER NY-6,
sheet no. 3.

1-018

1-019

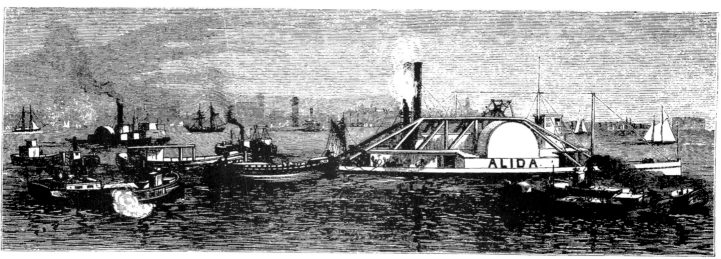

1-020

1-018. Erie Canal at Clinton Square, Syracuse, New York, ca. 1905. P & P, DPCC, LC-D4-18733.

1-019. Tour of the Erie Canal: Buffalo Jack. E. A. Abbey, delineator. From *Harper's New Monthly Magazine*, December 1873. LC, Harper's: AP2 .H3.

In 1873 a writer and artist from *Harper's New Monthly Magazine* took passage on a canal boat from New York City to Buffalo to gain insight into the lives of the 28,000 people who worked on the Erie Canal and its surroundings. This and the following illustrations are from the article in *Harper's* that detailed a seven-day canal trip from New York to Buffalo. Buffalo Jack was one of the helmsmen on the canal boat.

1-020. Tour of the Erie Canal: Making Up a Tow. E. A. Abbey, delineator. From *Harper's New Monthly Magazine*, December 1873. LC, Harper's: AP2 .H3.

The canal boat on which the *Harper's* writer and artist booked passage was first towed from New York City up the Hudson River to the entrance of the Erie Canal near Albany, across from Troy. *Niagara*, a steamer similar to the *Alida*, towed their canal boat, along with twenty to thirty boats, upriver at a speed of two miles per hour.

AT THE SHIPPING AGENT'S.

1-021

"THE CAPTAIN."

1-023

1-022

"BRAIN-WORK."

1-024

opposite

1- 021. Tour of the Erie Canal: At the Shipping Agent's. E. A. Abbey, delineator. From *Harper's New Monthly Magazine*, December 1873. LC, Harper's: AP2 .H3.

1-022. Tour of the Erie Canal: The Cabin. E. A. Abbey, delineator. From *Harper's New Monthly Magazine*, December 1873. LC, Harper's: AP2 .H3.

1-023. Tour of the Erie Canal: The Captain. E. A. Abbey, delineator. From *Harper's New Monthly Magazine*, December 1873. LC, Harper's: AP2 .H3.

1- 024. Tour of the Erie Canal: Brain-Work. E. A. Abbey, delineator. From *Harper's New Monthly Magazine*, December 1873. LC, Harper's: AP2 .H3.

this page

1-025. Tour of the Erie Canal: In the Forecastle. E. A. Abbey, delineator. From *Harper's New Monthly Magazine*, December 1873. LC, Harper's: AP2 .H3.

Access to the forecastle was by a 3-foot-square hatch in the deck. The men slept in the forecastle, described by the writer as "the smallest sleeping compartments in which men were ever herded." Here a helmsman, Buffalo Jack (left), is offering the writer a smell of his hair oil.

1-026. Tour of the Erie Canal: Wash-Day on the Canal Boats. E. A. Abbey, delineator. From *Harper's New Monthly Magazine*, December 1873. LC, Harper's: AP2 .H3.

According to the *Harper's* writer, the boatmen's duties were light while in tow on the Hudson River but the women were busy all day. The women wore dresses of brown calico with red sunbonnets that hid their features.

1-025

WASH-DAY ON THE CANAL-BOATS.

1-026

1-027

1-027. Tour of the Erie Canal: Entrance to the Canal at Troy. E. A. Abbey, delineator. From *Harper's New Monthly Magazine*, December 1873. LC, Harper's: AP2 .H3.

1-028. Tour of the Erie Canal: Canal Smithy. E. A. Abbey, delineator. From *Harper's New Monthly Magazine*, December 1873. LC, Harper's: AP2 .H3.

Once on the Erie Canal from the Hudson River, the canal boat had to ascend sixteen locks only a few hundred feet apart. Each of these locks was lined with wooden buildings used for trade with the boatmen. Past the locks, said the writer from *Harper's*, the canal boat on the Erie Canal entered a "dream-land of pastoral beauty."

1-029. Tour of the Erie Canal: The Raft. E. A. Abbey, delineator. From *Harper's New Monthly Magazine*, December 1873. LC, Harper's: AP2 .H3.

1-030. Tour of the Erie Canal: The Tramp. E. A. Abbey, delineator. From *Harper's New Monthly Magazine*, December 1873. LC, Harper's: AP2 .H3.

The accompanying text read: "The Canal Boat Captain yelled to the tramp, 'Beatin' yourn way down?' 'No Sir!,' replied the tramp, 'Can't beat the people in this locality much.' 'Where did you come from?' said the Captain. 'Saginaw; and walked eight hundred miles for a job,' said the tramp, ending the conversation."

1-028

CANAL SMITHY.

1-029

THE TRAMP.

1-030

1-031. Tour of the Erie Canal: Schenectady. E. A. Abbey, delineator. From *Harper's New Monthly Magazine*, December 1873. LC, Harper's: AP2 .H3.

1-032. Tour of the Erie Canal: Canal Grocery Store. E. A. Abbey, delineator. From *Harper's New Monthly Magazine*, December 1873. LC, Harper's: AP2 .H3.

1-033. Tour of the Erie Canal: Scow-Yard. E. A. Abbey, delineator. From *Harper's New Monthly Magazine*, December 1873. LC, Harper's: AP2 .H3.

The scow was the lowest class of vessel on the canal. Scows conveyed the least expensive forms of bulk cargo, such as sand, gravel, and coal. They were the cheapest boats to build; one observer described them as "a hole in the water lined with wood." The *Harper's* writer explained, "If a boatmen has a *bête noire*, it is a scow; if he would wound a rival, he calls his boat a scow; and to all that is despicable and contemptible he rarely applies any other than that contemned name."

1-031

1-032

1-033

1-034

1-035

1-034. Tour of the Erie Canal: Laid Up for the Winter, Atlantic Basin, Brooklyn. E. A. Abbey, delineator. From *Harper's New Monthly Magazine*, December 1873. LC, Harper's: AP2 .H3.

1-035. Canal boats in winter quarters in New York, ca. 1900–6. P & P, DPCC, LC-D4-16199.

The Erie Canal froze during the winter months. Canal boats were laid up in New York, Buffalo, or elsewhere.

1-036. Champlain Canal. J. P. Goodsell, Division Engineer; David Vaughan, draftsman, 1857. P & P, HAER, NY,46-WAFO,1-9.

1-037. Connection of the Champlain Canal with the Erie Canal, Waterford, New York. P & P, HAER, NY,46-WAFO,1-7.

1-038. Connection of the Champlain Canal with the Erie Canal, Waterford, New York. P & P, HAER, NY,46-WAFO,1-8.

The Champlain Canal connected White Hall on Lake Champlain with Albany. Constructed in conjunction with the Erie Canal, the Champlain Canal was completed by 1823. Twenty-one locks overcame a rise/fall of some 188 feet.

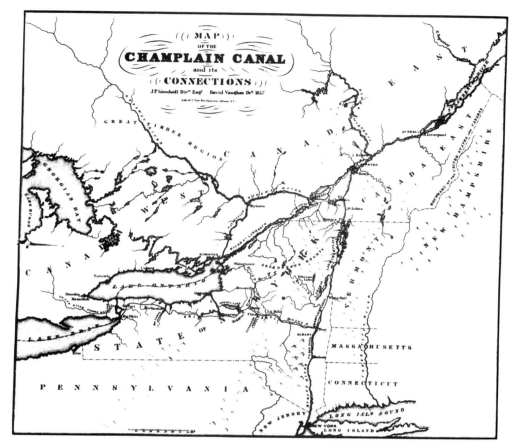

1-036

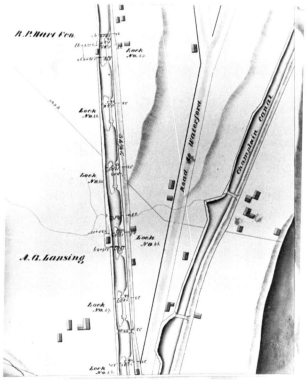

1-037

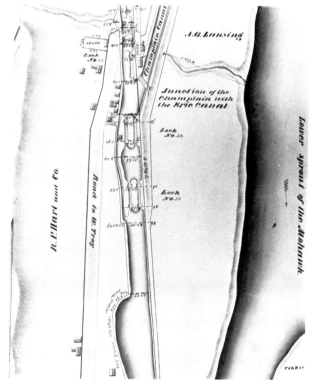

1-038

1-039

1-039. Waterford Locks, Champlain Canal, Waterford, New York. Jack E. Boucher, photographer, August 1969. P & P, HAER, NY, 46-WAFO,1-1.

1-040. DePuy House and lock, Delaware and Hudson Canal, High Falls, New York. Stanley P. Mixon, photographer, July 1940. P & P, HABS, NY,56-HIFA,1-1.

DePuy House was constructed before the canal, in 1797; the lock was built in 1825 and abandoned in 1899.

1-040

1-041. Delaware and Hudson Canal and Gravity Transportation System. Copy of an 1866 map, ca. 1923. From *A Century of Progress: History of the Delaware & Hudson Company 1823–1923.* P & P, HAER, PA,52-LACK,1-27.

1-042. Pennsylvania Main Line Canal. Paul R. Pinchot, delineator, 1988. P & P, HAER PA-106, sheet no. 1.

The Pennsylvania Main Line Canal was the State of Pennsylvania's response to the success of the Erie Canal. A canal/railroad link between Philadelphia and Pittsburgh, from east to west, it consisted of: the Columbia-Philadelphia Railroad, 81 miles long, connecting Philadelphia to the Main Division of the Pennsylvania Canal at Columbia,

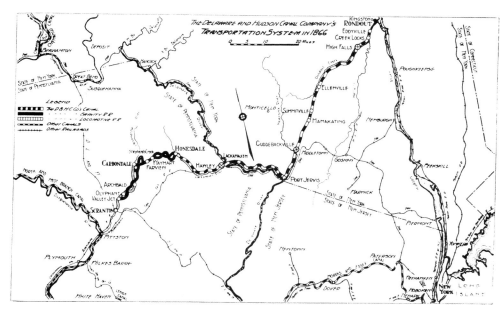

1-041

1-042

Pennsylvania; the Main Division (here identified as the Eastern and Juniata divisions), 172 miles long to Hollidaysburg, Pennsylvania, where it connected with the Allegheny Portage Railroad, 37 miles long across the Allegheny Mountains to the Western Division at Johnstown, Pennsylvania; and the Western Division, 104 miles to Pittsburgh.

1-043. Staircase of Locks 39–43, Black River Canal, Boonville Vic., New York. Jack E. Boucher, photographer, June 1970. P & P, HAER, NY,33-BOONV.V,1A-3.

Note the anchor and collar mounted on top of the coping wall of the lock. It held the upper end of the quoin post, the hinge for the lock gate.

1-043

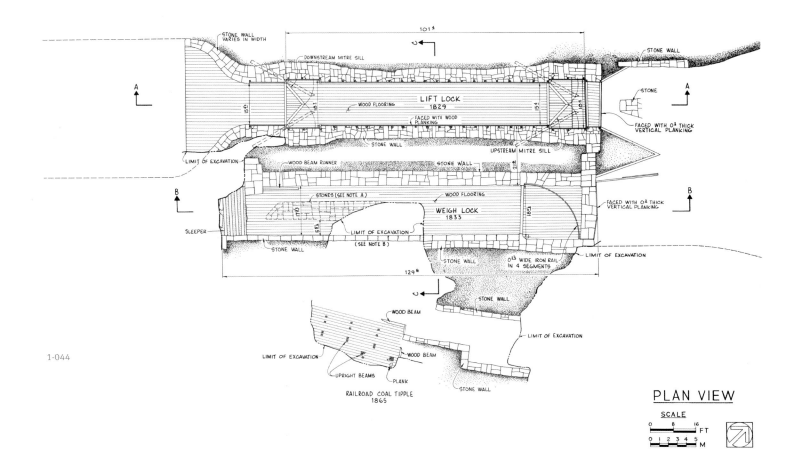

PLAN VIEW

SCALE

1-044

1-044. Plan of Allegheny lift lock 4 and weigh lock, Pennsylvania Canal, north shore of the Allegheny River, Pittsburgh, Pennsylvania. Paul R. Pinchot, delineator, 1988. P & P, HAER PA-106, sheet no. 2, detail.

Weigh locks weighed boats, providing the tare or empty weight, then the weight with cargo, in order to determine the amount of cargo carried and therefore the amount of toll to be paid.

1-045. Perspective of Allegheny lift lock 4 and weigh lock, Pennsylvania Canal, north shore of the Allegheny River, Pittsburgh, Pennsylvania. Paul R. Pinchot, delineator, 1988. P & P, HAER PA-106, sheet no. 4.

1-045

1-046. Main Division of the Pennsylvania Canal, near Huntington, Pennsylvania. A. Harral, illustrator. From William Cullen Bryant (ed.), *Picturesque America, or, The Land We Live In* (1894). LC-E168 .P5893.

1-047. Lilly Culvert at Allegheny Portage Railroad, Pennsylvania Main Line Canal, Lilly, Pennsylvania. Joseph Elliott, photographer, summer 1997. P & P, HAER, PA,11-LIL,1-2.

Constructed in 1832 and in use until 1857, Lilly Culvert was part of the Allegheny Portage Railroad system designed to haul canal boats over the Allegheny Mountains by means of ten inclined planes and stationary steam engines. Like most masonry canal structures, the foundation was on a wooden grillage, as shown here (compare 2-108–2-109; 4-114).

1-046

1-047

1-048

1-048. Hanging rock, road, railroad, canal, and Susquehanna River, North Branch of the Pennsylvania Canal near Danville, Pennsylvania, ca. 1890–1901. P & P, DPCC, LC-D4-12241.

The North Branch of the Pennsylvania Canal ran along the north shore of the North Branch of the Susquehanna from Northumberland, Pennsylvania, to about two miles below Wilkes-Barre, Pennsylvania, where it crossed the river and continued to the mouth of Lackawanna Creek, a total of 72 miles. An extension to the New York State line was begun in 1838 and opened in 1856.

1-049. North Branch of the Pennsylvania Canal, Hunlock, Pennsylvania, from William Cullen Bryant (ed.), *Picturesque America, or, The Land We Live In* (1894). LC-E168 .P5893.

1-050. Below the dam on the North Branch of the Pennsylvania Canal, Nanticoke, Pennsylvania, from William Cullen Bryant (ed.), *Picturesque America, or, The Land We Live In* (1894). LC-E168 .P5893.

1-051. North Branch of the Pennsylvania Canal, approaching Hunlock, Pennsylvania, ca. 1900–1906. P & P, DPCC, LC-D4-12212.

1-052

1-053. Interior of lockhouse, Lock 34, West Branch Canal, Lock Haven Vic., Pennsylvania. Rob Tucher, photographer, October 1991. P & P, HAER, PA,18-LOKHA.V,4B-5.

1-053

1-052. Lockhouse, Lock 34, West Branch Canal, Lock Haven Vic., Pennsylvania. Rob Tucher, photographer, October 1991. P & P, HAER, PA,18-LOKHA.V,4B-2.

1-053. Interior of lockhouse, Lock 34, West Branch Canal, Lock Haven Vic., Pennsylvania. Rob Tucher, photographer, October 1991. P & P, HAER, PA,18-LOKHA.V,4B-5.

The West Branch Canal of the Pennsylvania Canal extended 73 miles from Northumberland, Pennsylvania, west along the northern bank of the Susquehanna's West Branch to Farrandsville, Pennsylvania. The canal operated from 1834 to 1889. This lockhouse was constructed ca. 1834.

1-054. Lock 12, Bausman's Lock, Schuylkill Canal, Schuylkill Haven, Pennsylvania. Will Dunn, photographer, September 1982. P & P, HAER, PA,54-SCHUYH, 1A-1.

Built 1820–21, Bausman's Lock was part of the 108-mile-long Schuylkill Canal and river navigation connecting the towns of the upper Schuylkill River with Philadelphia. Bausman's Lock functioned until 1888.

1-055. Lock 36, Union Canal, Bernville Vic., Pennsylvania. Army Corps of Engineers photographer, ca. 1976. P & P, HAER, PA, 6-BERN. V,7-10.

This photograph shows the location of the anchor-and-collar mount that held the vertical quoin post, the lock gate's hinge. The quoin post would have been placed vertically in the space at lower right.

1-054

1-055

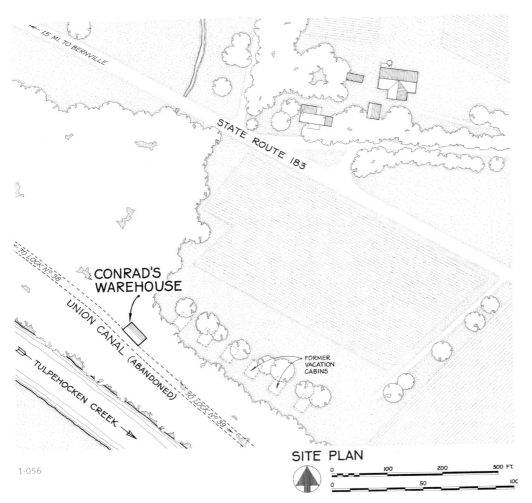

1-056. Site plan of Conrad's Warehouse, Union Canal, Bernville Vic., Pennsylvania. Robert Clarke, delineator, 1976. P & P, HAER PA-57, sheet no. 1, detail.

Constructed ca. 1830 between Locks 38 and 39 on the Union Canal, the canal warehouse is a rare survivor of the canal era in southeastern Pennsylvania.

1-057. Lock 37, Union Canal, Bernville Vic., Pennsylvania. Army Corps of Engineers photographer, ca. 1976. P & P, HAER, PA,6-BERN. V,7-16.

The Union Canal was 80 miles long and connected the Schuylkill River in the vicinity of Reading, Pennsylvania, with Middletown, Pennsylvania, on the Susquehanna. Completed in 1827, it had ninety-three locks of unusually small dimension—the lock chambers were 75 feet long and only 7½ feet wide. These small locks limited the canal to vessels with a capacity of approximately 25 tons—much less than the vessels of the Schuylkill River Navigation or the Pennsylvania Canal, which typically carried canal boats with a capacity of 60 tons or more.

1-056

1-057

1-058

1-059

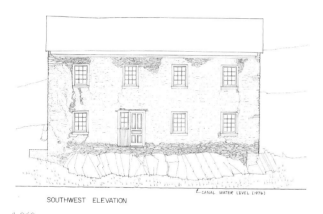

SOUTHWEST ELEVATION

1-060

1-061

1-058. Detail of Lock 37, Union Canal, Bernville Vic., Pennsylvania.
Army Corps of Engineers photographer, ca. 1976. P & P, HAER, PA,6-BERN. V,7-14.

Remnants of the wooden lock gate that was bolted to the masonry wall are visible.

1-059. Exterior, Conrad's Warehouse, Union Canal, Bernville Vic., Pennsylvania, ca. 1976.
P & P, HAER, PA,6-BERN. V,6-1.

1-060. Exterior elevation, Conrad's Warehouse, Union Canal, Bernville Vic., Pennsylvania.
Perry Benson, delineator, 1976. P & P, HAER PA–57, sheet no. 2, detail.

1-061. Interior, Conrad's Warehouse, Union Canal, Bernville Vic., Pennsylvania, ca. 1970s.
P & P, HAER, PA,6-BERN. V,6-6.

1-062

1-063

1-062. Aqueduct 3, Wiconisco Canal, Halifax Vic., Pennsylvania. Jet T. Lowe, photographer, 1999. P & P, HAER, PA,22-HAFX.V,1-2.

The Wiconisco Canal was a small, privately owned canal that carried coal from the Lykes Valley at Millersville, Pennsylvania, 12 miles to the eastern bank of the Susquehanna River at Clarks Ferry, Pennsylvania, where it met the Eastern Division of the Pennsylvania Canal. The canal continued to operate until 1890. Aqueduct 3 crossing Powell Creek, completed ca. 1840, was the largest of the three aqueducts on the canal.

1-063. Outlet lock, Lehigh River Navigation, Easton, Pennsylvania. Jet T. Lowe, photographer, 1979. P & P, HAER, PA,48-EATO,6A-1.

This outlet lock permitted boats to leave the Lehigh River Navigation, cross the Delaware River, and enter the Morris Canal on the Phillipsburg, New Jersey, side of the river. A masonry lock, it was covered with a concrete parging, or coating, at some date after its construction.

1-064. Saquit silk mill, south bank of the Lehigh Canal, Bethlehem, Pennsylvania. Jet T. Lowe, photographer, 1979. P & P, HAER, PA,39-BETH,3-1.

Mills frequently were constructed alongside or near canals. Surplus canal water provided the water power needed to drive the mills' machinery. The canals also provided transport for the mills' raw materials and finished products.

1-065. Detail of wood sheathing over the crib dam, Hamilton Street Dam, Lehigh Canal, Allentown, Pennsylvania. Robert G. Miller, photographer, July 1983. P & P, HAER, PA,39-ALLEN,3A-5.

Hamilton Street Dam is the seventh of eight dams constructed on the lower Lehigh River Navigation to form lock-and-pond navigation, permitting canal boats to navigate that section of the river. The dams were typically 6 to 16 feet high and constructed of wood "cribs" filled with stone and sheathed in wood (compare 2-127–2-130).

1-064

1-065

1-066

1-066. Guard lock 8 and lockhouse, Lehigh Canal, Glendon, Pennsylvania. Jet T. Lowe, photographer, 1979. P & P, HAER, PA,48-GLEN,2A-1.

The lock chamber (foreground), constructed in 1829, is 22 feet wide by 100 feet long. Here the lock gates are not operated by balance beams but by mechanisms, located on either side of the gate, which pulled the gates open or pushed them shut through struts.

1-067. Aquashicola Aqueduct ruins, Lehigh Canal, Allentown, Pennsylvania. Jet T. Lowe, photographer, 1969. P & P, HAER, PA,13-TOWLO,2-1.

One of four aqueducts built by the Lehigh Coal and Navigation Company, this consisted of a wooden trough and towpath supported on stone piers constructed on wood-crib foundations across Aquashicola Creek.

1-068. Lehigh Canal and environs, Walnutport, Pennsylvania. Jet T. Lowe, photographer, 1979. P& P, HABS, PA,48-WALNPO,3-1.

1-067

1-068

1-069. Mid-Atlantic states from Tanner's 1830 map, "Map of the Canals & Railroads of the United States." From George Armroyd, *A Connected View of The Whole Internal Navigation of The United States . . . With a Sheet Map* (1830). LC-TC623 .A72, detail.

This detail from Tanner's map shows the Morris Canal across the top of New Jersey. This canal was begun in 1825 and connected Phillipsburg, on the Delaware River opposite Easton, Pennsylvania, with Newark, New Jersey, a distance of 101 miles. The Delaware and Raritan Canal connected Bordentown, New Jersey, on the Delaware River, with New Brunswick, New Jersey, on the Raritan River, a distance of 37 miles. The Delaware and Raritan Canal was begun in 1832 and completed in 1840.

1-070. Ruins of a canal barge in the outer lock of the Delaware and Raritan Canal, New Brunswick, New Jersey. Jack E. Boucher, photographer, May 1978. P & P, HAER, NJ,12-NEBRO,18-7.

1-071. Outlet lock of the Delaware and Raritan Canal, Raritan River, New Brunswick, New Jersey. Jack E. Boucher, photographer, May 1978. P & P, HAER, NJ,12-NEBRO,18-1.

1-069

1-070

1-071

THE SOUTH
Delaware, Maryland, Virginia , North Carolina, South Carolina, Georgia

Before the Revolutionary War, Virginia and Maryland had prepared plans to use the James and Potomac Rivers as routes to the Ohio Territories (see IN-003). After the Revolutionary War a series of early canal projects were undertaken in the South: George Washington initiated the Potomac Canal in 1795; Benjamin Henry Latrobe proposed an extension to this canal to Washington, D.C., in 1802 (1-093 and 2-077); the State of Maryland began construction of a 9-mile canal, the Susquehanna Canal, along the northern shore of the Susquehanna River in 1783 (1-079, upper right), completed in 1801; in 1803 Latrobe was hired to design the Chesapeake and Delaware Canal (1-079, upper right, 1-072 and 1-073, see also 2-133 and 2-134); in 1793 construction began on the Dismal Swamp Canal (see 1-079, lower right, and 1-092); and in South Carolina the Santee Canal, first proposed in 1775, was opened in 1800 (1-100–1-101; see also IN-059 and IN-060). The success of the Erie Canal reinvigorated the James River and Kanawha Canal (1-080–1-087; see also IN-019, IN-064; 2-080) and led to the development of the Chesapeake and Ohio Canal Company to succeed the older Potomac Canal. Feeders to the Chesapeake and Ohio Canal were constructed, such as the Alexandria Canal (1-089–1-091; see also 2-075; 4-015–4-021); the Washington City Canal (1-094–1-097; see also 2-047–2-049); and the Goose Creek Canal (see 2-004). The Maryland Cross-cut Canal (1-078) was planned as a feeder canal but never constructed. In South Carolina following the end of the War of 1812, an ambitious project of river improvement and canal development was undertaken by the state (1-099).

opposite

1-072. Site plan of the Chesapeake and Delaware Canal Pump House, Chesapeake and Delaware Canal, Chesapeake City, Maryland. Janet Hochuli, delineator, 1977. P & P, HAER MD–39, sheet no. 1, detail.

The Chesapeake and Delaware Canal was originally constructed as a summit level canal—i.e., a canal that crosses a summit from one watershed to another. During the dry season there were continual problems keeping the canal watered at the summit, so steam-powered pumps were installed (see 2-133 and 2-134).

1-073. Basin and proposed northern course of Chesapeake and Delaware Canal, Elk River Vic., Maryland. Benjamin Henry Latrobe, delineator, 1803. G & M, neg. no. 1044.

Benjamin Henry Latrobe was engaged in the early planning of the Chesapeake and Delaware Canal, 1803 to 1806. His plans were not constructed; a more southerly route for the canal opened in 1829.

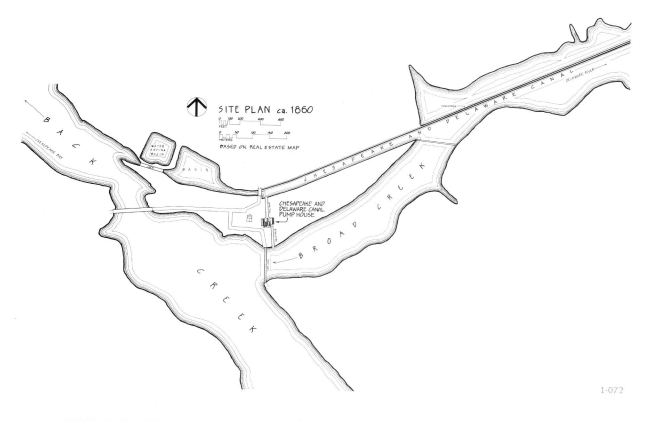

SITE PLAN ca. 1860

BASED ON REAL ESTATE MAP

1-072

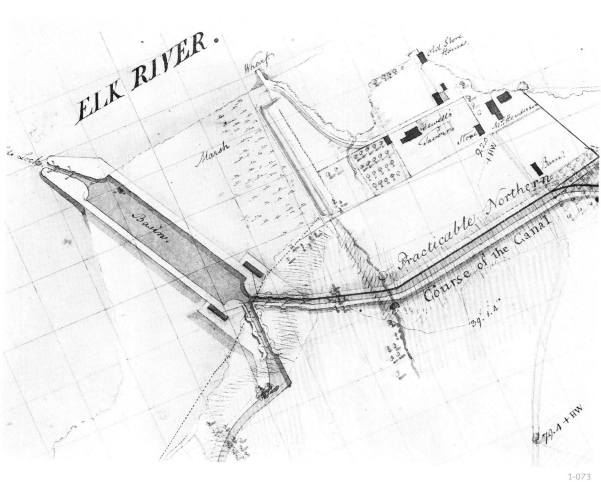

1-073

1-074

1-075

1-076

1-074. Coxey's Army on the Chesapeake and Ohio Canal, Maryland, April 1894. P & P, LC-USZ62-92477.

Jacob Coxey, an Ohio businessman, led an "Industrial Army" to Washington, D.C., in 1894 to protest the federal government's inaction in the face of a depression and to demand that the government ease unemployment by creating jobs to build roads and other public works. The Chesapeake and Ohio Canal was one means of transportation that Coxey's Army utilized to get to Washington.

1-075. Monocacy Aqueduct, Chesapeake and Ohio Canal, Dickerson Vic., Maryland. William Henry Jackson, photographer, ca. 1892. P & P, DPCC, LC-D43-T01-1776.

The Chesapeake and Ohio Canal was begun in 1828 in Washington, D.C., and reached Cumberland, Maryland, in 1850—a distance of 184 miles. The Chesapeake and Ohio Canal Company constructed eleven aqueducts along the canal: the Monocacy Aqueduct was the largest.

1-076. Mule team and canal boat on the Conococheague Aqueduct, Chesapeake and Ohio Canal, Williamsport, Maryland, ca. 1903. P & P, DPCC, LC-D4-16566.

Aqueduct 5, the Conococheague Aqueduct, across Conococheague Creek, was the second largest of the eleven aqueducts on the Chesapeake and Ohio Canal. It was constructed 1833–34. This photograph was taken before the upstream spandrel wall failed. Compare with IN-046 and IN-047.

1-077. Dam 4 looking from Maryland toward West Virginia, Chesapeake and Ohio Canal, Sharpsburg Vic., Maryland. Jet Lowe, photographer, September 1980. P & P, HAER, WVA,2-SHEP,V,1-9.

One of the two masonry dams along the Chesapeake and Ohio Canal (for Dam 5, see 2-131), Dam 4 was constructed from 1857–61 to replace a timber crib dam from 1832–34 which was located immediately upstream. Dam 4 was initially 630 feet long between abutments and 715 feet long overall; its length increased to 810 feet in 1915 with the construction of an electric power plant, shown on the West Virginia shore. The dam is 18 feet wide at its base, 12 feet wide at the top, and 20 feet high.

1-078. Plan for the Maryland Cross Cut Canal. E. W. Bridges and F. Lucas, Jr., delineators, ca. 1823. G & M, neg. no. 1544.

In the early 1820s Baltimore was the largest exporter of flour in the United States, flour primarily received from the Susquehanna River valley. But rival merchants in Philadelphia threatened to divert the Susquehanna valley agricultural produce there. Access to the agricultural products of the Potomac River valley was seen as an answer to this threat. Beginning with Robert Mills's plan of 1820, a series of studies was planned to connect Baltimore with the Potomac River. None of these plans proved practical because of the ridge that separates Baltimore from the Potomac valley. Frustrated with their inability to develop a canal to the Potomac, the Baltimore merchants turned to a new invention: the railroad.

1-077

1-078

1-079

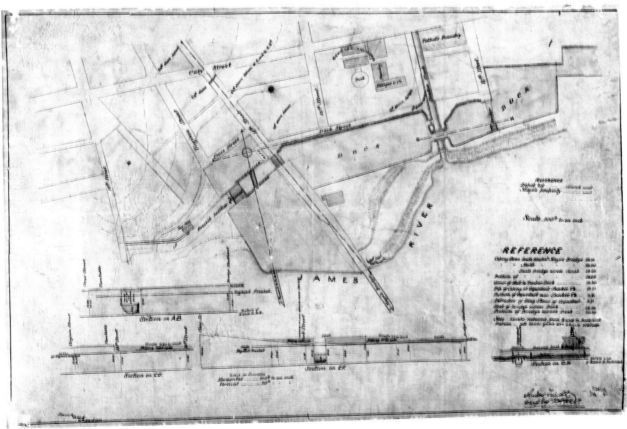

1-080

opposite

1-079. "A Map of the Internal Improvements of Virginia." Claudius Crozet, principal engineer, 1848. G & M, RR307.

The State of Virginia, through its Board of Public Works, was extremely aggressive in developing internal improvements throughout the state and in particular the main east-west route of the James River and Kanawha Canal. The canal became the nation's fourth east-west commerce route, after the Erie Canal, the Pennsylvania Main Line Canal, and the Chesapeake and Ohio Canal. Claudius Crozet was principal engineer.

1-080. Site plan and sections of the canal and docks, James River and Kanawha Canal, Richmond, Virginia. Andrew Talcott, delineator, 1851. G & M, neg. no. 2929.

this page

1-081. James River and Kanawha Canal, Richmond, Virginia. J. Filmer, illustrator. From William Cullen Bryant (ed.), *Picturesque America, or, The Land We Live In* (1894). LC-E168 .P5893.

1-082. James River and Kanawha Canal and the James River at Richmond, Virginia, as seen from above Richmond. From William Cullen Bryant (ed.), *Picturesque America, or, The Land We Live In* (1894). LC-E168 .P5893.

Compare with IN-064.

1-081

1-082

1-083

1-084

1-085

1-083. James River and Kanawha Canal with ruins of the Gallego Mills beyond, Richmond, Virginia, 1865. P & P, LC-B8171-3172.

1-084. Canal basin and James River and Kanawha Canal with Virginia State Capitol behind, Richmond, Virginia. Andrew J. Russell, photographer, 1865. P & P, LC-USZC4-7956.

1-085. African American Civil War refugees on canal boats on the James River and Kanawha Canal, Richmond, Virginia. Alexander Gardner, photographer, 1865. P & P, LC-B817-7617.

1-086. James River and Kanawha Canal and the James River above Richmond, Virginia. From William Cullen Bryant (ed.), *Picturesque America, or, The Land We Live In* (1894). LC-E168 ,P5893.

1-087. James River Kanawha Canal and the James River near the mouth of the North River, from Edward Beyer, *Album of Virginia* (1858). RBSCD, F227.B48.

1-086

1-087

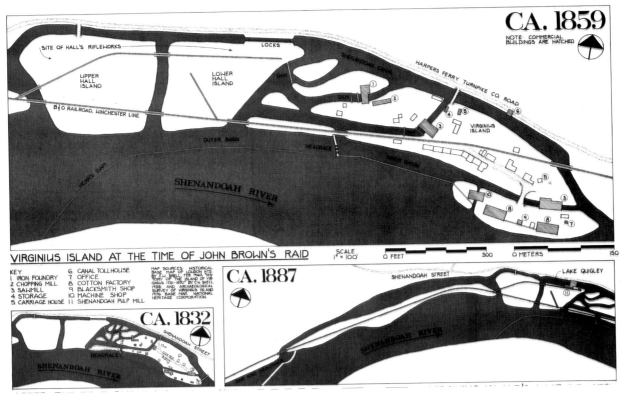

CA. 1859

NOTE: COMMERCIAL BUILDINGS ARE HATCHED

SITE OF HALL'S RIFLEWORKS

LOCKS

UPPER HALL ISLAND

LOWER HALL ISLAND

DAM

SHENANDOAH CANAL

HARPERS FERRY TURNPIKE CO. ROAD

B & O RAILROAD, WINCHESTER LINE

DAM

VIRGINIUS ISLAND

OUTER BASIN

HEARS DAM

HEADRACE

INNER BASIN

SHENANDOAH RIVER

VIRGINIUS ISLAND AT THE TIME OF JOHN BROWN'S RAID

SCALE 1" = 100'

0 FEET — 500

0 METERS — 150

KEY
1 IRON FOUNDRY
2 CHOPPING MILL
3 SAWMILL
4 STORAGE
5 CARRIAGE HOUSE
6 CANAL TOLL HOUSE
7 OFFICE
8 COTTON FACTORY
9 BLACKSMITH SHOP
10 MACHINE SHOP
11 SHENANDOAH PULP MILL

MAP SOURCES: HISTORICAL BASE MAP OF LOUDON HTS. BY C.H. SNELL, FEB. 1960, "HISTORY OF THE ISLAND OF VIRGINIUS 1751-1870" BY C.H. SNELL, 1958, AND ARCHAEOLOGICAL SURVEY OF VIRGINIUS ISLAND 1976 BASE MAP, NATIONAL HERITAGE CORPORATION

CA. 1832

SHENANDOAH STREET

HEADRACE

SHENANDOAH RIVER

CA. 1887

SHENANDOAH STREET

LAKE QUIGLEY

SHENANDOAH RIVER

1-088

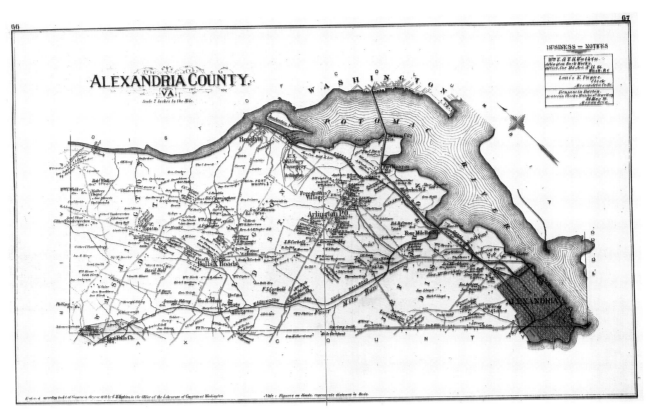

ALEXANDRIA COUNTY.

VA.

Scale 2 Inches to the Mile.

BUSINESS — NOTICES

WASHINGTON

POTOMAC RIVER

Rosslyn

U.S. Military Cemetery

Arlington

Freedmans Village

Arlington P.O.

Four Mile Run

Balls X Roads

OHIO RAILROAD

Four Mile Run

Mile Run

ALEXANDRIA

COUNTY

Falls Ch.

Note: Figures on Roads represents distances in Rods.

1-089

opposite

1-088. Evolution of the power canal at Harper's Ferry, Virginia (now West Virginia). Joanna Downs, Brian D. Bartholomew, Samuel Gaine, and Isabel Yang, delineators, 1987–88. P & P, HAER WV-35, sheet no. 2.

The original Shenandoah Canal, shown in the lower left-hand corner of this drawing, evolved into a power canal for the industries of Virginius Island, Harper's Ferry.

1-089. Map of the Alexandria Canal, Virginia. Griffith Morgan Hopkins, surveyor and compiler. From G. M. Hopkins, *Atlas of Fifteen Miles Around Washington* (1879). G & M, neg. no. 2826.

Constructed 1831–42, the Alexandria Canal connected the Chesapeake and Ohio Canal at Georgetown, Washington, D.C. (top center of the drawing), with Alexandria, Virginia (lower right), a distance of seven miles. (The canal is incorrectly identified on this map as the Chesapeake and Ohio Canal.)

this page

1-090. Hydrographic map of the Potomac River near Georgetown, Washington, D.C., showing the siting of the Potomac Aqueduct of the Alexandria Canal. Captain William Turnbull and Lieutenant Maskell C. Ewing, delineators, 1832. P & P, HAER, DC, GEO,1-1.

To connect Alexandria, Virginia, to the Chesapeake and Ohio Canal required construction of a 1,600-foot-long aqueduct (including approaches) across the Potomac River. The original siting (shown on the map as a double solid line in the center of the drawing) was established by Benjamin Wright and Nathan Roberts, engineers of the Chesapeake and Ohio Canal Company.

1-091. Potomac Aqueduct, Alexandria Canal, Georgetown, Washington, D.C. George N. Barnard, photographer, ca. 1862–65. P & P, LC-B8171-0288.

The Chesapeake and Ohio Canal, with a mule crossover bridge, is in the foreground. Captain William Turnbull constructed a wooden structure to hold the trough of the aqueduct and the towpath, which was mounted on eight masonry piers and two masonry abutments.

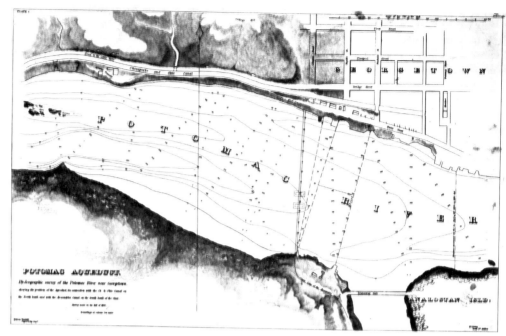

1-090

1-091

1-092

1-092. Dismal Swamp Canal, showing connections with Chesapeake Bay and Currituck, Albemarle, and Pamlico Sounds. D. S. Walton, civil engineer and delineator, 1867. G & M, G3881 .P53 1867.W3.

The 23-mile-long Dismal Swamp Canal connected Deep Creek, Virginia, with South Mills, North Carolina. Originally authorized by the Virginia Assembly in 1787, construction began in 1793 and limited navigation began in 1805. This canal provided an inland water link between Chesapeake Bay to Albemarle Sound and Pamlico Sound. Shippers could not only avoid the hazardous voyage around Cape Hatteras but also, as was the case during the Revolutionary War and the War of 1812, hostile naval vessels. Today the canal, although enlarged, still serves the same function as a link in the intracoastal waterway along the Atlantic seaboard.

1-093. Proposed Potomac Canal extension from the Potomac Canal at Little Falls, Potomac River, to the Navy Yard on the Eastern Branch (Anacostia River) at Washington, D.C. Benjamin Henry Latrobe, delineator, December 1802. G & M, G3852.W28G45 s07 .L3 Vault, section II.

This drawing shows the area immediately west of Georgetown, Washington, D.C., along the Potomac River. This canal was never constructed.

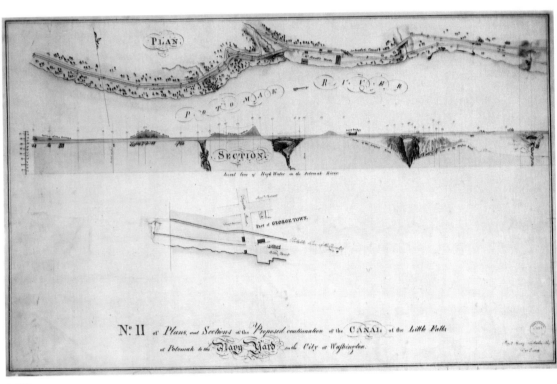

1-093

1-094. Washington City Canal, Washington, D.C. From Nicholas King, *A Map of the City of Washington* (1818). G & M, neg. no. 1080.1.

The Washington City Canal connected Tiber Creek (immediately below the White House on the map) with the Eastern Branch (Anacostia River) through a route that passed in front of the U.S. Capitol (center). Constructed 1810–12, the Washington City Canal was about a mile long. Little used commercially, it eventually turned into an open sewer and was filled in during the 1870s.

1-095. Plan of the groundwork and piling for the wood locks, Washington City Canal, Washington, D.C. Benjamin Henry Latrobe, delineator, ca. 1810. P & P, LC-USZC4-49.

Benjamin Henry Latrobe was chief engineer of the Washington City Canal and prepared a number of drawings for it, particularly the wood locks. This drawing shows the pilings at right, typically used for the foundations of canal locks. On that foundation a super-structure (at left) for the wooden canal locks would be constructed.

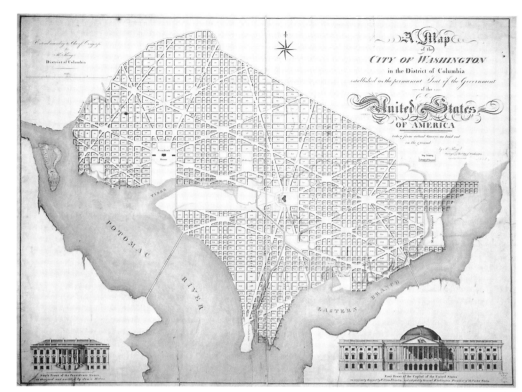

1-094

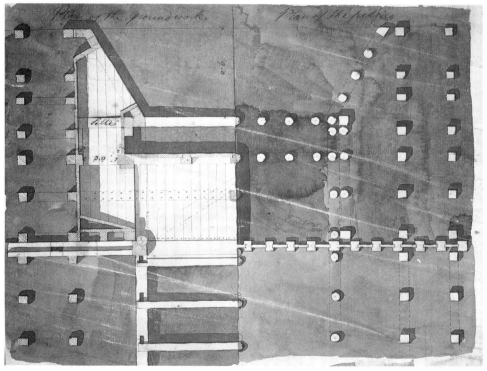

1-095

1-096

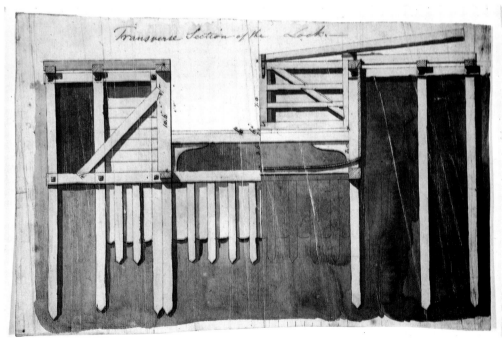

1-097

this page
1-096. Longitudinal section of the upper gate and plan of the lock floor for the wooden locks of the Washington City Canal, Washington, D.C. Benjamin Henry Latrobe, delineator, ca. 1810. P & P, LC-USZC4-48.

1-097. Transverse section of the lock, Washington City Canal, Washington, D.C. Benjamin Henry Latrobe, delineator, ca. 1810. P & P, LC-USZC4-50.

opposite
1-098. Rough hydrographic map of the North Carolina Junction Canal. William Tatham, delineator, 1807. G & M, G3901 .P5 1807 .T Vault.

This map shows a system of existing and proposed canals and routes that would effectively utilize Albemarle Sound for inland navigation.

1-099. Map of South Carolina showing canals and roads. H. S. Tanner, delineator, 1833. G & M, neg. no. 2641.

Following the end of the War of 1812, the state legislature of South Carolina embarked on an ambitious program of developing water routes throughout the state by improving existing waterways and developing bypass canals where needed. Most of these routes were abandoned by the 1830s.

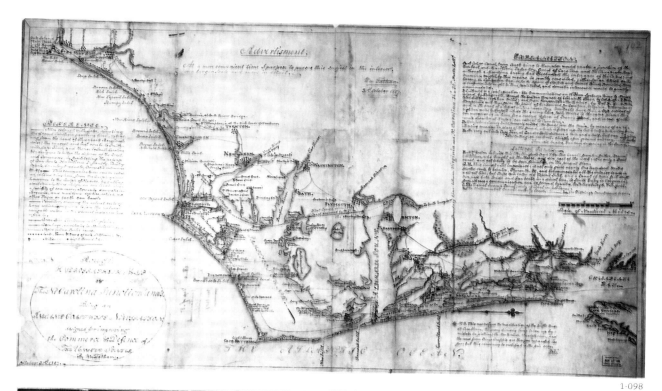

1-098

1-099

1-100

1-100. Frierson's Lock, Santee Canal, South Carolina, ca. 1930s. P & P, HABS, SC,8-____,1-3.

The Santee Canal connected the Santee River with the Cooper River and had two double locks and eight single locks to overcome an elevation of 69 feet above the Cooper River and 34 feet above the Santee River. Lock chambers were small, measuring 10 feet in width by 60 feet in length. A typical 56-foot-long Santee Canal boat could carry eighty to a hundred bales of cotton and paid $20 for passage through the canal. See also IN-059 and IN-060.

1-101. Frierson's Lock, Santee Canal, South Carolina, ca. 1930s. P & P, HABS, SC,8-____,1-4.

The sign on the tree reads, "Frierson's Lock, Built 1800." The construction of the Santee Canal opened a route to export agricultural products, primarily cotton, from the inland portion of South Carolina to Charleston. The brick masonry locks shown here were unusual in American canal lock construction. See also IN-059 and IN-060.

1-101

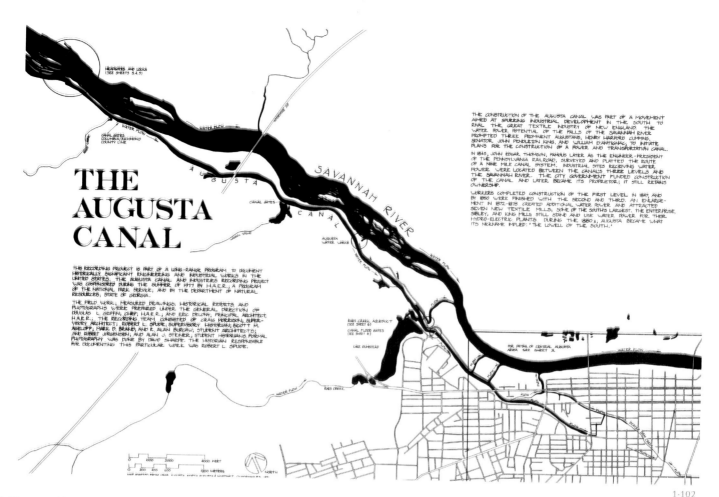

THE AUGUSTA CANAL

1-102

1-102. Site map of Augusta Canal, Savannah River, Georgia. Craig Morrison, delineator, 1977. P & P, HAER GA-5, sheet no. 1.

In 1844 engineer John Edgar Thompson, then chief engineer of the Georgia Railroad, laid out this 9-mile-long canal. Construction on this section was completed by 1850. After the Civil War this canal was enlarged to provide power for a variety of industries in Augusta.

1-103. Plan and elevation of lift gate mechanism for head gates and bypass lock, Augusta Canal, Augusta Vic., Georgia. Scott M. Ageloff and R. Alan Burcaw, delineators, 1977. P & P, HAER GA-5, sheet no. 5.

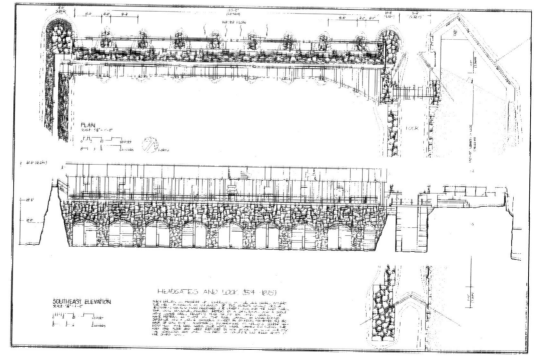

1-103

THE MIDWEST
Ohio, Indiana, Illinois, Kentucky

The opening of the Erie Canal had the same effect on Ohio that it had on many other states—a massive canal construction effort was undertaken that was to result, by 1850, in over 1,000 miles of canals and slackwater navigation within Ohio. The largest of these were the Ohio and Erie Canal, 308 miles, from the Ohio River, at Portsmouth, to Cleveland on Lake Erie (1-105–1-108; see also IN-038; 2-006, 2-023, 2-025, 2-051, 2-101–2-104, 2-115) and the Miami and Erie, 249 miles, from Cincinnati on the Ohio River to Toledo (see 1-109; see also IN-020). Although most of these canals were of the narrow lock type prevalent in the East, some, such as the Muskingum River improvement (see 1-110) had locks large enough to accommodate Ohio River steamers.

1-104. "Map of Ohio Canals." Captain Hiram M. Chittenden, delineator, and A. H. Sawyer, draftsman, ca. 1905. C. C. Huntington, *History of the Ohio Canals: Their Construction, Cost, Use and Partial Abandonment* (1905). LC-TC624.O3 043.

Ohio's extensive canal system included the Miami and Erie Canal, 249 miles long, connecting Cincinnati on the Ohio River to Toledo, Ohio, on Lake Erie, and the Ohio and Erie Canal, the largest of the Ohio canals, at 308 miles, from Portsmouth, Ohio, on the Ohio River to Cleveland on Lake Erie. The Hocking Canal was a feeder canal to the Ohio and Erie Canal, running 56 miles from Carroll, Ohio, on the Ohio and Erie Canal, to Athens, Ohio. The Muskingum River improvement stretched 91 miles, from the Ohio and Erie Canal through Zanesville, Ohio, to the Ohio River. Smaller canals included the Walhonding Canal (a 25-mile extension northwest from the Ohio and Erie Canal at Roscoe, Ohio, along the Walhonding River), the Cincinnati and Whitewater Canal (a 90-mile-long canal that extended from Cincinnati up the Whitewater Creek into Indiana), the Sandy and Beaver Canal (a 73-mile canal from Bolivar, Ohio, on the Ohio and Erie Canal to the mouth of Beaver Creek at the Ohio-Pennsylvania border), the Pennsylvania and Ohio Canal (a 93-mile canal from Akron, Ohio, along the Walhonding River to its junction with the Pennsylvania and Erie Canal), and others.

MAP OF OHIO CANALS
PROPOSED, EXISTING AND ABANDONED

Drawn from Map and Data prepared by Capt Hiram M. Chittenden Corps of Engineers, U.S.A.

1-104

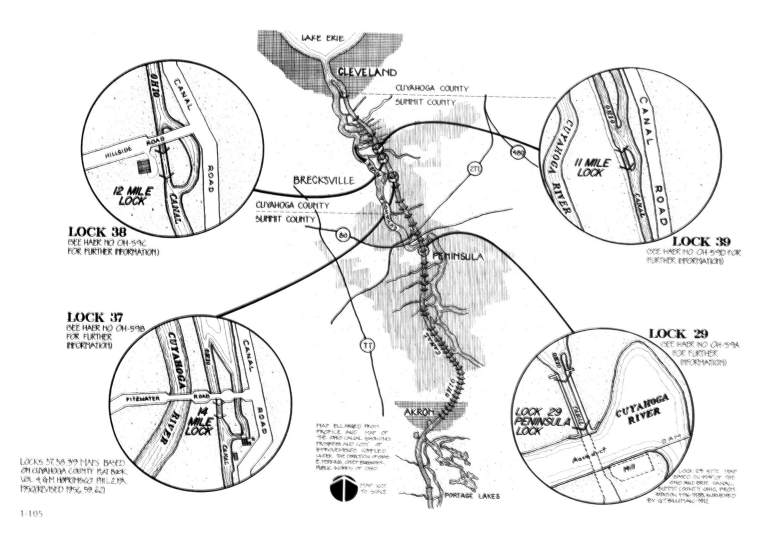

LAKE ERIE

CLEVELAND

CUYAHOGA COUNTY
SUMMIT COUNTY

BRECKSVILLE

CUYAHOGA COUNTY
SUMMIT COUNTY

PENINSULA

AKRON

PORTAGE LAKES

12 MILE LOCK

OHIO CANAL

HILLSIDE ROAD

OHIO CANAL

LOCK 38
(SEE HAER NO OH-59C
FOR FURTHER INFORMATION)

11 MILE LOCK

CUYAHOGA RIVER

OHIO CANAL

CANAL ROAD

LOCK 39
(SEE HAER NO OH-59D FOR
FURTHER INFORMATION)

LOCK 37
(SEE HAER NO OH-59B
FOR FURTHER
INFORMATION)

14 MILE LOCK

CUYAHOGA RIVER

OHIO CANAL

FITZWATER ROAD

CANAL ROAD

LOCKS 37,38,39 MAPS BASED
ON CUYAHOGA COUNTY PLAT BOOK
VOL 4, G.M. HOPKINS CO PHIL 2, PA.
1950 (REVISED 1956, 59, 62)

MAP ENLARGED FROM
PROFILE AND MAP OF
THE OHIO CANAL SHOWING
PROGRESS AND COST OF
IMPROVEMENTS COMPILED
UNDER THE DIRECTION OF GEO.
E. PERKINS, CHIEF ENGINEER,
PUBLIC WORKS OF OHIO

MAP NOT
TO SCALE

LOCK 29
(SEE HAER NO OH-59A
FOR FURTHER
INFORMATION)

LOCK 29
PENINSULA
LOCK

OHIO CANAL

CUYAHOGA RIVER

DAM

Aqueduct

Mill

LOCK 29 SITE MAP
BASED ON MAP OF THE
OHIO AND ERIE CANAL,
SUMMIT COUNTY OHIO, FROM
STATION 1146-1133, SURVEYED
BY G.T. SILLIMAN 1912

1-105

1-105. Sites between Cleveland and Akron, Ohio, Ohio and Erie Canal, Ohio. William F. Conway, delineator, 1986. P & P, HAER OH-59, sheet no. 1. detail.

The Ohio and Erie Canal connected Cleveland on Lake Erie, with Portsmouth, Ohio, on the Ohio River, a distance of 308 miles. The canal was constructed 1825–32.

In Indiana, stretching 450 miles from Toledo to Evansville, the Wabash and Erie Canal was the longest canal in America. Begun in 1832, it was not completed until the middle of the century. The lower portion of the canal closed in 1860; the upper part operated until 1874, when it succumbed to flood damage and railroad competition (1-115 and 1-116; see also 2-016). The Whitewater Canal was privately owned and extended northwest from Cincinnati into Indiana (see 2-068–2-072). Across from Indiana, on the Kentucky side of the Ohio River, was the Louisville and Portland Canal, a canal designed to provide safe passage for Ohio River steamboats around the falls at Louisville (1-013, 1-111–1-113; 2-123). In Illinois, the Illinois and Michigan Canal extended 97 miles southwest from Chicago (1-117–1-120; see also 2-007, 2-027, 2-036, 2-041, 2-055–2-057, 2-063, 2-096–2-100).

1-106

1-106. Lock 39 and spillway, Ohio and Erie Canal, Valley View, Ohio. Louise Taft Cawood, photographer, July 1986. P & P, HAER, OHIO,18-VAVI,4-5.

A spillway is an overflow device for excess water, similar to a bypass flume but usually larger.

1-107. Lock 29, Ohio and Erie Canal, Peninsula, Ohio. Louise Taft Cawood, photographer, July 1986. P & P, HAER, OHIO, 77-PEN, 2-2.

1-108. Lock 28 ("Deep Lock"), Ohio and Erie Canal, Peninsula Vic., Ohio. Jet T. Lowe, photographer, May 1985. P & P, HAER, OHIO, 77-PEN,V,6-1.

Called "Deep Lock" because of its 16-foot lift, about twice the normal lift of locks, this lock was originally constructed of masonry and repaired with concrete 1905–6.

1-107

1-108

1-109. Staircase of lift locks, Miami and Erie Canal, Loramie Portage Vic., Lockington, Ohio. Perry E. Borchers, photographer, February 1959. P & P, HABS, OHIO, 75-LOCK,1-1.

The Miami and Erie Canal was created in 1849 by legislative designation combining three earlier canals: the Miami Canal, the Miami Extension Canal, and the Wabash and Erie Canal.

1-110. Muskingum River improvement, Muskingum County, Ohio. From William Cullen Bryant (ed.), *Picturesque America, or, The Land We Live In* (1894). LC-E168 .P5893.

The Muskingum River improvement was authorized by the Ohio legislature in 1836 to provide an additional connection between the Ohio and Erie Canal and the Ohio River (besides the Ohio and Erie Canal main stem), as well as to provide transportation for the town of Zanesville and the Muskingum valley. The locks, 150 to 175 feet long and 34 to 36 feet wide, were larger than those of other Ohio canals, to accommodate Ohio River steamboats.

1-109

1-110

1-111

1-112

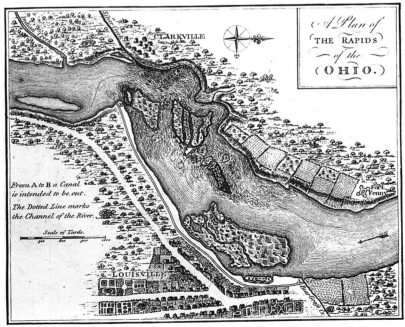

1-113

this page

1-111. Louisville and Portland Canal, Ohio River, Louisville, Kentucky, ca. 1906. P & P, DPCC, LC-D4-19364.

Although only 2 miles long, the Louisville and Portland Canal is still in use, operated by the Corps of Engineers and used by Ohio River barges. It provides Ohio River traffic with a bypass of the 24-foot fall in the Ohio River at Louisville. The original canal, 50 feet wide, was designed by Benjamin Wright and was completed in 1830. Not wide enough for the steamboats on the Ohio, it was enlarged to 90 feet after the Civil War.

1-112. Louisville and Portland Canal, Ohio River, Louisville, Kentucky, ca. 1906. P & P, DPCC, LC-D4-19362.

A stern-wheeler riverboat sits in the lock.

1-113. Plan of the Rapids of Ohio, showing location of what was to become the Louisville and Portland Canal, Louisville, Kentucky. Thomas Hutchins, delineator, 1778. G & M, neg. no. 547.

opposite

1-114. Indiana canals. H. S. Tanner, delineator, 1831. G & M, neg. no. 1364.

The proposed Wabash and Erie Canal was not yet begun at the time of the publication of this map. Construction on the Wabash and Erie Canal began in 1832 in Fort Wayne, Indiana, in the northeastern part of the state. The canal proceeded across the state to Loganport, Lafayette, and Covington and then down to Terre Haute and eventually to Evansville, Indiana, on the Ohio River, by 1853. At 458 miles from Toledo to Evansville, this was the longest canal in America. It didn't last long, however, due to flood damage and railroad competition.

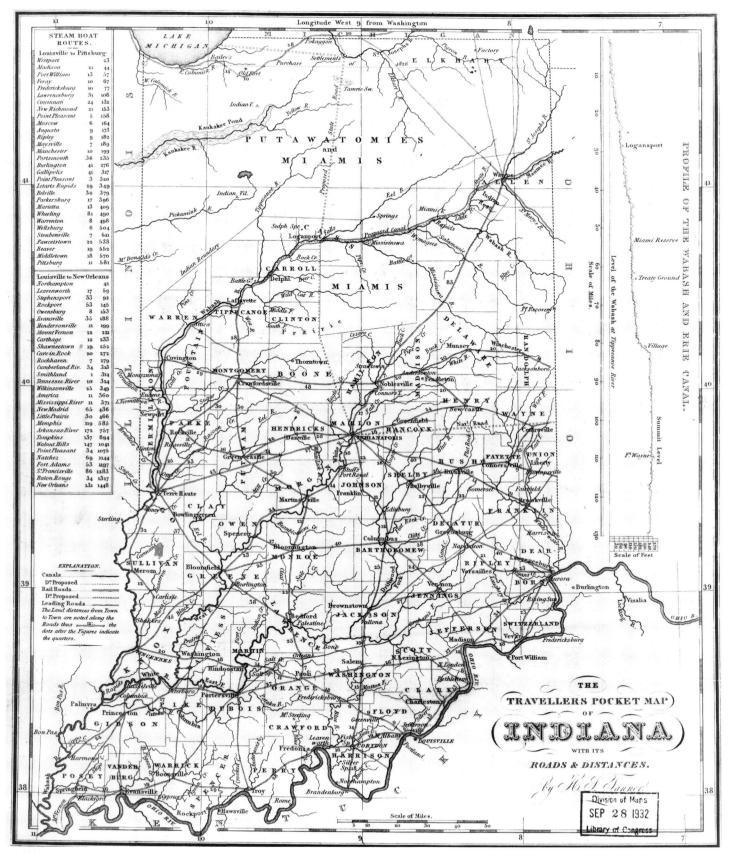

1-114

1-115

1-116

1-115. Timber crib foundation under the west bay of Lock 2, Wabash and Erie Canal, 8 miles east of Fort Wayne, Indiana. Thomas W. Salmon II, photographer, May 1992. P & P, HAER, IND,2-NEHA.V,1-6 .

1-116. Lock 2 (Gronauer Lock), Wabash and Erie Canal, 8 miles east of Fort Wayne, Indiana. Thomas W. Salmon II, photographer, May 1992. P & P, HAER, IND,2-NEHA.V,1-3 .

This photograph shows the lock chamber, 15 feet wide and approximately 100 feet long, beginning at the miter gates in the foreground, after excavation by archaeologists in 1992.

1-117. Map of the Illinois canals, from James W. Putnam, *The Illinois and Michigan Canal: A Study in Economic History* (1918). LC-TC625 .I 2P8.

The Illinois and Michigan Canal was begun in 1836 and, despite the economic panic of 1837, was completed by 1848. The canal extended 97 miles from the Chicago River, near Chicago, to the Illinois River at Peru, Illinois.

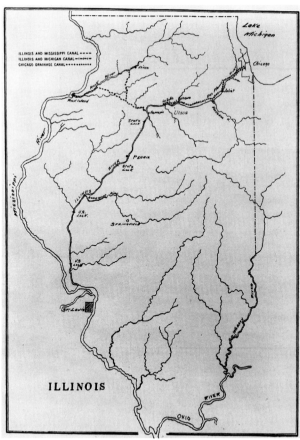

1-117

1-118. Illinois and Michigan Canal, from *Frank Leslie's Illustrated Newspaper*, v. 7, no. 178 (April 30, 1859). P & P, LC-USZ62-126972.

1-119. Lock of the Illinois and Michigan Canal, Channahon Vic., Illinois. Copy of an undated photograph, 1936. P & P, HABS, ILL,99-CHA.V,1, 1A-1.

1-120. Lock 2 of the Illinois and Michigan Canal, Lockport, Illinois. Jet T. Lowe, photographer, 1979. P & P, HAER, ILL,99-LOCK,2-9.

1-118

1-119

1-120

CANAL STRUCTURES

The canal prism and the canal boat are the two most basic elements of a canal, but other structures were required to make the canals function. First and foremost were the locks to move boats from one level to another. Dry docks, a type of lock, were needed to repair canal vessels. Lock fittings such as gates and hinges tended to follow European prototypes. Water emptied from locks through valves of various types, such as butterfly, screw, and paddle valves. Men and women, sometimes families, operated the locks and had to be housed; they collected tolls in buildings sited next to the locks (living quarters and office sometimes combined).

Canals had to cross streams and rivers: aqueducts—bridges for canal boats— were built to meet this need. Culverts, a small form of aqueduct, also carried the canal over waterways. Bridges allowed roads to cross canals. Occasionally, a canal could not avoid a hill or mountain and ran through the obstacle by means of a tunnel.

Dams were another necessity, diverting river waters to the canal or impounding water in reservoirs for canal use.

Finally, there were the boats themselves. On the one hand, canal vessels were standardized—canals were very expensive and the companies that promoted and built them preferred not to take chances on untried methods or models. But on the other hand, there was a very large variance in the actual details of building canal boats.

LOCKS

Locks were the heart and soul of canals. The lock, the invention of which is attributed to Leonardo da Vinci, was a hydraulic device for lifting or lowering large and heavy canal boats from one level to another (2-003; see IN-004–IN-005). Typically, locks were narrow (15 to 18 feet wide) and long (70 to 100 feet between gates). The lift of a lock was 8 to 10 feet, usually the same for all locks because the water released by a higher lock was required to fill a lower lock. Although the lift lock was the most common form of lock, other hydraulically activated locks were also used (2-018).

Lock foundations were critical to the longevity of the structure. The three types of foundations were rock, in rock formations; inverted masonry arches in relatively stable soils (2-005, upper right; see IN-031); and pilings topped by a wood grillage in soft soils (see 1-095–1-097). The lock walls could be wood (2-016; see 1-095–1-097, 1-115), a combination or composite of wood and masonry (2-012, 2-060), or masonry (2-009–2-011; see 1-007, 1-039; 3-078; 4-001, 4-003, 4-004, 4-138, 4-140), including brick (see IN-059; 1-100 and 1-101).

When a lock was full, the water in it tended to balance the earth pressure on its walls. But when the lock was empty, the two lock walls acted as retaining walls and required sufficient strength to hold back the earth behind. Canal engineers provided for that strength by stepping the wall: making the lowest portion of the wall the thickest. Or they built very thick walls throughout (2-002). They also used counterforts, like buttresses, but acting in tension to hold the wall back (2-008, plan; see IN-033). Also used were cramps, or clamps—large masonry clips that looked like staples and increased wall strength by holding together adjacent masonry blocks (2-015).

Lock walls were equipped with recesses so that open gates would not block canal boats in passage (2-010, 2-011, 2-044). Sometimes locks were equipped with lift gates instead of swing gates (2-018, 2-032). The gate (2-024–2-029) or chamber (IN-034) or both were fitted with valves that, when opened, permitted the draining or filling of the lock (2-039). At either end of the opening of the lock, wing walls provided a transition between the lock and the adjoining canal banks (2-001, 2-056; see 1-120; 4-070, 4-081, 4-086, 4-095).

2-001. At the lock. S. G. McCutchen, engraver, 1879. *Harper's Weekly*, December 20, 1879. P & P, LC-USZ62-35602.

2-002. Sections and plan of the masonry inlet lock at Cherbourg, France, ca. 1763. From Charles Vallancey, *A Treatise on Inland Navigation* (1763). RBSCD, TC744.V17.

Americans received their canal technology from England, and the English received their canal technology from Europe, particularly France. But the Americans did not have the masons that would permit perfect replication of the great French canals. Rather, Americans built simplified versions of their European cousins, either in wood or masonry. This elaborate canal structure, the great sluice at Cherbourg, is an inlet lock. The plan view (Fig. 2, center) shows the sea to the right and the harbor to the left; a single set of lock gates (left) permits ships to enter or leave the harbor when the tide and water level in the harbor are equal. The lock gates (Fig. 1, top, and Fig. 3, bottom) are identical to canal lock gates constructed in America. The masonry structure of the lock is shown (Fig. 2, center) as well as how the cut stone along the top of the lock is keyed into the rubble masonry beneath to provide greater strength (Figs. 4 and 5, bottom left). The longitudinal elevation of this lock (Fig. 1) shows that the approaches on both sides of the lock are built on pilings but that the actual lock itself is on a masonry foundation.

2-001

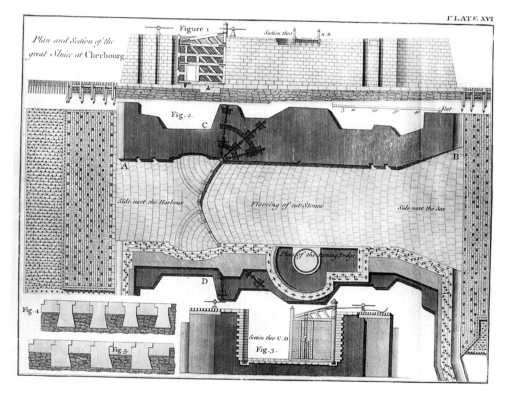

2-002

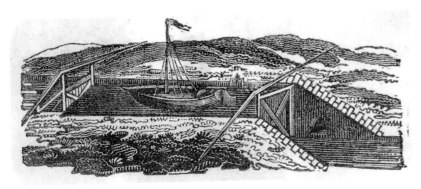

2-003

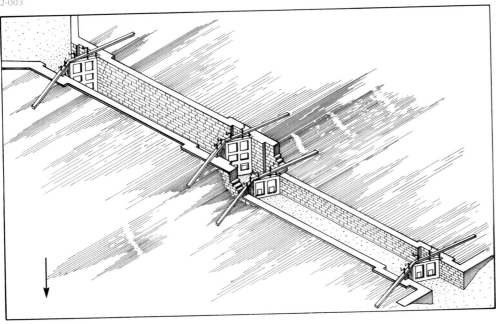

2-004

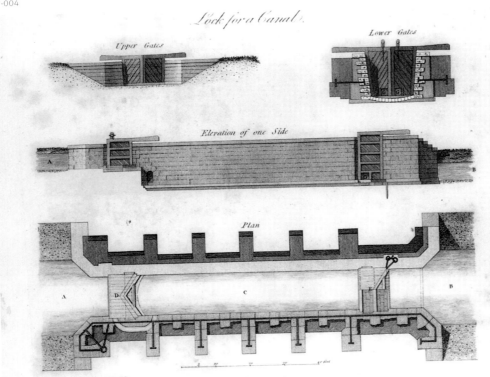

Lock for a Canal.

Upper Gates

Lower Gates

Elevation of one Side

Plan

2-005

2-003. Early American depiction of a boat passing through a canal lock, from Elkanah Watson, *History of the Rise, Progress and Existing Condition of the Western Canals in The State of New-York, from September 1788, to . . . 1819 . . .* (1820). LC, TC624.N7 W3.

2-004. Clapham's Double Lock on the Goose Creek Canal, Leesburg Vic., Virginia. C. J. Sotera, delineator, 1985. P & P, HAER, VA-39, sheet no. 1, detail.

This staircase consisting of two locks was the most important structure on the Goose Creek Canal, a 20-mile river navigation designed to provide access for Loudon, Fauquier, and Prince William Counties, Virginia, to the Chesapeake and Ohio Canal along the Potomac River. It was completed in 1850, when canals were beginning to succumb to railroad competition; only one boat is known to have traversed the entire length of the navigation. The company was dissolved in 1857.

2-005. Elevations and plan view of a typical masonry lock, from J. Phillips, *A General History of Inland Navigation* (1792). RBSCD, TC744 .P53.

The protruding masonry structures in the plan are counterforts holding the sidewalls of the lock. Reinforcement, presumably iron, is shown in the plan and section. The elevation of the lower gates indicates that the lock is constructed on an inverted masonry arch foundation.

2-006. Sections and plan of Lock 38, Ohio and Erie Canal, Valley View, Ohio. Marcy Schulte, delineator, 1986. P & P, HAER OH-59-C, sheet no. 1.

A typical masonry lock, Lock 38 was constructed in 1826–27 and reconstructed in 1905–6. As shown in the plan, the upper level of the lock would be to the left of this lock and the lower level to the right. The curved lift wall of the lock can be seen in the plan immediately to the right of the balance beams of the upper gates. The plan shows lock recesses for both the upper and the lower locks. Section C-C shows the sloping batter of the lock walls, used to help withstand the pressure of the earth.

2-007. Sections and plan view of lock and lockhouse, Illinois and Michigan Canal, Channahon Vic., Illinois. Harold Hugh Sriver, delineator, May 1936. P & P, HABS IL-157, sheet no. 2, detail.

The wood pilings, driven to bedrock, for the foundation of this lock can be seen in the longitudinal section.

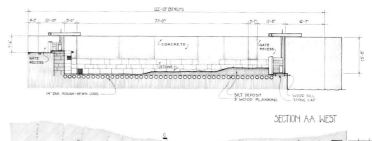

SECTION A-A WEST

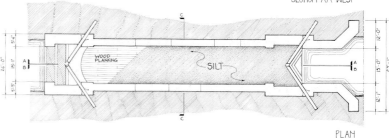

PLAN

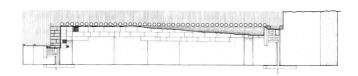

SECTION B-B EAST

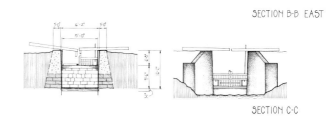

SECTION C-C

2-006

LONGITUDINAL SECTION

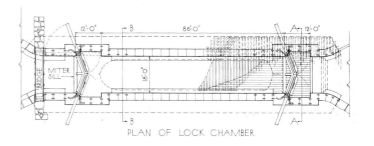

PLAN OF LOCK CHAMBER

TYPICAL CANAL BARGE

2-007

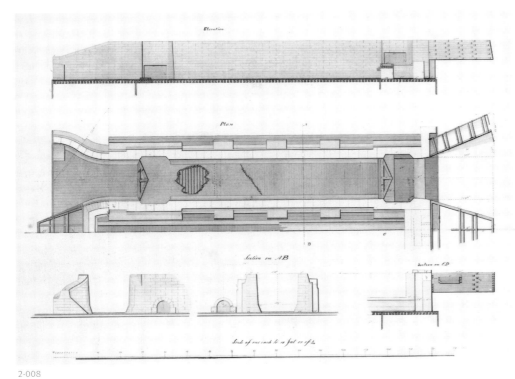

2-008

2-009

2-010

2-008. Elevation and plan view of a typical lock on the Erie Canal (enlarged), New York. Charles E. Jesup, delineator, 1858. G & M, G 3802 .E 7 1858 .S vault.

The wood planking used on the floor of the lock chamber is shown and, in the cutaway, the joists below. Typically, joists were mounted as a grillage on the top of wooden piles first driven into the soil as part of the preparation of the lock construction. The plan also depicts the miter sills at the bottom of the lock gates. This drawing was prepared as a student exercise at the U.S. Military Academy to teach an understanding of lock construction and to improve engineering drawing ability.

2-009. The top of the hollow quoin at Lock 24, Blackstone Canal, Millville, Massachusetts. Martin Stupich, photographer, 1987. P & P, HAER, MASS,14-MILV,2-3.

2-010. Lock wall and gate recesses, Lock 34, Chesapeake and Ohio Canal, Harper's Ferry Vic., Maryland. Jack E. Boucher, photographer, 1958. P & P, HABS, MD,22-HARF.V,8-4.

See also 4-081.

2-011. The gate recess of Empire Lock 29, Erie Canal (enlarged), Fort Hunter, New York. Jack E. Boucher, photographer, 1969. P & P, HAER, NY,29.FORHU,2C-3.

Although the lock gate is gone, the gate recess is obvious. In the left-hand side of the recess is the hollow quoin—the stack of masonry blocks with a concavity to receive the quoin post. At the top, where the top of the quoin post would have fitted into the balance beam, remnants of the anchor and collar are visible. (The function of the concavity through the lower four courses of masonry in the middle of the recess is unknown.)

2-012. Section and plan of a typical composite lock, Delaware and Hudson Canal, New York and Pennsylvania. Edwin D. LeRoy, delineator, drawing from the original 1827 plans, ca. 1945. P & P, LOT 2516 (H), Blueprint #5 (LeRoy #265).

2-013. Sections, elevation, and plan of a lift lock, Louisville and Portland Canal, Louisville, Kentucky. Edward Watts, engineer, November 1856. G & M, G3701 .P53 1856 .B7 TIL.

The locks of the Louisville and Portland Canal were much larger than the typical canal lock of the time in order to accommodate river steamboats. Most canal locks ranged from 15 to 18 feet wide; the locks of the Louisville and Portland Canal were 50 feet wide, extended to 90 feet after the Civil War. In the 1920s these locks were again widened, to 110 feet.

2-011

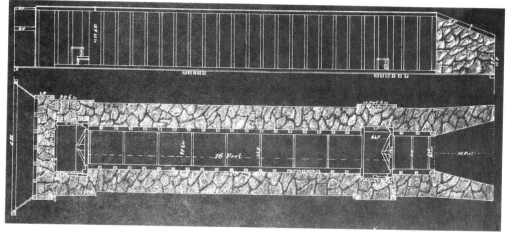

2-012

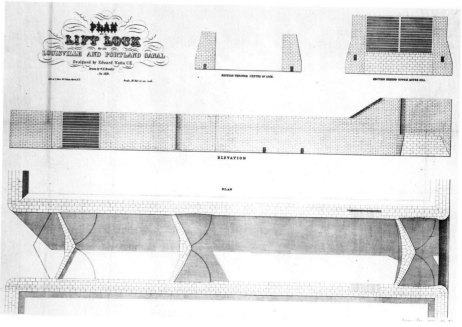

2-013

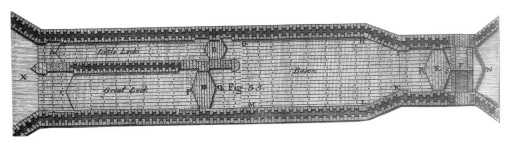

2-014

2-014. Plan of a double masonry lock, from Charles Vallancey, *A Treatise on Inland Navigation* (1763). RBSCD, TC744.V17.

Double locks allowed ascending and descending boats to be accommodated at the same time, decreasing the transit time in a lift lock. Double locks like those shown here, one large and one small, were also used to provide for different-sized boats, saving water otherwise wasted down the canal.

2-015. Iron cramps, or clamps, used to secure adjacent masonry blocks, usually the lock coping stones or topmost layer, Bald Eagle Cross-Cut Canal Lock, Lock Haven, Pennsylvania. Rob Tucher, photographer, October 1991. P & P, HAER, PA, 18-LOKHA, 9-4.

2-016. Mortise-and-tenon construction of the lock crib of Lock 2, Wabash and Erie Canal, New Haven Vic., Indiana. Thomas W. Salmon II, photographer, May 1992. P & P, HAER, IND,2-NEHA.V,1-4.

2-015

2-016

2-017. Longitudinal section, plan, and cross section of a stop lock, Dam 4, Chesapeake and Ohio Canal, Williamsport Vic., Maryland. A. Gutterson and D. McGrew, measurers; D. McGrew and Pick, delineators, ca. 1939. P & P, HABS MD-57-H, sheet no. 10.

A stop lock prevented water from entering a select reach of the canal by lowering planks into a predetermined portion of the canal prism. This stop lock is somewhat unusual as it has a housing to protect the planks.

2-018. Hydraulic lock of the Delaware and Raritan Canal, Kingston, New Jersey. John H. Harvey, delineator, July 1937. P & P, HABS NJ-359, sheet no. 11, detail.

Although double lock gates with miter sill were the most common form of gate mechanism, hydraulic lift locks like this one were successfully used on a number of canals.

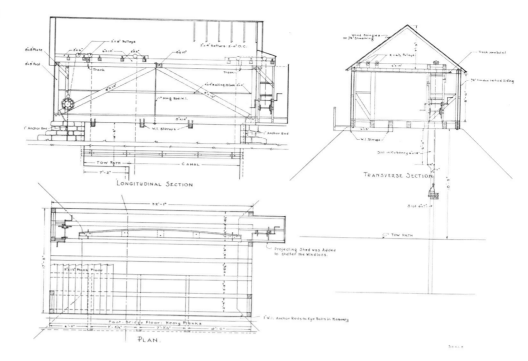

2-017

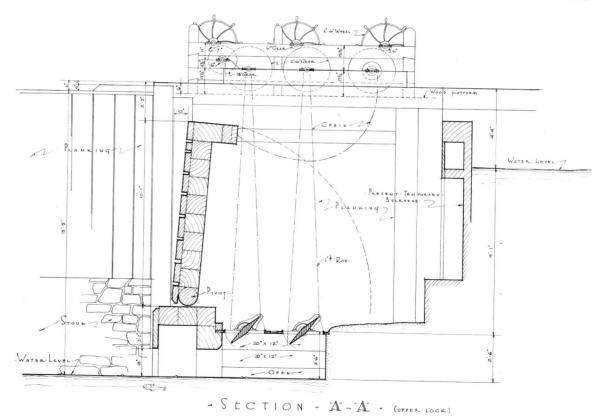

2-018

DRY DOCKS

Dry docks—locks emptied of water—permitted work on the hull of a canal boat (2-019–2-022).

2-019

2-019. Canal boat in dry dock. S. G. McCutchen, engraver, 1879. From *Harper's Weekly*, December 20, 1879. P & P, LC-USZ62-35602.

2-020. Dry dock at Lock 35, Chesapeake and Ohio Canal, Harper's Ferry Vic., Maryland. Jack E. Boucher, photographer, April 1959. P & P, HABS, MD,22-HARF.V,6-3.

Lock 35 is parallel to and behind the dry dock. In the distance is the Potomac River. Unloaded canal boats were floated into the dry dock and blocked on top of the concrete sills, then water was let out of the lock at the east end (left).

2-020

2-021. Dry dock at Lock 35, Chesapeake and Ohio Canal, Harper's Ferry Vic., Maryland. Jack E. Boucher, photographer, April 1959. P & P, HABS, MD,22-HARF.V,6-2.

The construction of the concrete sills in this undated structure indicates that the dry dock was built in the latter years of the Chesapeake and Ohio Canal, which closed in 1924. The need to construct dry docks had been discussed by the company's board of directors almost from the beginning of the canal.

2-022. Plan and sections of the dry dock at Lock 35 of the Chesapeake and Ohio Canal, Harper's Ferry Vic., Maryland. J. E. Replogle, delineator. P & P, HABS MD-885, sheet no. 1.

2-021

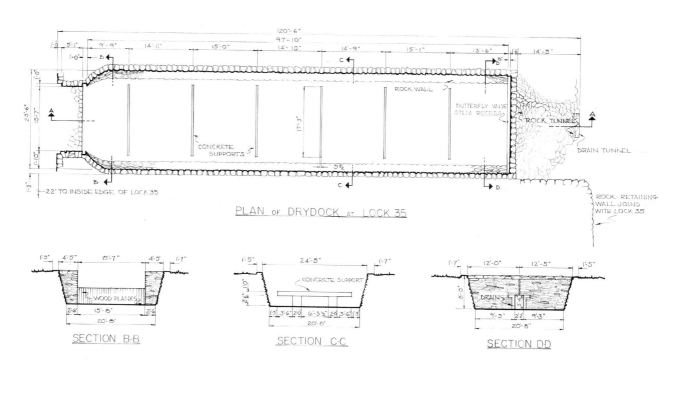

PLAN of DRYDOCK at LOCK 35

SECTION B-B

SECTION C-C

SECTION D-D

SECTION A-A

2-022

LOCK GATES

The gates on either end of the lock chamber were usually made of stout timber (2-023–2-027, 2-031; see IN-035–IN-038). At the bottom they pressed against a miter sill, a strong wooden isosceles triangle–shaped structural frame (2-042–2-046; see IN-042, IN-043, and IN-063).

The hinge posts of the gates were pressed by water pressure into the concavity within the lock wall called the hollow quoin (2-011 and 2-012). The hinges were held to the top of the lock walls by the ironwork anchor and collar (see 2-033–2-035; IN-039, IN-41). Mounted at the top of the gate were balance beams or gate sweeps, large wooden members to open and close the gates (2-023, 2-025; see IN-063).

2-023. Perspective of typical lock gates, Ohio and Erie Canal, Ohio. Alan J. Rutherford, delineator, 1987. P & P, HAER OH-60, sheet no. 1.

The levers mounted on the balance beams opened valves in the gates.

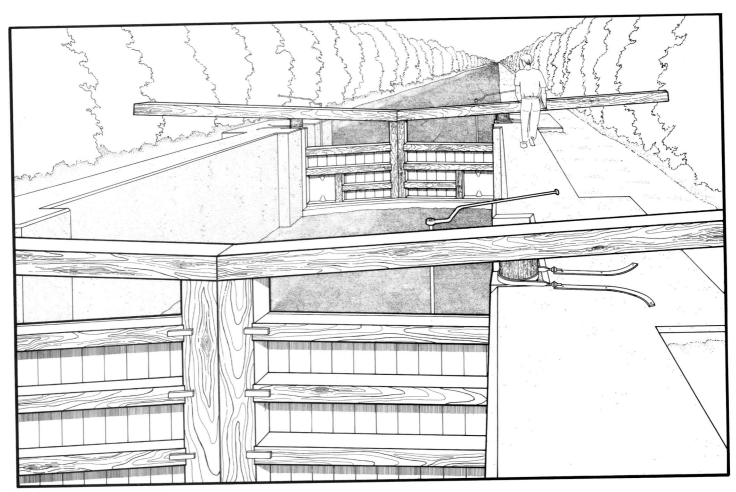

2-023

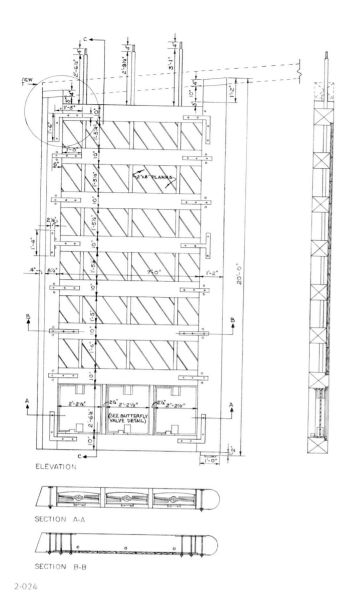

SECTION A-A

SECTION B-B

2-024

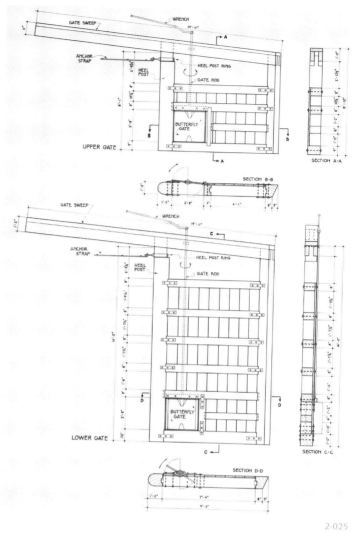

2-025

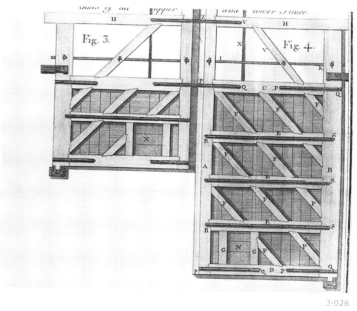

2-026

2-024. Typical lock gate, Chesapeake and Ohio Canal, Maryland. C. H. Lavers, Jr., delineator, ca. 1970. P & P, HABS MD-767, sheet no. 1, detail.

This elevation of a lock gate shows rails, miter post, and quoin post. The planking is diagonal, to help resist racking of the lock gate (compare with 2-025).

2-025. Typical gate details, Ohio and Erie Canal, Valley View Vic., Ohio. Alan J. Rutherford, delineator, 1987. P & P, HAER OH-60, sheet no. 2, detail.

The balance beam is shown on top of both the short, upper gate and the long, lower gate. In both cases the vertical member on the right is the miter post; the vertical member on the left (upon which the balance beam is balanced) is the quoin post. The horizontal gate components are rails. Planking is attached to the rails and posts. Here the planking is vertical. At the bottom of both gates are butterfly gates, or valves, so called because they loosely resemble a butterfly. The gate shown in 2-024 has three valves to speed the emptying of the lock.

2-026. Elevation of upper and lower lock gates, from Charles Vallancey, *A Treatise on Inland Navigation* (1763). RBSCD, TC744.V17.

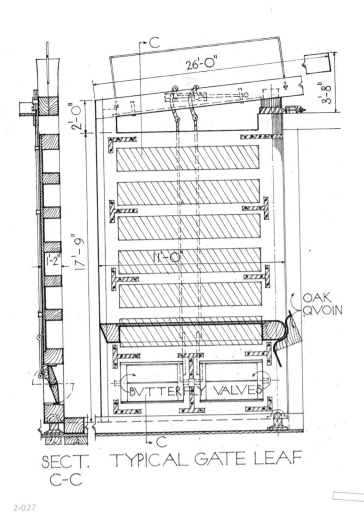

SECT. C-C   TYPICAL GATE LEAF

2-027

2-027. Typical lock gate, Illinois and Michigan Canal, Channahon Vic., Illinois. Harold Hugh Sriver, delineator, May 1936. P & P, HABS IL-157, sheet no. 2, detail.

Very similar to the gates shown in 2-104 and 2-105, this gate differs in that a single lever operated both butterfly valves or gates at the base of the gate. For a photograph of this lock gate, see 2-056.

2-028. Typical lock gate, Delaware and Hudson Canal, New York and Pennsylvania. Edwin D. LeRoy, delineator, ca. 1945. P & P, LOT 2516 (H), Blueprint #1 (LeRoy #269).

2-029. Lock gate, Delaware and Raritan Canal, Kingston, New Jersey. John H. Harvey, delineator, ca. 1937. P & P, HABS NJ-359, sheet no. 12, detail.

This drawing shows a bank of valves or paddle gates in a lock gate. Paddle gates do not turn, as butterfly valves do, but resemble a paddle moving up and down on the surface of the gate.

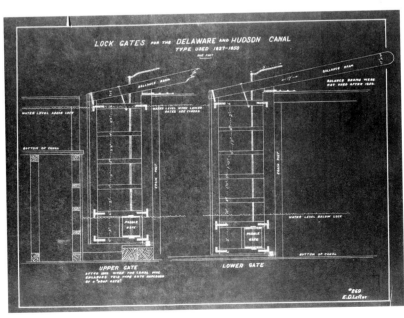

2-028

ELEVATION OF GATE (LOWER LOCK)

2-029

2-030. Operating mechanism of the lock gates, Champlain and Hudson Canal, Saratoga, New York. Jack E. Boucher, photographer, 1959. P & P, HABS, NY,46-SAR,2-4.

Levers operate wickets in the leaves of the gates, allowing water to enter the chamber. Similar levers are shown in 2-023.

2-031. Components of a lock gate, Augusta Canal, Augusta, Georgia. Copy, July 1977, from original drawings in the Office of City Engineer, ca. 1872. P & P, HAER, GA,123-AUG,41-34.

2-032. Elevation of a lift gate, Augusta Canal, Augusta, Georgia. Copy, July 1977 from original drawings in the Office of City Engineer, ca. 1845. P & P, HAER, GA,123-AUG,41-32.

2-030

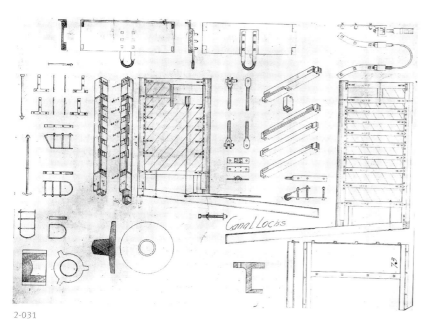

2-031

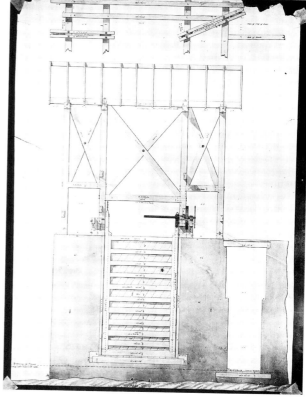

2-032

2-033

2-034

2-033. Detail of the anchor and collar on Lock 44, Chesapeake and Ohio Canal, Williamsport Vic., Maryland. Jack E. Boucher, photographer, 1959–60. P & P, HABS, MD,22-WILPO.V,4-3.

The top of the quoin post, also called a hinge post or heel post, is topped by a tenon to be inserted into the shaped cavity, the mortise, in the balance beam, not present in this photograph (see 2-036). Note the top of the bolts, driven as much as 12 inches into the masonry. The collar could be removed if it was necessary to do work on the quoin post.

2-034. Gate hinge, Lock 35, Chesapeake and Ohio Canal, Harper's Ferry Vic., Maryland. Jack E. Boucher, photographer, 1959. P & P, HABS, MD,22-HARF.V,9-3.

2-035. Plan of anchor and collar, Delaware and Raritan Canal, Kingston, New Jersey. John H. Harvey, delineator, July 1937. P & P, HABS NJ-359, sheet no. 13, detail.

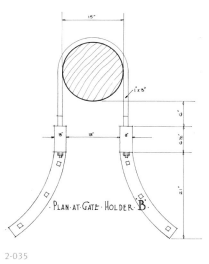

2-035

2-036. Gate hinge with the balance beam mounted on top of the quoin post, with anchor and collar in place, Illinois and Michigan Canal, Channahon Vic., Illinois. Harold Hugh Sriver, photographer, May 1936. P & P, HABS, ILL,99.CHA.V,1,1A-8.

2-037. Axonometric drawing of typical lower lock gate machinery, Delaware and Hudson Canal, New York and Pennsylvania. Edwin D. LeRoy, delineator, April 1945. P & P, LOT 2516 (H), Blueprint #10 (LeRoy #200–344).

This machinery came into use in 1850 when balance beams, considered cumbersome, were discarded. The "goon neck" referred to in the drawing is the collar, the metal strap that secures the post to the top of the masonry lock (2-033–2-038). This strap is adjustable so canal workers could tighten or loosen the gate or take down the gate assembly for maintenance, repair, or replacement.

2-038. Vertical view, plan, and section of anchor and collar connection to the quoin post of a typical lock gate, Delaware and Hudson Canal, New York/Pennsylvania. Edwin D. LeRoy, delineator, ca. 1945. P & P, LOT 2516 (H), Blueprint #3 (LeRoy #270).

2-036

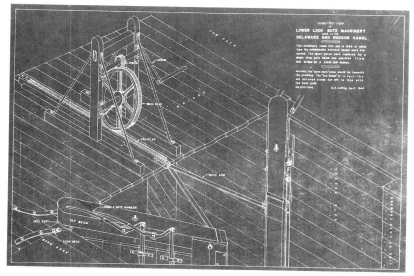

2-037

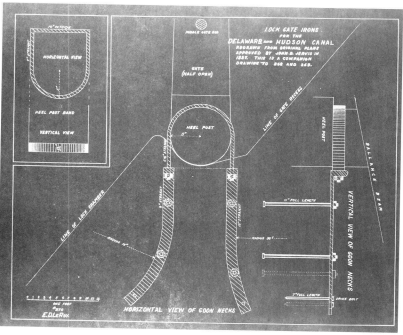

2-038

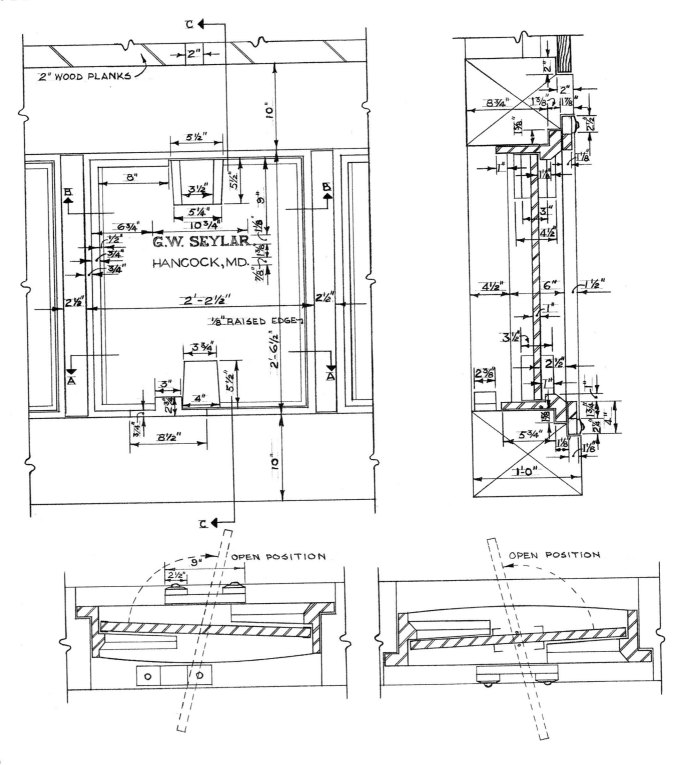

2-039

2-039. Details of typical butterfly valves used in the lock gates of the Chesapeake and Ohio Canal, Maryland.

C. H. Lavers, Jr., delineator, ca. 1970. P & P, HABS MD-767, sheet no. 1, detail.

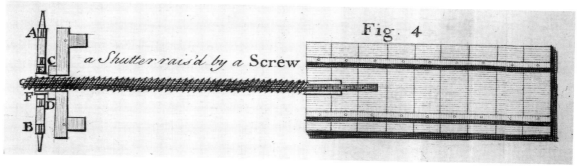

2-040

2-041

2-040. Plan of a screw valve, from Charles
Vallancey, *A Treatise on Inland Navigation*
(1763). RBSCD, TC744.V17.

2-041. Gate-mounted valve control levers,
Illinois and Michigan Canal, Channahon
Vic., Illinois. Carl Magro, photographer, May
1936. P & P, HABS, ILL,99-CHA.V,1,1A-7.

MITER SILLS

If the lock was the heart and soul of a canal, then the miter sill, at the base of the lock gates, was the heart and soul of the lift lock. The apex of the wooden, isosceles triangle–shaped miter sill always faced upstream. As water bore against the lock gates, the lock gates pressed against the miter sill and provided a tight seal.

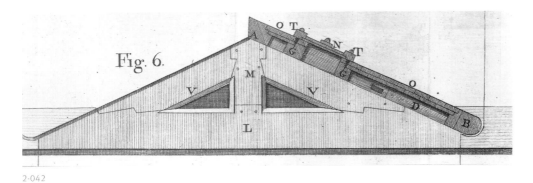

2-042

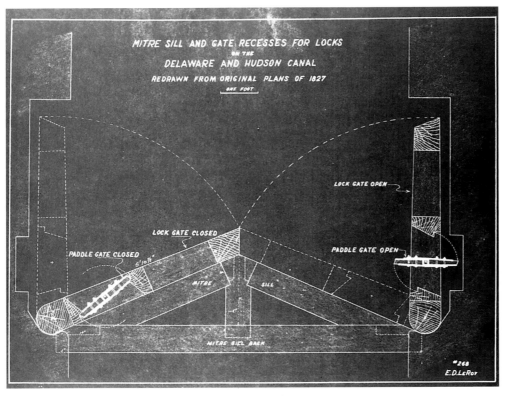

2-043

2-042. Plan view of a miter sill, from Charles Vallancey, *A Treatise on Inland Navigation* (1763). RBSCD, TC744.V17.

2-043. Miter sill, Delaware and Hudson Canal, New York and Pennsylvania. Edwin D. LeRoy, delineator, drawing from the original 1827 plans, ca. 1945. P & P, LOT 2516 (H), Blueprint #4 (LeRoy #268).

2-044. Miter sill, Lock 3, Chesapeake and Ohio Canal, Georgetown, Washington, D.C. George Eisenman, photographer, 1967. P & P, HABS, DC,GEO.25-10.

The top of the lift wall can be seen below the miter sill (bottom right). The lift wall extends downward from the bottom of the upper level to the bottom of the lower level and is therefore approximately equal to the lift of the lock. Also visible are the balance beams and gate recesses for the upper gates of this lock (right and left middle). The large black object (left) is the end of the left balance beam.

2-045. Miter sill, Lock 55, Chesapeake and Ohio Canal, Hancock Vic., Maryland. Jack E. Boucher, photographer, 1959–60. P & P, HABS, MD,22-HAN.V,5-3.

2-046. Miter sill, Lock 2, Wabash and Erie Canal, New Haven Vic., Indiana. Thomas W. Salmon II, photographer, May 1992. P & P, HAER, IND,2-NEHA.V,1-13.

2-044

2-045

2-046

LOCKHOUSES

Travel on canals could be by day or night, so it was imperative for the lockkeeper and his family to live in the immediate vicinity of the lock that they tended. Although travel on the canal was slow, delays at the lock were frowned upon. The call, "Heyyy, lock ready!" told the lockkeeper that a boat was approaching and that the captain expected the lock gates to be open on his arrival.

An early form of lockhouses was a modest one-and-a-half-story symmetrical masonry block facing the lock (2-047–2-049, 2-062; see also 4-030–4-032, 4-035, 4-037, 4-039, 4-041, 4-043, 4-055, 4-062, 4-069, 4-070, 4-089–4-091, 4-107, and 4-108). This design probably originated on the Erie Canal and was brought south to other canals by its engineers; certainly these lockhouses appear to have been designed to withstand the rigors of a northeastern winter. These lockhouses were usually built to a standard design, with a centrally located entrance, a central chimney, and small windows. There is no particular operational reason for a lockhouse's standard design, except perhaps for windows in gables, which gave a view of approaching boats up and down the canal. Most commonly, lockhouses were of wood-frame construction and reflected regional architectural influences (2-050–2-052, 2-055–2-061, 2-063; 1-052, 1-053, 1-066; 4-087, 4-088, 4-109, 4-110, 4-112, 4-119, 4-134–4-137, 4-137, 4-139, 4-141.).

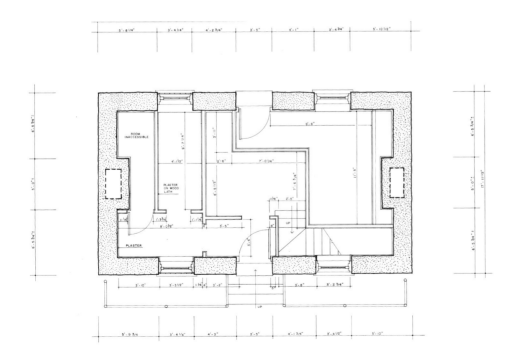

2-047. Floor plan of the lockhouse, Washington City Canal, Washington, D.C. Steve Wynn, delineator, 1993–94. P & P, HABS DC-36, sheet no. 2.

2-047

2-048. North elevation, lockhouse,
Washington City Canal, Washington, D.C.
Steve Wynn, delineator, 1993–94. P & P,
HABS DC-36, sheet no. 4.

2-049. Lockhouse, Washington City Canal,
Washington, D.C. Albert S. Burns, photogra-
pher, 1934–35. P & P, HABS, DC,WASH,12-
(DLC/PP-95:DC-7)4.

The lockhouse at 17th Street and
Constitution Avenue, N.W., still standing
and only a few blocks from the White House,
is the last remaining vestige of the
Washington City Canal (see 1-094).

2-048

2-049

2-050

2-050. Lockhouse, West Branch of the Pennsylvania Canal, Lock Haven, Pennsylvania. Rob Tucher, photographer, October 1991. P & P, HAER, PA,18-LOKHA.V,4-4.

2-051. Lockhouse, Lock 38, Ohio and Erie Canal, Valley View, Ohio. Louise Taft Cawood, photographer, July 1986. P & P, HAER, OHIO,18-VAVI,3-1.

2-052. Lockhouse at Gillis's Lock, Middlesex Canal, Wilmington, Massachusetts. Arthur C. Haskell, photographer, ca. 1930s. P & P, HABS, MASS,9-____,8-1.

2-051

2-052

2-053. Lockhouse, Lock 44, Lehigh Canal,
Freemansburg, Pennsylvania. Jet T. Lowe,
photographer, 1979. P & P, HAER, PA,48-
FREEB,1A-1.

2-054. Lockhouse, Lock 23, Lehigh Canal,
Walnutport, Pennsylvania. Jet T. Lowe, pho-
tographer, 1979. P & P, HAER, PA,48-
WALPO,1A-1.

2-053

2-054

2-055

2-055. Lockhouse, Lock 6, Illinois and Michigan Canal, Channahon, Illinois. Jet T. Lowe, photographer, 1986. P & P, HAER, ILL,99-CHA,2-2.

The iron wheel in the foreground probably controls a valve built into the lock walls for emptying or filling the lock.

2-056. Lockhouse, Illinois and Michigan Canal, Channahon Vic., Illinois. Harold Hugh Sriver, photographer, May 1936. P & P, HABS, ILL,99-CHA.V,1,1A-3.

See 2-027 for a drawing of this lock gate.

2-057. Lockhouse, Lock 1, Illinois and Michigan Canal, Lockport, Illinois. Jet T. Lowe, photographer, 1979. P & P, HAER, ILL,99-LOCK,2-8.

2-056

2-057

2-058. Southwest elevation of lockhouse, Delaware and Raritan Canal, New Brunswick, New Jersey. Kagan and Stewart, architects, P.C., delineators, 1985. P & P, HAER NJ-60-B, sheet no. 7.

2-059. Lockhouse, Delaware and Raritan Canal, New Brunswick, New Jersey. Jack E. Boucher, photographer, 1978. P & P, HABS, NJ,12-NEBRU,13-1.

2-058

2-059

2-060

2-061

2-060. Lockhouse, Delaware and Raritan Canal, Kingston, New Jersey. Nathaniel R. Ewan, photographer, November 1936. P & P, HABS, NJ,12-PLABO.V,3-2.

2-061. Lockhouse, Delaware and Raritan Canal, New Brunswick, New Jersey. Jack E. Boucher, photographer, 1978. P & P, HAER, NJ,12-NEBRU,13-B-3.

2-062. Lockhouse, Lock 25, Chesapeake
and Ohio Canal, Seneca Vic., Maryland. Jack
E. Boucher, photographer, December 1960.
P & P, HABS, MD,16____,31A1.

2-063. Lockhouse, Illinois and Michigan
Canal, Channahon Vic., Illinois. Harold Hugh
Sriver, photographer, May 1936. P & P,
HABS, ILL,99-CHA.V,1,1A-9.

2-062

2-063

TOLLHOUSES

Tollhouses were another type of building seen along canals. They sometimes also provided housing for the company's employees.

2-064

2-065

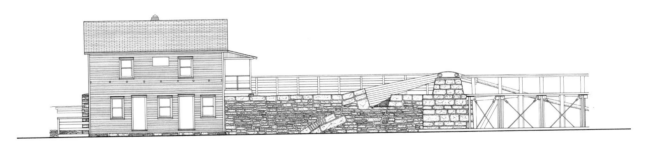

2-066

2-064. Tollhouse, Delaware Aqueduct, Delaware and Hudson Canal, Lackawaxen, Pennsylvania. Jet T. Lowe, photographer, 1988. P & P, HAER, NY,53-MINFO,1-(DLC/PP-96:NY-1)1.

2-065. Tollhouse, Delaware and Raritan Canal, Kingston, New Jersey. Nathaniel R. Ewan, photographer, November 1936. P & P, HABS, NJ,12-PLABO.V,3-5.

2-066. Elevation of the tollhouse and approach to the Delaware Aqueduct, Delaware and Hudson Canal, Lackawaxen, Pennsylvania. Brian D. Bartholomew, Anne Guerette, Elizabeth F. Knowlan, Scott Barber, delineators, 1988. P & P, HAER NY-205, sheet no. 1, detail.

AQUEDUCTS

In early canal schemes, boats were locked down from the canal to the level of the water-way to be crossed, ferried across, and locked back up to the canal level on the other side. This was usually unsatisfactory: it was slow and locks were expensive and subject to flood damage. Dams frequently had to be built to impound water to permit boats to cross. Aqueducts over the intersecting stream or river, although expensive, delayed through-traffic less and were less susceptible to flood damage.

Aqueducts made of wood on masonry piers were most common because timber and carpenters were abundant (2-067–2-075; see IN-045, IN-062; 1-003, 1-005, 1-067, 1-091, 3-116; 4-017, 4-018, 4-058, 4-059). Masonry aqueducts were expensive but durable (2-076–2-086; see IN-015, IN-021, IN-044, IN-046–IN-048; 1-017, 1-062, 1-075, 1-076; 4-056, 4-057, 4-064–4-068, 4-071–4-072, 4-092–4-093, 4-099, 4-100, 4-120, 4-121, 4-131, 4-132, 4-142). As the nineteenth century advanced, iron canal troughs and steel canal troughs were used (2-096–2-104). In one notable case, a suspension bridge carried the aqueduct (2-088–2-095).

2-067. Section and plan of a wood aqueduct, from Charles Vallancey, *A Treatise on Inland Navigation* (1763). RBSCD, TC744.V17.

Although termed an aqueduct, this structure runs under the canal and would usually be referred to as a culvert.

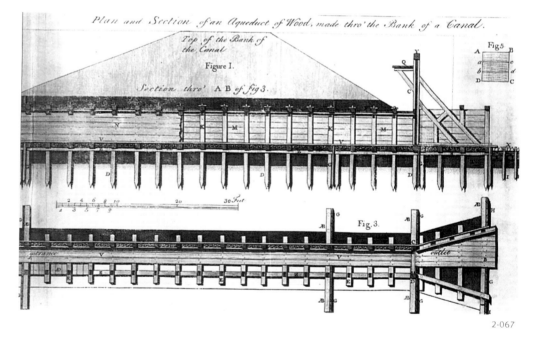

2-067

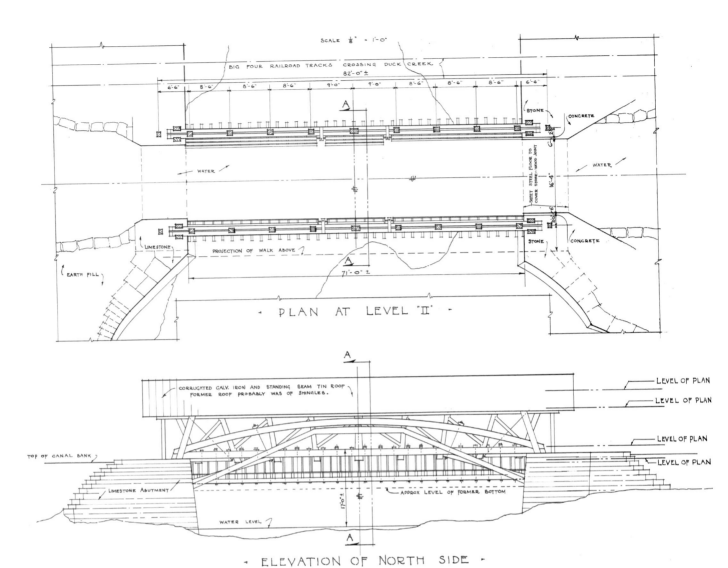

BIG FOUR RAILROAD TRACKS CROSSING DUCK CREEK
82'-0" ±

6'-6" 8'-6" 8'-6" 8'-6" 9'-0" 9'-0" 8'-6" 8'-6" 8'-6" 6'-6"

A

STONE
CONCRETE

SHEET STEEL FLOOR TO COVER STONE—WOOD JOINT

WATER   WATER

16'-4"

PROJECTION OF WALK ABOVE

LIMESTONE

A

STONE   CONCRETE

EARTH FILL

71'-0" ±

- PLAN AT LEVEL "II" -

A

CORRUGATED GALV. IRON AND STANDING SEAM TIN ROOF
FORMER ROOF PROBABLY WAS OF SHINGLES.

LEVEL OF PLAN
LEVEL OF PLAN

TOP OF CANAL BANK

LEVEL OF PLAN
LEVEL OF PLAN

LIMESTONE ABUTMENT

APPROX LEVEL OF FORMER BOTTOM

1'-0"±

WATER LEVEL

A

- ELEVATION OF NORTH SIDE -

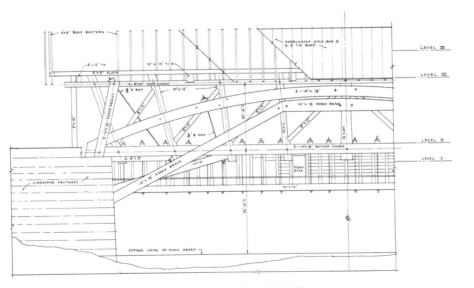

3 x 4" ROOF RAFTERS

CORRUGATED GALV. IRON & S.S TIN ROOF

LEVEL IV

8 x 12" TIE
8 x 9" PLATE

12" x 14" TIE

LEVEL III

2 4" 0 ROD
10" x 12"
2 - 10" x 18"

2 - 10" x 18 ADDED BRACE

2 - 10" x 18 BOTTOM CHORD

LEVEL II

LIMESTONE ABUTMENT

2 - 8 x 8"

10" x 18 ADDED BRACE

FLOOR GATE

LEVEL I

16'-0"

10" x 12"

APPROX LEVEL OF DUCK CREEK

NORTH SIDE ELEVATION

2-068. Plan and north elevation, Whitewater Canal Aqueduct, Whitewater Canal, over Duck Creek, Metamora, Indiana. John R. Kelley, delineator, April 1934. P & P, HABS IN-24-20, sheet no. 1.

2-069. North elevation of detail, Whitewater Canal Aqueduct, Whitewater Canal, over Duck Creek, Metamora, Indiana. John R. Kelley, delineator, April 1934. P & P, HABS IN-24-20, sheet no. 3.

2-070. Whitewater Canal Aqueduct, Whitewater Canal, over Duck Creek, Metamora, Indiana. John R. Kelley, photographer, March 1934. P & P, HABS, IND,24-METMO,1-1.

The Whitewater Canal was constructed north from Cincinnati, Ohio, into the Whitewater Valley in Indiana. The first aqueduct at this location was constructed in 1843 but washed out in 1847; this aqueduct replaced it shortly thereafter. Few covered aqueducts were constructed in the United States: this is the only known surviving example.

2-071. North elevation of the Whitewater Canal Aqueduct, Whitewater Canal, over Duck Creek, Metamora, Indiana. John R. Kelley, photographer, March 1934. P & P, HABS, IND,24-METMO,1-2.

2-072. Interior, Whitewater Canal Aqueduct, Whitewater Canal, over Duck Creek, Metamora, Indiana. John R. Kelley, photographer, March 1934. P & P, HABS, IND,24-METMO,1-3.

Shown are the aqueduct prism (bottom left), the wood truss structure, and the sheathing beyond, to protect the wooden structure from the elements. The wooden braces (shown from bottom left to top right) may have been temporary braces for the structure to prevent collapse—at the time of this photograph the structure was very definitely leaning (see 2-070).

2-070

2-071

2-072

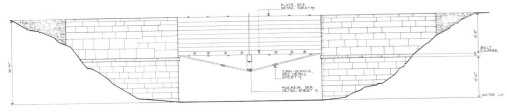

WEST ELEVATION

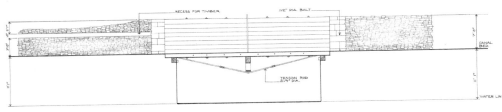

SECTION A-A

2-073

2-074

2-075

2-073. West elevation and longitudinal section of Broad Run Creek Aqueduct, Chesapeake and Ohio Canal, Lock 25 Vic., Maryland. C. Gustave Wormuth, delineator, August 1961. P & P, HABS MD-741, sheet no. 3.

2-074. West elevation of Broad Run Creek Aqueduct, Chesapeake and Ohio Canal, Lock 25 Vic., Maryland. Jack E. Boucher, photographer, 1959–60. P & P, HABS, MD,16-MARB.V,1-1.

Broad Run Creek Aqueduct is one of the few wooden aqueducts to survive. Sometimes called Broad Run Trunk, it was initially constructed as a masonry culvert by the Chesapeake and Ohio Canal Company (culvert 44). The culvert was a double 16-foot span, the only double-span culvert on the canal. In 1846 the original construction was washed out and replaced with a wooden trunk. It was replaced in 1856, burned in the Civil War, and was subsequently replaced. It is the only wooden aqueduct on the Chesapeake and Ohio Canal, although records indicate that other wooden aqueducts were contemplated by the canal company, including one across the Monocacy River, the largest river crossing of the canal.

2-075. Aqueduct Bridge, Alexandria Canal, across the Potomac River from Georgetown (seen in the distance), ca. 1868–77. From the files of the Peabody Room, Georgetown Public Library. P & P, HABS, DC,GEO,1-15.

The Aqueduct Bridge was the most important structure of the Alexandria Canal, a 7-mile feeder canal linking the Chesapeake and Ohio Canal in Georgetown to Alexandria, Virginia (see 1-020, 1-021; 4-015–4-018). The aqueduct crossed the Potomac River immediately upstream of the present Key Bridge at Georgetown. Constructed between 1833 and 1843, the Alexandria (or Potomac) Aqueduct was considered a "stupendous engineering achievement" of the nineteenth century. Major William Turnbull, engineer, designed the wooden superstructure on masonry piers to carry boats across the river.

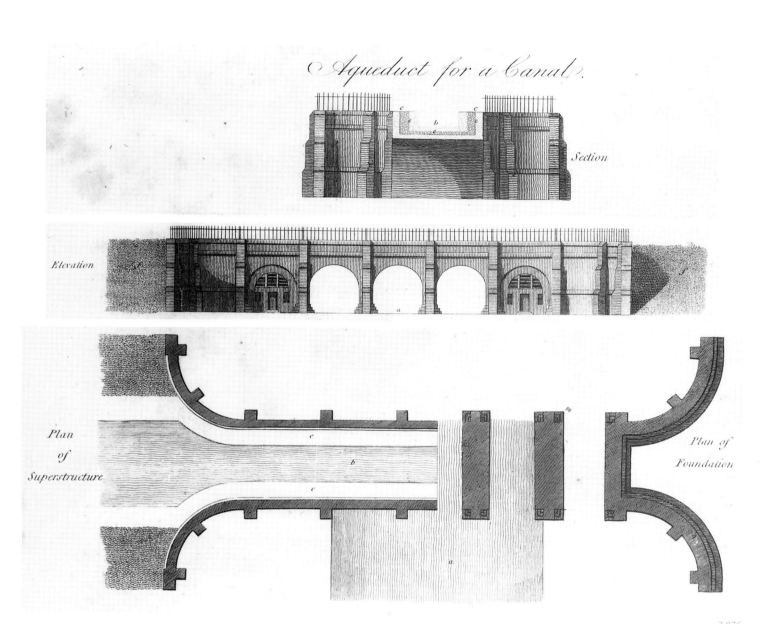

Aqueduct for a Canal.

Section

Elevation

Plan
of
Superstructure

Plan of
Foundation

2-076

2-076. Section, elevation, and plan of an ornate masonry aqueduct for a canal, from J. Phillips, *A General History of Inland Navigation* (1792), RBSCD, TC744 .P53.

Wood aqueducts predominated in the United States, masonry aqueducts in Europe. Shown at regular intervals in the plan view are buttresses that assist the structure in resisting the outward water pressure of the water within the canal. Compare with 2-005.

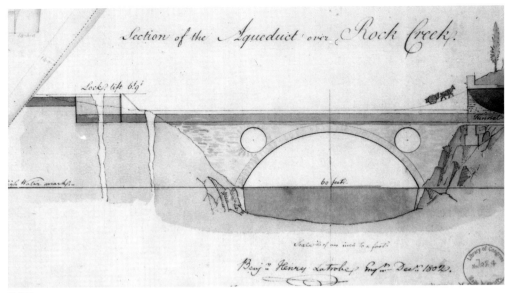

2-077

2-078

2-079

2-077. Elevation of a proposed masonry aqueduct over Rock Creek, Potomac Canal Extension, Georgetown, Washington, D.C. Benjamin Henry Latrobe, delineator, December 1802. G & M, G3852 .W28G45 s07 .L3 Vault, detail.

2-078. Aqueduct Bridge at Little Falls, Erie Canal, Little Falls, New York. J. Eights, delineator. From Cadwallader D. Colden, *Memoir, Prepared at the Request of a Committee at the Celebration of the Completion of the New York Canals* (1825). RBSCD, TC624 .N7 C6.

2-079. Aqueduct Bridge at Rochester, Erie Canal, Rochester, New York. J. Eights, delineator. From Cadwallader D. Colden, *Memoir, Prepared at the Request of a Committee at the Celebration of the Completion of the New York Canals* (1825). RBSCD, TC624 .N7 C6.

2-080. North elevation, Lickinghole Creek Aqueduct, James River and Kanawha Canal, Goochland Vic., Virginia. James J. Depasquale, delineator, summer 1970. P & P, HAER VA-10, sheet no. 1, detail.

This aqueduct was built in 1827 and had a 57-foot span.

2-081. Rae's Creek Aqueduct, Augusta Canal, Augusta, Georgia, 1850. Mark Brand and Craig Morrison, delineators, 1977. P & P, HAER GA-5, sheet no. 6, detail.

Compare the semicircular arches of this aqueduct, each a 30-foot span, with the flat arch of Lickinghole Creek Aqueduct, James River and Kanawha Canal (2-080). The relatively flat arch of the Lickinghole Creek Aqueduct provides a greater span but less strength.

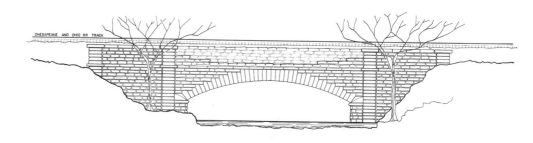

2-080

2-081

2-082

2-082. Schoharie Creek Aqueduct, Erie Canal (enlarged), Fort Hunter, New York. Jack E. Boucher, photographer, August 1969. P & P, HAER, NY,29-FORHU,2A-6.

Built downstream of the original Erie Canal crossing of Schoharie Creek, Schoharie Aqueduct was constructed in 1839–41, when the canal was enlarged. Masonry arches carried the towpath, and a wooden trunk, long since deteriorated, carried the prism of the canal over Schoharie Creek.

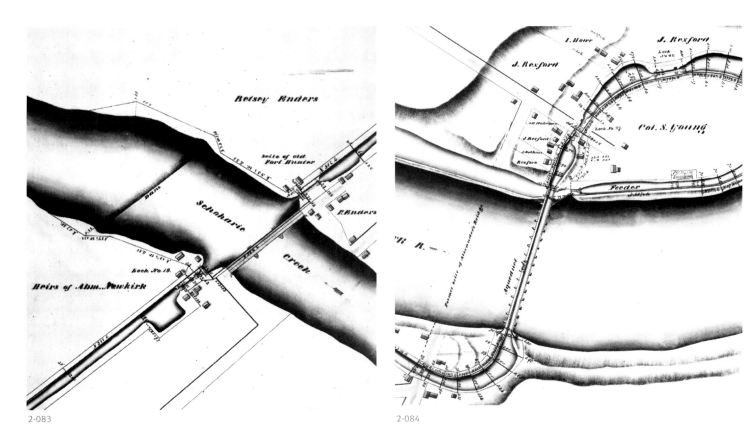

2-083

2-084

2-085

2-083. Site plan, Schoharie Creek Crossing, Schoharie Aqueduct, Erie Canal (enlarged) at Fort Hunter, New York, ca. 1839–41. P & P, HAER, NY,FORHU,2A-28, detail.

2-084. Site plan, Upper Mohawk River Aqueduct, Mohawk River, Erie Canal (enlarged), Rexford, New York, ca. 1839–41. P & P, HAER, NY,46-REXFO,1-5, detail.

2-085. Genesee River Aqueduct over the Genesee River, Erie Canal (enlarged), Rochester, New York, ca. 1900–1906. P & P, DPCC, LC-D4-10847.

2-086. Upper Mohawk River Aqueduct,
Mohawk River, Erie Canal (enlarged), at
Rexford, New York. Jack E. Boucher, photog-
rapher, August 1969. P & P, HAER, NY,46-
REXFO,1-1.

The Upper Mohawk River Aqueduct, also
called the Rexford Aqueduct, was completed
in 1842 as part of the program to enlarge
the Erie Canal. It replaced the original
Rexford Aqueduct constructed in 1828. The
aqueduct continued in operation until
1916, when the New York Barge Canal was
opened. A major portion of the aqueduct
was removed in 1918.

2-087. Fence detail, Monocacy Aqueduct,
Chesapeake and Ohio Canal, Dickerson Vic.,
Maryland. Jack E. Boucher, photographer,
April 1959. P & P, HABS, MD, 11-_____,
3-15.

2-088

2-089

2-090

this page

2-088. Looking downstream at the Delaware Aqueduct, Delaware and Hudson Canal, Lackawaxen, Pennsylvania. David Plowden, photographer, 1969–70. P & P, HAER, PA,52-LACK,1-4.

Suspension bridge aqueducts are very rare in canal construction. Constructed in 1847–48 by John A. Roebling under contract to the Delaware and Hudson Canal Company, this aqueduct spanning the Delaware River was one of four suspension aqueducts built for the company. It consisted of three spans of approximately 131 feet each, and one span of 142 feet. This structure is America's oldest existing suspension bridge. After the canal was abandoned, the aqueduct was converted into a highway bridge.

2-089. Upstream face of the center pier, Delaware Aqueduct, Delaware and Hudson Canal, Lackawaxen, Pennsylvania. David Plowden, photographer, 1969–70. P & P, HAER, PA,52-LACK,1-6.

2-090. Suspension bridge decking, Delaware Aqueduct, Delaware and Hudson Canal, Lackawaxen, Pennsylvania. David Plowden, photographer, 1969–70. P & P, HAER, PA,52-LACK,1-7.

opposite

2-091. Plan and northwest elevation, Delaware Aqueduct, Delaware and Hudson Canal, Lackawaxen, Pennsylvania. Eric Delony, delineator, 1969. P & P, HAER PA-1, sheet no. 2, detail.

2-092. Longitudinal section of Pier 3, the west abutment, and a view (based on design drawings) of the west anchorage, Delaware Aqueduct, Delaware and Hudson Canal, Lackawaxen, Pennsylvania. Eric Delony and Robert M. Vogel, delineators, 1969. P & P, HAER PA-1, sheet no. 3.

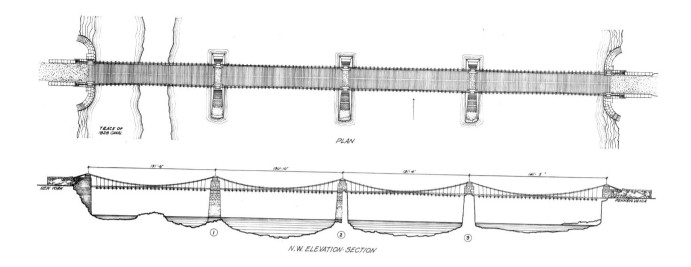

TRACE OF
1828 CANAL

PLAN

131'-6"   130'-10"   131'-6"   141'-5"

NEW YORK

PENNSYLVANIA

① ② ③

N.W. ELEVATION·SECTION

2-091

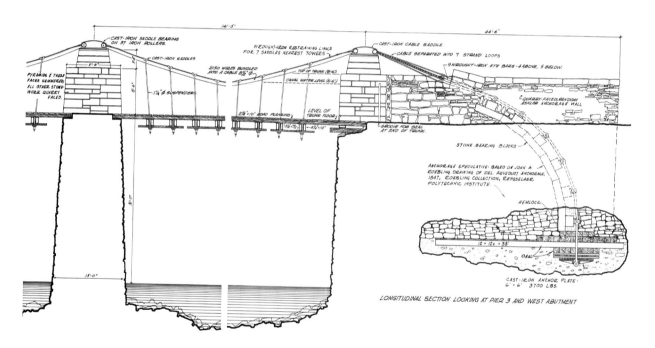

141'-5"   44'-6"

CAST-IRON SADDLE BEARING
ON 37 IRON ROLLERS.

CAST-IRON SADDLES

WROUGHT-IRON RESTRAINING LINKS
FOR 7 SADDLES NEAREST TOWERS.

CAST-IRON CABLE SADDLE

CABLE SEPARATED INTO 7 STRAND LOOPS.

9'-6"

PYRAMIDS & THESE
FACES HAMMERED
ALL OTHER STONE
WORK QUARRY
FACED.

8'-6"

2150 WIRES BUNDLED
INTO A CABLE 8½" Ø

1¼" Ø SUSPENDERS.

TOP OF TRUNK (8'-6")

CANAL WATER LEVEL (8'-6")

9 WROUGHT-IRON EYE BARS - 4 ABOVE, 5 BELOW.

QUARRY-FACED RANDOM
ASHLAR ANCHORAGE WALL

2½"·10" ROAD PLANKING

LEVEL OF
TRUNK FLOOR

GROOVE FOR SEAL
AT END OF TRUNK.

STONE BEARING BLOCKS

ANCHORAGE SPECULATIVE: BASED ON JOHN A.
ROEBLING DRAWING OF DEL. AQUEDUCT ANCHORAGE,
1847, ROEBLING COLLECTION, RENSSELAER
POLYTECHNIC INSTITUTE.

50'-0"

HEMLOCK

13'-0"

12"·12"·33'

OAK

CAST-IRON ANCHOR PLATE
6'·6' 3700 LBS.

LONGITUDINAL SECTION LOOKING AT PIER 3 AND WEST ABUTMENT

2-092

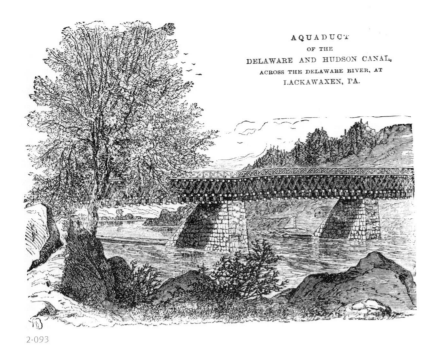

AQUADUCT
OF THE
DELAWARE AND HUDSON CANAL,
ACROSS THE DELAWARE RIVER, AT
LACKAWAXEN, PA.

2-093

2-093. Scenic view, Delaware Aqueduct, Delaware and Hudson Canal, Lackawaxen, Pennsylvania. From *Erie Route* (1887). P & P, HAER, PA,52-LACK,1-21.

2-094. Delaware Aqueduct, Delaware and Hudson Canal, Lackawaxen, Pennsylvania. Delaware and Hudson Canal Company photograph, 1898. P & P, HAER, PA,52-LACK,1-24.

Shown shortly after the canal ceased operation in late 1898, the prism is empty, not yet converted to a highway bridge.

2-095. Suspension cables and the saddle on the towers of the Delaware Aqueduct, Delaware and Hudson Canal, Lackawaxen, Pennsylvania. David Plowden, photographer, 1969–70. P & P, HAER, PA,52-LACK,1-14.

The metal saddles carried the suspension cables over the tops of the towers and distributed the load of the cables to prevent the masonry atop the towers and immediately below the cables from being crushed.

2-094

2-095

2-096. Au Sable Creek Aqueduct, Illinois and Michigan Canal, Morris Vic., Illinois. Jet T. Lowe, photographer, 1986. P & P, HAER, ILL,32-MOR.V,1-2.

This steel plate–girder aqueduct was constructed in 1927–28 to replace the original 1847 wood truss aqueduct.

2-097. South elevation, Au Sable Creek Aqueduct, Illinois and Michigan Canal, Morris Vic., Illinois. Jet T. Lowe, photographer, 1986. P & P, HAER, ILL,32-MOR.V,1-1.

2-096

2-097

2-098

2-098. Steel plate–girder trough, Fox River Aqueduct, Illinois and Michigan Canal, Ottawa, Illinois. Martin Stupich, photographer, 1988. P & P, HAER, ILL,50-OTWA, 5-9.

2-099. Interior of the canal trough, Fox River Aqueduct, Illinois and Michigan Canal, Ottawa, Illinois. Martin Stupich, photographer, 1988. P & P, HAER, ILL,50-OTWA, 5-5.

2-099

2-100. Fox River Aqueduct from the west
bank of the Fox River, Illinois and Michigan
Canal, Ottawa, Illinois. Martin Stupich, photographer, 1988. P & P, HAER, ILL,50-OTWA,
5-1.

2-101

2-102

2-101. Tinker Creek Aqueduct, Ohio and Erie Canal, Valley View, Ohio. Louise Taft Cawood, photographer, July 1986. P & P, HAER, OHIO,18-VAVI,5-4.

2-102. Wood trough and waste gates, Tinker Creek Aqueduct, Ohio and Erie Canal, Valley View, Ohio. Louise Taft Cawood, photographer, July 1986. P & P, HAER, OHIO, 18-VAVI,5-2.

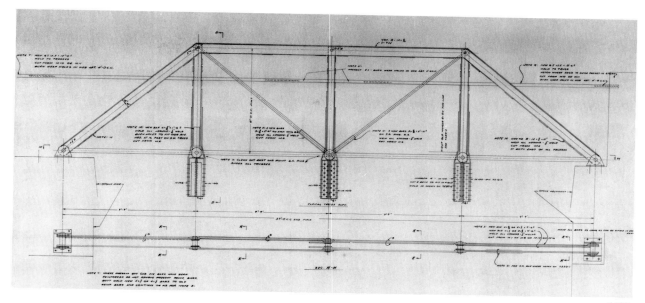

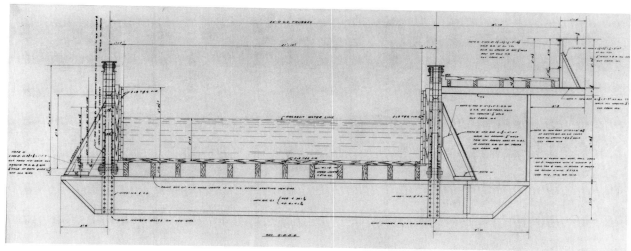

2-103. Fabrication drawing of steel truss for the aqueduct, Tinker Creek Aqueduct, Ohio and Erie Canal, Valley View, Ohio. Cuyahoga Works, American Steel and Wire Company, delineators, 1950. Copy, July 1986. P & P, HAER, OHIO,18-VAVI,5-7.

2-104. Cross section, Tinker Creek Aqueduct trough, Ohio and Erie Canal, Valley View, Ohio. Cuyahoga Works, American Steel and Wire Company, delineators, 1950. Copy, July 1986. P & P, HAER, OHIO,18-VAVI,5-8.

CULVERTS AND WASTE WEIRS

Culverts were usually constructed to channel water under the canal. Sometimes substantial structures in their own right, they were usually masonry arch structures (2-107–2-109; see also 4-060, 4-063, 4-114–4-115) constructed on a wooden grillage foundation (2-108–2-109; see also 1-047; 4-114). Waste weirs were structures that, when opened, allowed water to be drained from the canal. They also discharged excess water, thus acting as a safety valve.

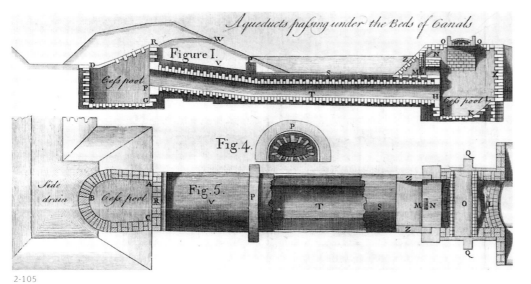

2-105

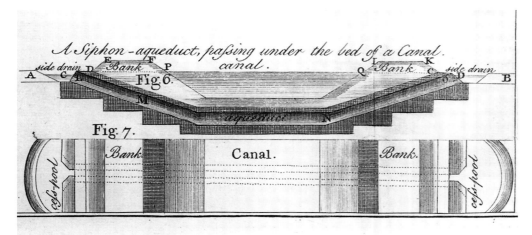

2-106

2-105. Section and plan of a canal culvert, from Charles Vallancey, *A Treatise on Inland Navigation* (1763). RBSCD, TC744.V17.

2-106. Section and plan of a culvert that siphoned water from one side of the canal to the other, from Charles Vallancey, *A Treatise on Inland Navigation* (1763). RBSCD, TC744.V17.

Canal structures built in Europe in the eighteenth and nineteenth centuries tended to be more sophisticated than those built in America at the same time. One example is siphons—used in Europe to pass water under the canal but hardly ever used in America. Siphons differ from open air culverts in that they can raise the outflow to a higher level, but they had to be constructed to withstand the water pressure.

2-107. Northwest facade of the canal culvert headwall of Ten Mile Run Culvert, Delaware and Raritan Canal, East Millstone Vic., New Jersey. Anthony Masso, photographer, 1968. P & P, HAER, NJ,18-MILE.V,2-2.

2-108. Lilly Culvert, Allegheny Portage Railroad, Lilly, Pennsylvania. Joseph Elliott, photographer, 1997. P & P, HAER, PA,11-LIL, 1-5.

2-109. West elevation, Bens Creek Culvert, Allegheny Portage Railroad at Cassandra, Pennsylvania. Joseph Elliott, photographer, 1997. P & P, HAER, PA,11-CLASS,1-2.

Note the wood floor. Also see 1-047; 4-114.

2-107

2-108

2-109

2-110

2-110. River side of the waste weir, Lock 27, Chesapeake and Ohio Canal, Dickerson Vic., Maryland. Jack E. Boucher, photographer, 1959. P & P, HABS, MD,16-DICK.V,5-1.

The river side of a waste weir is typically protected with wing walls and an apron to prevent the discharging water from under-cutting the canal embankment.

2-111. Canal side of the waste weir, Lock 27, Chesapeake and Ohio Canal, Dickerson Vic., Maryland. Jack E. Boucher, photographer, 1959. P & P, HABS, MD,16-DICK.V,5-2.

2-111

BRIDGES

Canals frequently cut through valuable bottom land, and bridges were sometimes necessary to give property owners access. Bridges were required particularly in urban areas, and sometimes they served the canal owners' needs—for example, mule crossover bridges (see 1-091) when the towpath changed from one side of the canal to the other.

Because a minimum clearance had to be maintained over a canal for boat passage and a gradual rise was required on both sides of the bridge, masonry bridges (2-112–2-114; see also 4-008, 4-009; 4-011) were expensive. Wood truss (see 1-081, 1-091; 3-070, 3-088, 3-092, 3-107, 3-111) and metal truss bridges (2-115; see also 4-060, 4-096, 4-133) were less expensive but still required substantial engineering approaches. Movable bridges, in contrast, did not: with lift bridges, the bridge decking was raised or drawn out of the way of boat traffic (2-116, 2-119; see 3-112, 3-113, 3-148, 3-109, 3-110; 4-097), while with swing, turning, or pivot bridges, the bridge deck was swung or rotated out of the way (2-117, 2-118, 2-120–2-123). Road culverts under the canal were expensive alternatives (see 3-071). Some canal companies used ferries across the canal to transport hay wagons and similar cargoes, but not very successfully.

2-112. Masonry arch bridge over the Middlesex Canal, Medford, Massachusetts. Undated photograph. P & P, HABS, MASS,9-____,10-1.

2-112

Bridge for a Canal.

2-113

2-113. Elevation and plan of a masonry arch bridge for a canal, from J. Phillips, *A General History of Inland Navigation* (1792). RBSCD, TC744 .P53.

2-114. Wisconsin Avenue Bridge, a masonry arch bridge, over the Chesapeake and Ohio Canal, Georgetown, Washington, D.C., ca. 1910–20. P & P, DPCC, LC-D4-73253.

A team of mules and driver are towing the canal boat under the bridge.

2-115. Metal truss bridge over a lock, Ohio and Erie Canal, Coshocton, Ohio. Joseph Elliott, photographer, 1992. P & P, HAER, OHIO,16-COSH,1-2.

2-116. Lift bridge over a canal, from J. Phillips, *A General History of Inland Navigation* (1792). RBSCD, TC744 .P53.

2-114

2-115

2-116

2-117

2-118

2-117. Canal boat passing a swing bridge. S. G. McCutchen, engraver. From *Harper's Weekly*, December 20, 1879. P & P, LC-USZ62-35602.

2-118. Swing bridge over the Delaware and Raritan Canal, Kingston, New Jersey. Nathaniel R. Ewan, photographer, 1936. P & P, HABS, NJ,12-PLABO.V,3-1.

2-119. Plan, section, and elevation of a lift bridge, from Charles Vallancey, *A Treatise on Inland Navigation* (1763). RBSCD, TC744.V17.

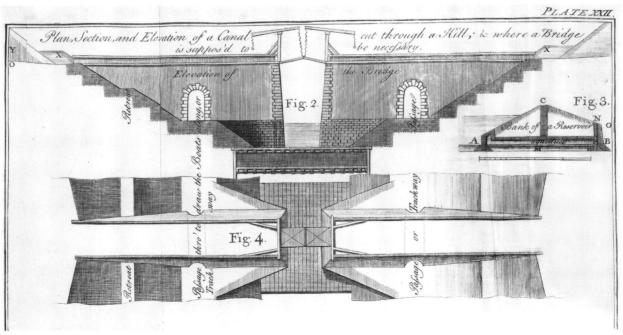

2-119

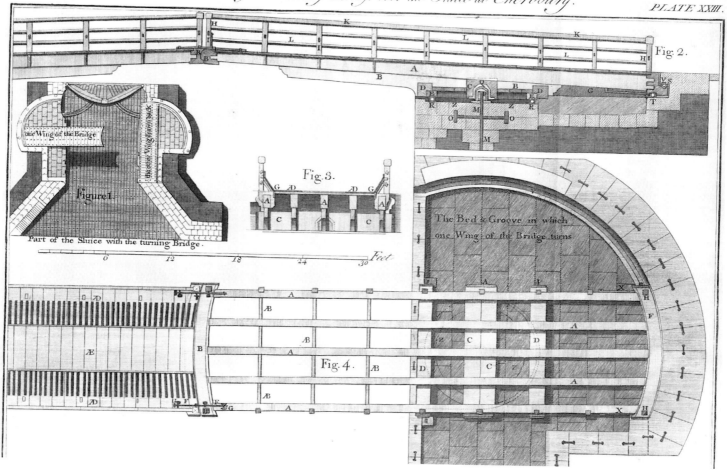

Fig. 2.

one Wing of the Bridge

the other Wing drawn back

Figure 1.

Part of the Sluice with the turning Bridge.

Fig. 3.

The Bed & Groove in which one Wing of the Bridge turns

0   12   18   24   30   Feet

Fig. 4.

2-120

2-120. Elevation, plan, and section of the swing or turning bridge over the sluice at Cherbourg, France, from Charles Vallancey, *A Treatise on Inland Navigation* (1763). RBSCD, TC744.V17.

2-121. Plan and section of a canal swing bridge, from Charles Vallancey, *A Treatise on Inland Navigation* (1763). RBSCD, TC744.V17.

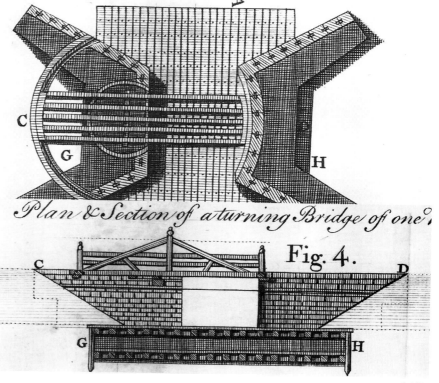

Plan & Section of a turning Bridge of one

Fig. 4.

2-121

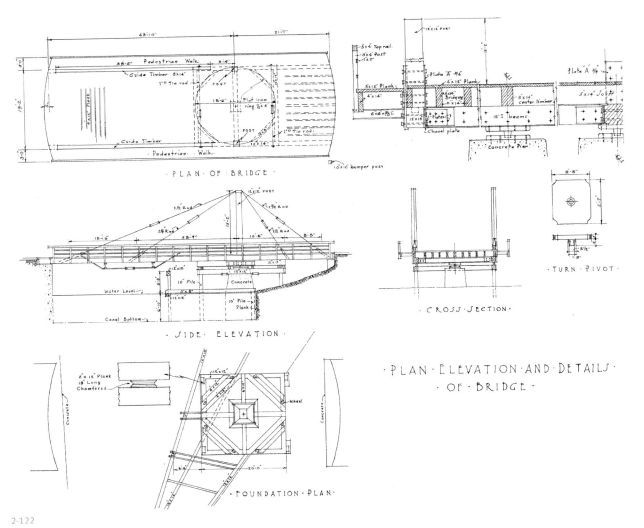

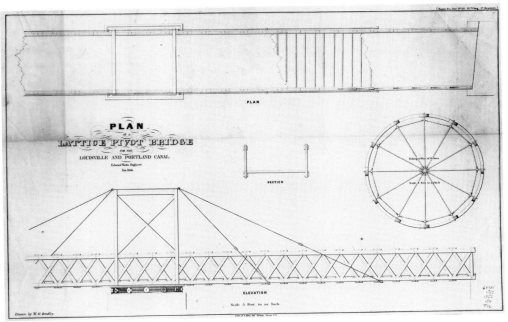

2-122. Plan, elevation, section, and foundation plan of the swing bridge, Delaware and Raritan Canal, Kingston, New Jersey. John A. Kehoe, delineator, 1937. P & P, HABS NJ-359, sheet no. 7.

2-123. Plan, section, and elevation of a swing bridge, Louisville and Portland Canal, Louisville, Kentucky. Edward Watts, engineer, November 1856. G & M, G3701 .P53 1856 .B7 TIL.

This bridge was designed for the enlargement of the locks on the Louisville and Portland Canal. Because the canal lock was sized for riverboats, the bridge had to be designed for a greater span than usual. Tension cables tied to the central truss tower helped prevent the lattice trusses from sagging at the end of the bridge. The weight of this bridge had to be supported by rollers arranged in a circle around the central truss tower (right).

TUNNELS

Tunnels were rare on canals because they were very expensive to build. Sometimes, however, canal engineers could not otherwise avoid hills and mountains in the path of the canal. When tunnels had to be built, they were bored from each end and also from positions inside the tunnel reached from vertical shafts, as with the Paw Paw Tunnel (see 4-128).

2-124

2-124. South portal of the Paw Paw Tunnel, Chesapeake and Ohio Canal, Oldtown Vic., Maryland. Jack E. Boucher, photographer, 1960. P & P, HABS, MD,1-OLDTO.V,4-7.

One of the engineering accomplishments of the Chesapeake and Ohio Canal Company, the Paw Paw Tunnel is 3,118 feet long and was constructed to avoid the double bend of the Potomac River and a length of 6 miles by that route. The tunnel took fourteen years to build and opened in 1850 (see 4-126, 4-128).

2-125. Longitudinal section, Thames and Medway Tunnel, England, from William Strickland, *Reports on Canals, Railways, Roads and Other Subjects, made to The Pennsylvania Society for the Promotion of Internal Improvement* (1826). RBSCD, TA57 .S91.

2-126

2-126. Thames and Medway Tunnel, England, from William Strickland, *Reports on Canals, Railways, Roads and Other Subjects, made to The Pennsylvania Society for the Promotion of Internal Improvement* (1826). RBSCD, TA57 .S91.

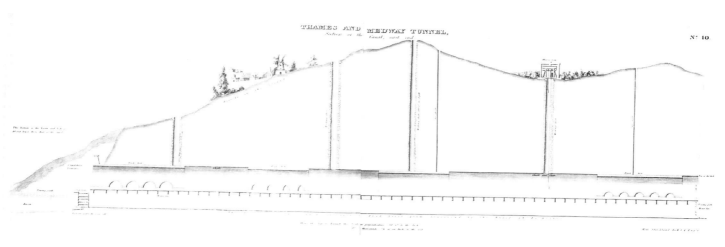

2-125

DAMS

Dams were used in all kinds of canals. In river navigation projects, they were used to impound water, usually for mills. Boats passed them by means of flash locks, a portion of the dam that could be opened to allow the craft to descend on a flood, or flash, of water. Dams in lock-and-pond navigation schemes were usually traversed by means of a lift lock (see IN-009–IN-010). In stillwater canals dams diverted water from the river to the canal or impounded water in a reservoir. The most common river dams were timber cribs: wooden boxes or cribs filled with rock rubble and stone and their interstices filled with tamped loose soil (see IN-050 and IN-051). Framed timber dams required less timber than a dam made of logs (2-119 and 2-130). Masonry dams were much more durable than either timber crib or framed timber dams but were also much more expensive (2-131, 2-132; see also IN-008; 1-077).

2-127

2-127. Hamilton Street Dam, Lehigh Canal, Allentown, Pennsylvania. Robert G. Miller, photographer, July 1983. P & P, HAER, PA, 39-ALLEN, 3A-10.

Timber crib dams were frequently sheathed in wood to prevent erosion of their rubble fill by the river. The larger timber members held the dam together, and thinner wood sheathing protected the rubble-filled interior against water erosion. (See also IN-049– IN-051; 1-065).

2-128. Detail, Hamilton Street Dam, Lehigh Canal, Allentown, Pennsylvania. Robert G. Miller, photographer, July 1983. P & P, HAER, PA,39-CATSN,3A-7.

2-129. Section of framed timber dam across the Schuylkill River at Plymouth, Pennsylvania, by the Schuylkill River Navigation Company. From Edward Wegmann, *The Design and Construction of Dams* (1899). LC, TC540 .W4.

Constructed in 1819 to create lock-and-pond navigation, the 12-by-16-inch timbers at the bottom of this dam were secured to the river bottom and the frame was built on these sills. Thick planking was secured on the upstream side and a slope of clay and stone was placed against this face. This type of dam could be built without a cofferdam to keep the water from the work (see IN-023, 4-019). It may not look as substantial as a masonry or timber crib dam, but this particular dam survived for thirty-nine years, and the company replaced it with a similar dam.

2-130. Section of framed timber dam across the Schuylkill River at Plymouth, Pennsylvania, by the Schuylkill River Navigation Company. From Edward Wegmann, *The Design and Construction of Dams* (1899). LC, TC540 .W4.

2-128

No 1. OLD DAM AT PLYMOUTH.
SCHUYLKILL NAV. CO.

2-129

No 3. NEW DAM AT PLYMOUTH
SCHUYLKILL NAV. CO.

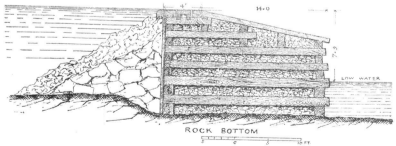

2-130

2-131. Dam 5, Chesapeake and Ohio Canal, Fort Frederick Vic., Maryland. Jack E. Boucher, photographer, 1959. P & P, HABS, MD,22-FOFR.V,4-1.

First constructed in 1833–35 as a timber crib dam by Thomas Purcell, engineer, Dam 5 was 706 feet long and 20 feet high. It diverted water from the Potomac to a 20-mile stretch of the Chesapeake and Ohio Canal, to Dam 4 downstream. Dam 5 was damaged by a series of floods in 1840, 1847, and 1857, when work began on a replacement masonry gravity dam 711 feet long and 21 to 22 feet tall. The Civil War delayed the completion of this dam; it was finished in 1873. It is one of the two "High Rock" dams (i.e., masonry dams over 5 feet tall) along the Chesapeake and Ohio Canal. For the other High Rock dam, Dam 4, see 1-077.

2-132. Attack on Dam 5, Chesapeake and Ohio Canal, Williamsport Vic., Maryland. From *Frank Leslie's Illustrated Newspaper*, February 18, 1862. MRC, Leslie's: Microfilm 02282.

In December 1861, Confederate forces (far side of the Potomac River) launched an unsuccessful attack on Dam 5. Union forces used the canal lock (center foreground) and lockhouse (right foreground) to defend themselves.

LIFT WHEELS

2-133. Half-section and half-elevation of the lift wheel and steam engine, Chesapeake and Delaware Canal, Chesapeake City, Maryland. Robert Levy, delineator, 1977. P & P, HAER, MD-39, sheet no. 5.

The Chesapeake and Delaware Canal was plagued with low water at its summit, between St. George's, Delaware, and Chesapeake City, Maryland. The company installed a steam-driven pump in 1837, replaced in 1851–52 by a 175-horsepower steam engine (right). This drove the lift wheel (left), nearly 40 feet in diameter and capable of lifting 200,000 cubic feet of water per hour 14 feet from Back Creek to the summit. A second engine, almost identical to the first, was added in 1854. These two machines continued to operate until 1927, when a sea-level Chesapeake and Delaware Canal was constructed. These machines are believed to be the oldest American stationary steam engines extant on their original foundations.

2-134. Front elevation of engines and lift wheel, Chesapeake and Delaware Canal, Chesapeake City, Maryland. Janet Mochuli, delineator, 1977. P & P, HAER, MD-39, sheet no. 4.

Shown are the 1851–52 engine (left), lift wheel (center), and the 1854 engine (right).

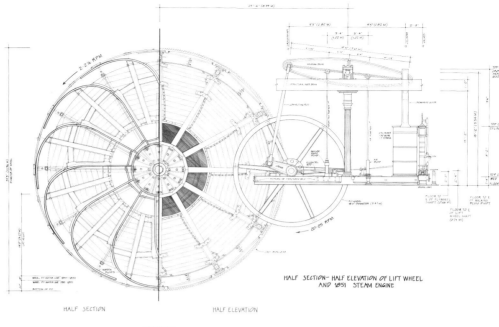

HALF SECTION — HALF ELEVATION OF LIFT WHEEL AND 1851 STEAM ENGINE

HALF SECTION   HALF ELEVATION

LIFT WHEEL

2-133

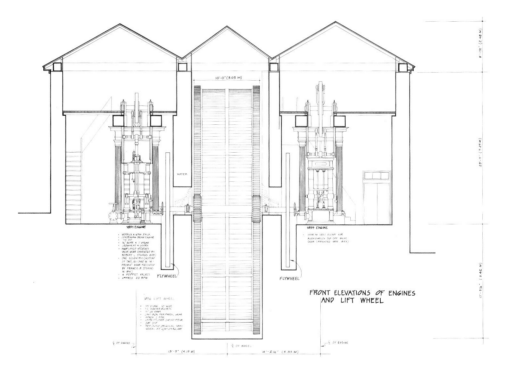

FRONT ELEVATIONS OF ENGINES AND LIFT WHEEL

2-134

BOATS

Most canal boats were made of wood, so very few of them have survived: we know them only from illustrations. Boats built for river navigation reflected the conditions of the river. On the broad but shallow Susquehanna, where almost all traffic was one way downstream at the time of spring floods, rafts and arks predominated (see IN-006, IN-007, IN-012). Usually flat-bottomed and constructed of 2-inch planking without iron or caulking, these vessels were broken apart at the end of their journey. In the upstream reaches of the James and Potomac Rivers, long, narrow boats (such as bateaux, or Potomac River sharpers, with pointed ends and covered with hoops and tarpaulins, like Conestoga wagons), requiring little draft, were used (2-141; see also IN-064; 1-081, 1-086). With the advent of stillwater canals, boats were designed and constructed with the smallest element of the canal—the lock—in mind. Unlike the boats built for one-way passage, these boats were more substantial and were intended for a long life, perhaps twenty years or more. The finest of them were the packet boats for passenger travel (2-136; see also IN-013, IN-018, IN-019; 1-015, 1-016) and excursion boats (2-140; see also 3-147). Other boats were intended for the repair and maintenance of canals (2-142; see also 3-151) or to deliver freight (2-135–2-139; see also 3-154). The most basic vessel was the scow, which hauled bulk cargoes (2-142; see also 1-033). Some canal boats provided living quarters for the crew.

Boats for river navigation were carried downriver by the current and poled or towed upriver (2-138; see also IN-013). Stillwater canal boats were almost always towed by mules or horses and always attended by a driver, sometimes a child, to ensure that the animals did not stop to graze along the towpath (2-139; see also IN-007, IN-020, IN-025, 1-019; 4-017). Frequently the animals lived aboard the canal boat (2-040A). Sometimes oars were used (2-138; see also IN-019). Numerous attempts were made to power stillwater canal boats with engines. These efforts usually ended in failure as the wake of the boat tended to erode the canal banks. Until the canals' demise in the beginning of the twentieth century, mules and horses were the preferred motive power.

2-135. Canal boat on the Chesapeake and Ohio Canal, unidentified location, Maryland. Herbert E. French, photographer, ca. 1909–24. P & P, LC-USZ62-131447.

2-136. Illustration of canal boats on the Erie Canal, New York, from Cadwallader D. Colden, *Memoir, Prepared at the Request of a Committee at the Celebration of the Completion of the New York Canals* (1825). RBSCD, TC624 .N7 C6.

2-137. Canal boats on the Erie Canal, Rochester, New York, ca. 1900–1906. P & P, DPCC, LC-D4-17931.

2-135

2-136

2-137

2-138

2-138. Poling a boat on the Augusta Canal, Augusta, Georgia. William Goater, artist, July 1977. From *Frank Leslie's Illustrated Newspaper*, August 14, 1880. P & P, HAER, GA,123-AUG,41-39.

The lowlands of Georgia and South Carolina were ideal for shallow-draft vessels that could be poled through the low waters (center). In the cotton country of these states, where roads didn't exist or were frequently impassable, such small vessels were used to ship cotton to the port cities of Savannah and Charleston for transshipment overseas.

2-139. Canal boat on the Chesapeake and Ohio Canal, entering the lock at Great Falls, Maryland. Herbert E. French, photographer, ca. 1912. P & P, LC-USZ62-10149.

2-140. School children on an outing, Chesapeake and Ohio Canal, Georgetown, Washington, D.C. Benjamin Frances Johnson, photographer, ca. 1899. P & P, LC-USZ62-4551.

2-139

2-140

2-141

2-141. Canal boat on the Augusta Canal, Augusta, Georgia, from *Art Work of Augusta* (1894). P & P, HAER, GA,123-AUG,41-24.

2-142. Boats used on the Augusta Canal, Augusta, Georgia. Craig Morrison, delineator, 1977, based on original working drawings in the Office of the City Engineer, Augusta, Georgia. P & P, HAER GA-5, sheet no. 8.

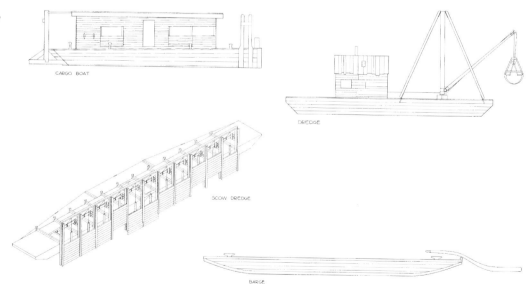

CARGO BOAT

DREDGE

SCOW DREDGE

BARGE

2-142

MORRIS CANAL

The hills of northern New Jersey separated one of the greatest sources of coal, in northeastern Pennsylvania, from one of the largest markets for coal, the New York metropolitan area. Three routes were devised to overcome this obstacle: above the hills in Pennsylvania and New York (the Delaware and Hudson Canal), below them across the narrow girth of New Jersey (the Delaware and Raritan Canal), and over them (the Morris Canal).

Work began on the Morris Canal in 1825. When completed, it comprised twenty-three inclined planes (as well as twenty-three locks 95 to 100 feet long and 11 feet wide, with a lift of 8 to 12 feet); canal boats were hauled over the hills separating Phillipsburg, New Jersey, in the west, and Jersey City in the east, overcoming an increase in elevation of 716 feet between Phillipsburg and the canal summit and a decrease in elevation of 914 feet between the canal summit and Jersey City. The distance between these two cities was a little over 100 miles, which could be traversed by boat in five days. The inclined planes were powered by Scotch turbines from water impounded in Lake Hopatcong at the summit and elsewhere.

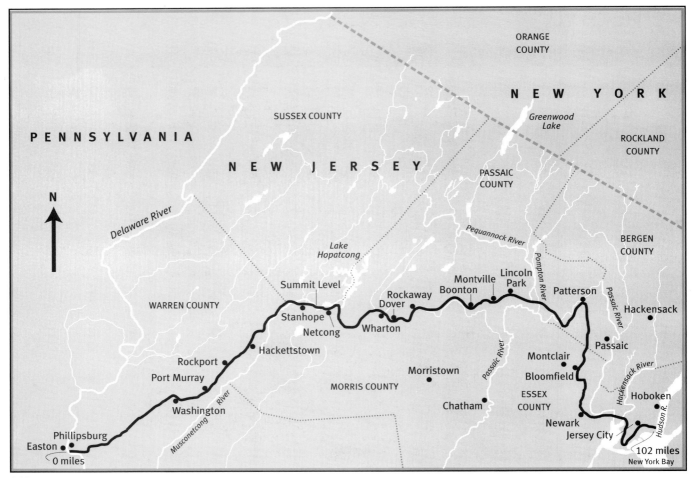

3-001

3-001. Morris Canal, New Jersey.

Stretching across northern New Jersey, the Morris Canal linked the anthracite fields of northeastern Pennsylvania with the New York Metropolitan market. A series of water-powered inclined planes hauled coal-laden canal boats 716 feet in vertical elevation from Phillipsburg to the canal summit at Lake Hopatcong and then lowered the boats 914 vertical feet to sea level in New York Harbor.

Competition from railroads hurt the canal, and in 1922 it passed into the hands of the State of New Jersey. Its structures were dismantled or replaced, and its remains have largely been obliterated from the landscape. With a few exceptions, mainly in rural areas (3-020–3-022, 3-024–3-026, 3-030), the canal can only be experienced in the images that survive. This section is arranged by mileage as originally designated by the canal company: the entrance from the Delaware River at Phillipsburg is mile zero while the basin at Jersey City is mile 102. Where mileage is not given, the location falls between the mileage given for illustrations before and after.

3-002. Elevation of a canal boat in the cradle (also called a car or carriage), used to haul canal boats up and down inclined planes, and plan of the cradle. Morris Canal, New Jersey. From David Stevenson, *Sketch of the Civil Engineering of North America* (1859). James Andrews, delineator. P & P, HAER, NJ,21-PHIL.V,1-6.

3-003. Views of Inclined Plane II East, Morris Canal, Bloomfield, New Jersey. *Scientific American*, May 20, 1882. LC TI.S5.

The inclined planes of the Morris Canal were considered one of the engineering wonders of the nineteenth century and were frequently described and depicted in the magazines and journals of the day. Inclined Plane II East was 1,600 feet long and overcame a difference in elevation of 60 feet. Transit time was four minutes.

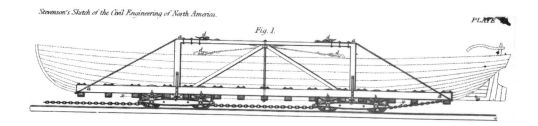

Stevenson's Sketch of the Civil Engineering of North America.

PLATE

Fig. 1.

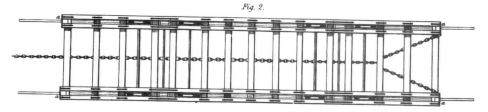

Fig. 2.

Boat car used on the inclined planes at the Morris Canal.

3-002

HYDRAULIC LIFT ON THE MORRIS CANAL, AT BLOOMFIELD, N. J.

3-003

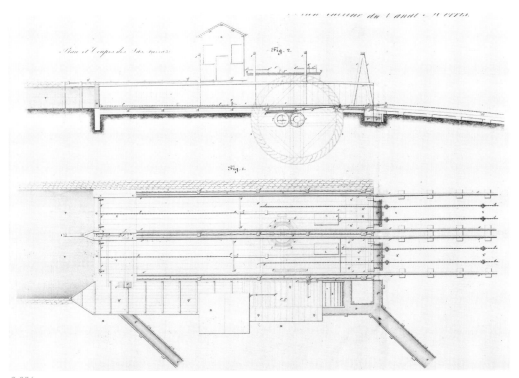

3-004

3-004. Elevation and plan, top, and power-house of a typical double-tracked inclined plane, Morris Canal, New Jersey. From Michel Chevalier, *Histoire et Description des Voies de Communication aux États-Unis et des Travaux d'art Qui en Dépendent*, 1841–42. LC TA 23. C52.

3-005. Elevation and section of a typical inclined plane powerhouse, Morris Canal, New Jersey. *Engineering* (July 31, 1868). LC TA1 .E55.

The penstock (right) brings water to the powerhouse where it falls vertically into the Scotch turbine (bottom), which turns the drive shaft (center), which turns the pulleys (center), which pull the cable (right), which, in turn, hauls the canal boat and cradle up or down the inclined plane. Used water is discharged back into the lower level of the canal (left) .

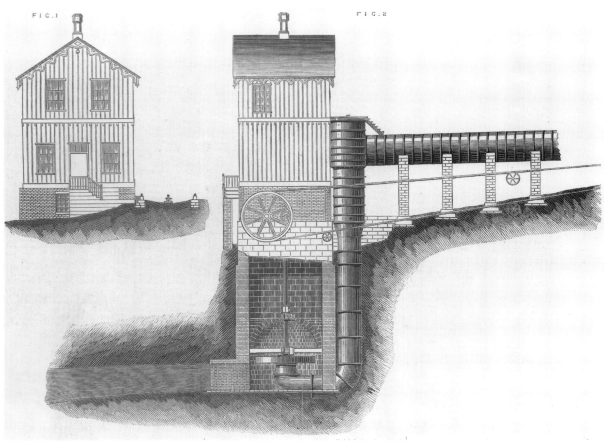

3-005

3-006. Bottom of a typical Scotch turbine, Morris Canal, Hopatcong Vic., New Jersey. Jack E. Boucher, photographer, 1970. P & P, HAER, NJ,21-PHIL,1-L-2.

The water from the penstock entered the turbine at the bottom and exited through the arms shown in the middle, thus turning the wheel.

3-007. Top of a typical Scotch turbine, Morris Canal, Hopatcong Vic., New Jersey. Jack E. Boucher, photographer, 1970. P & P, HAER, NJ,21-PHIL,1-L-2.

The main shaft shown here rotated and turned the machinery that pulled the traction rope that hauled the cradles and boats up and down the inclined plane. The water entered from below so that the upward pressure of the water balanced the weight of the wheel, vertical shaft, and bevel gear, relieving friction on bearings. The operating efficiency of this turbine from Plane 3 East was tested in 1926. The engineers conducting the tests concluded that the performance of wheel, gearing, drum, and cable designed a century earlier was almost as good as the machinery designed in the twentieth century.

3-006

3-007

3-008

3-009

3-008. Hinged canal boat in its cradle at the top of an inclined plane, Morris Canal, New Jersey. From Canal Society of New Jersey, late nineteenth/early twentieth century. P & P, HAER, NJ,21-PHIL, 1-161.

The Morris Canal boats were constructed in sections to assist their transit at the summit of the inclined planes (3-013). The cradles were built in two sections, each 36 feet long. Each cradle rode on four pairs of 30-inch-diameter double-flanged wheels. The cradles were equipped with powerful brakes that could be applied from the top of the cradle.

3-009. Canal boat in its cradle, possibly at Plane 4 East, Morris Canal, Netcong Vic., New Jersey. From Canal Society of New Jersey, late nineteenth/early twentieth century. P & P, HAER, NJ,21-PHIL,1-63.

At the top of the inclined plane was a hump, a mound of earth to hold the water at the upper level. This photograph shows the canal boat in its cradle passing over the hump. Both boat and cradle were hinged to facilitate passage over it.

3-010. Exterior of the West Portal, Morris Canal, from the Delaware River at Phillipsburg, New Jersey (0 miles). Jack E. Boucher, photographer, 1970. P & P, HAER, NJ,21-PHIL,1-A-2.

Canal boats were hauled across the Delaware River from the Lehigh River at Easton, Pennsylvania.

3-011. Plane 11 West, Morris Canal, Phillipsburg, New Jersey. From Canal Society of New Jersey, late nineteenth/early twentieth century. P & P, HAER, NJ,21-PHIL,1-4.

Immediately after entering the Morris Canal at the Delaware River, the canal traveler traversed the first of eleven inclined planes on the western division of the canal. Plane 11 West had a vertical lift of 35 feet and a gradient of one in twelve. This view shows the powerhouse (left), the hauling cable and rails (foreground), the cradle for the canal boat (middle right), the portal to the Delaware River, and the Delaware River (far right, under the railroad trestle).

3-012. Coal chutes built by the Lehigh Valley Railroad, Port Delaware, Morris Canal, Phillipsburg, New Jersey. From Canal Society of New Jersey, late nineteenth/early twentieth century. P & P, HAER, NJ,21-PHIL,1-6.

Port Delaware, the canal basin of the Morris Canal at Phillipsburg, began at the top of Plane 11 West.

3-010

3-011

3-012

3-013

3-014. Canal boats, Morris Canal, Port Delaware, Phillipsburg, New Jersey. From Canal Society of New Jersey, late nineteenth/early twentieth century. P & P, HAER, NJ,21-PHIL,1-7.

The coal chutes of the Lehigh Valley Railroad can be seen behind the boats, which appear to be empty: they are riding high in the water awaiting their next load. The delineation between hinged sections is visible on the side of the boat in the foreground.

3-014. Toll collector's house at the northwest end of the Port Delaware Basin, Morris Canal, Port Delaware, Phillipsburg, New Jersey. From Canal Society of New Jersey, late nineteenth/early twentieth century. P & P, HAER, NJ,21-PHIL,1-8.

3-015. Cooper's Furnace, Morris Canal, Phillipsburg Vic., New Jersey (1.4 miles). From Canal Society of New Jersey, late nineteenth/early twentieth century. P & P, HAER, NJ,21-PHIL,1-9.

3-014

3-015

3-016. Lock 9 West, Morris Canal, Green's Bridge, New Jersey (2.3 miles). From Canal Society of New Jersey, late nineteenth/early twentieth century. P & P, HAER, NJ,21-PHIL,1-11.

3-017. Lock 8 West and lockhouse, Morris Canal, Phillipsburg Vic., New Jersey (2.6 miles). From Canal Society of New Jersey, late nineteenth/early twentieth century. P & P, HAER, NJ,21-PHIL,1-12.

3-018. Plane 10 West, Morris Canal, Phillipsburg Vic., New Jersey (3.1 miles). Copy of photograph by William Cone, ca. 1900. P & P, HAER, NJ,21-PHIL.V,1-1.

Plane 10 West had a vertical lift of 44 feet and a gradient of one in ten.

3-016

3-017

3-018

3-019

3-020

3-019. Looking down Plane 10 West, Morris Canal, Phillipsburg Vic., New Jersey (3.1 miles). Copy of photograph by William Cone, ca. 1900. P & P, HAER, NJ,21-PHIL.V,1-2.

The track of the inclined plane (left) and the canal basin at the bottom of the inclined plane (top center) can be seen.

3-020. Plane 10 West, Morris Canal, Phillipsburg Vic., New Jersey (3.1 miles). Jack E. Boucher, photographer, 1970. P & P, HAER, NJ,21-PHIL.V,1-3.

Plane 10 West as it appeared in 1970. Originally, heavy timbers were secured to the stone sleepers, shown, and the rails spiked to the timbers.

opposite

3-021. A canal building, perhaps the plane tender's house, near Plane 10 West, Morris Canal, Phillipsburg Vic., New Jersey (3.1 miles). Jack E. Boucher, photographer, 1970. P & P, NJ,21-PHIL.V,1-8.

3-022. A former hotel along the Morris Canal, Phillipsburg Vic., New Jersey. Jack E. Boucher, photographer, 1970. P & P, HAER, NJ,21-PHIL,1-B-1.

3-023

3-023. Plane 9 West, Morris Canal, Phillipsburg Vic., New Jersey (4.5 miles). From Canal Society of New Jersey, late nineteenth/early twentieth century. P & P, HAER, NJ,21-PHIL,1-13.

A partially submerged cradle is visible in the foreground; the powerhouse is at the top of the inclined plane (left).

3-024. Looking up to the summit of Plane 9 West, Morris Canal, Phillipsburg Vic., New Jersey (4.5 miles). Jack E. Boucher, photographer, 1970. P & P, HAER, NJ,21-PHIL,1-D-2.

Plane 9 West had a vertical lift of 100 feet—the largest lift of the planes on the canal. Its gradient was one in eleven.

3-025. Morris Canal, Rockport Vic., New Jersey. Jack E. Boucher, photographer, 1970. P & P, HAER, NJ,21-PHIL,1-H-1.

3-024

3-025

3-026. Morris Canal, Rockport Vic., New Jersey. Jack E. Boucher, photographer, 1970. P & P, HAER, NJ,21-PHIL,1-H-2.

3-026

3-027

3-028

3-027. Morris Canal, Stewartsville, New Jersey (8.1 miles). From Canal Society of New Jersey, late nineteenth/early twentieth century. P & P, HAER, NJ,21-PHIL,1-E-1.

3-028. Morris Canal, Broadway Vic., New Jersey. From Canal Society of New Jersey, late nineteenth/early twentieth century. P & P, HAER, NJ,21-PHIL,1-15.

3-029. Morris Canal, Greene's Mill Vic., New Jersey. From Canal Society of New Jersey, late nineteenth/early twentieth century. P & P, HAER, NJ,21-PHIL,1-F-1.

3-030. Morris Canal, Greene's Mill Vic., New Jersey. Jack E. Boucher, photographer, 1970. P & P, HAER, NJ,21-PHIL, 1-F-2.

3-031. Lockhouse, Greene's Mill, Morris Canal, Stewartsville Vic., New Jersey. Jack E. Boucher, photographer, 1970. P & P, HAER, NJ,21-PHIL,1-F-3.

3-029

3-030

3-031

3-032

3-033

opposite

3-032. Looking down Plane 7 West, Morris Canal, Washington Vic., New Jersey (14.8 miles). From Canal Society of New Jersey, late nineteenth/early twentieth century. P & P, HAER, NJ,21-PHIL,1-16.

Plane 7 West had a vertical lift of 73 feet and a gradient of one in ten. The flume that carried the water to the penstock, where it descended to the turbine, is at left.

3-033. Looking up Plane 7 West, Morris Canal, Washington Vic., New Jersey (14.8 miles). From Canal Society of New Jersey, late nineteenth/early twentieth century. P & P, HAER, NJ,21-PHIL,1-17.

The powerhouse is on the right.

this page

3-034. Morris Canal and canal boat, Brass Castle, near Port Washington, New Jersey. From Canal Society of New Jersey, late nineteenth/early twentieth century. P & P, HAER, NJ,21-PHIL,1-18.

3-035. Morris Canal, Port Colden Vic., New Jersey. From Canal Society of New Jersey, late nineteenth/early twentieth century. P & P, HAER, NJ,21-PHIL,1-20.

3-036. Lock 6 West, Morris Canal, Port Colden, New Jersey. From Canal Society of New Jersey, late nineteenth/early twentieth century. P & P, HAER, NJ,21-PHIL,1-21.

3-034

3-035

3-036

3-037

3-038

3-039

3-037. Lock gate, Lock 6 West, Morris Canal, Port Colden, New Jersey. From Canal Society of New Jersey, late nineteenth/early twentieth century. P & P, HAER, NJ,21-PHIL,1-22.

3-038. Just east of Lock 6 West, Morris Canal, Port Colden, New Jersey. From Canal Society of New Jersey, late nineteenth/early twentieth century. P & P, HAER, NJ,21-PHIL,1-23.

3-039. Looking up Plane 6 West, Morris Canal, Port Colden, New Jersey (17.9 miles). From Canal Society of New Jersey, late nineteenth/early twentieth century. P & P, HAER, NJ,21-PHIL,1-25.

Plane 6 West was one of the three double-tracked inclined planes on the canal. Its vertical lift was 50 feet, its gradient one in ten. A cradle is halfway up the right-hand plane pathway. The tailrace, the water that has passed through the turbine, is on the right.

3-040. Tailrace and inclined plane, Plane 6 West, Morris Canal, Port Colden, New Jersey (17.9 miles). From Canal Society of New Jersey, late nineteenth/early twentieth century. P & P, HAER, NJ,21-PHIL,1-26.

Compare the tailrace with that shown for Plane 2 East (3-074–3-076).

3-041. Head of Plane 6 West, Morris Canal, Port Colden, New Jersey (17.9 miles). From Canal Society of New Jersey, late nineteenth/early twentieth century. P & P, HAER, NJ,21-PHIL,1-27.

The structure in the middle is a water-powered sawmill. The canal tender's house is to the left.

3-042. Head of Plane 6 West, Morris Canal, Port Colden, New Jersey (17.9 miles). From Canal Society of New Jersey, late nineteenth/early twentieth century. P & P, HAER, NJ,21-PHIL,1-28.

The powerhouse for Plane 6 West is in the center.

3-040

3-041

3-042

3-043

3-044

3-045

3-043. Morris Canal, Great Meadows Vic., New Jersey. From Canal Society of New Jersey, late nineteenth/early twentieth century. P & P, HAER, NJ,21-PHIL,1-30.

3-044. Morris Canal, Great Meadows Vic., New Jersey. From Canal Society of New Jersey, late nineteenth/early twentieth century. P & P, HAER, NJ,21-PHIL,1-31.

3-045. Morris Canal, Hackettstown Vic., New Jersey. From Canal Society of New Jersey, late nineteenth/early twentieth century. P & P, HAER, NJ,21-PHIL,1-32.

3-046. Morris Canal west of Hackettstown, New Jersey. From Canal Society of New Jersey, late nineteenth/early twentieth century. P & P, HAER, NJ,21-PHIL,1-34.

3-047. Morris Canal east of Hackettstown, New Jersey. From Canal Society of New Jersey, late nineteenth/early twentieth century. P & P, HAER, NJ,21-PHIL,1-35.

3-048. Bridge crossing Morris Canal east of Hackettstown, New Jersey. From Canal Society of New Jersey, late nineteenth/early twentieth century. P & P, HAER, NJ,21-PHIL,1-36.

More than 200 bridges crossed the Morris Canal—about two per mile.

3-046

3-047

3-048

3-049

3-050. Morris Canal at Guard Lock 5 West, Saxton Falls, New Jersey (30.6 miles). From Canal Society of New Jersey, late nineteenth/early twentieth century. P & P, HAER, NJ,21-PHIL,1-I-1.

Guard locks protected the main canal from variations in water levels in rivers and reservoirs that provided water to the canal, while allowing boats to pass from the canal to the reservoir or river.

3-050. Morris Canal at Guard Lock 5 West, Saxton Falls, New Jersey (30.6 miles). From Canal Society of New Jersey. Jack E. Boucher, photographer, 1970. P & P, HAER, NJ,21-PHIL,1-I-2.

3-050

3-051. Morris Canal, Waterloo Vic., New Jersey. From Canal Society of New Jersey, late nineteenth/early twentieth century. P & P, HAER, NJ,21-PHIL,1-J-1.

3-052. Morris Canal, Waterloo Vic., New Jersey. From Canal Society of New Jersey, late nineteenth/early twentieth century. P & P, HAER, NJ,21-PHIL,1-J-3.

3-053. Morris Canal, Waterloo Vic., New Jersey. From Canal Society of New Jersey. Jack E. Boucher, photographer, 1970. P & P, HAER, NJ,21-PHIL,1-J-4.

3-051

3-052

3-053

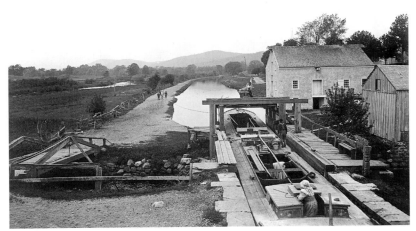

3-054

3-054. Lock, possibly Lock 4 West, Morris Canal, Waterloo Vic., New Jersey (31.5 miles), ca. 1900. P & P, DPCC, LC-D4-12035.

3-055. Canal boat in its boat cradle on an inclined plane, possibly Plane 4 West, Morris Canal, Waterloo Vic., New Jersey (34.2 miles), ca. 1900. P & P, DPCC, LC-D4-12037.

3-056. Basin and the foot of an inclined plane, possibly Plane 3 West, Morris Canal, Waterloo Vic., New Jersey (34.9 miles), ca. 1890–1900. P & P, DPCC, LC-D4-12036.

3-055

3-056

3-057. Cassedy's Store, Morris Canal, Waterloo Vic., New Jersey. Jack E. Boucher, photographer, 1970. P & P, HAER, NJ,21-PHIL,1-K-2.

3-058. Cassedy's Store, Morris Canal, Waterloo Vic., New Jersey. Jack E. Boucher, photographer, 1970. P & P, HAER, NJ,21-PHIL,1-K-3.

At the peak of the gable is a cantilevered strut for mounting a hoist to load canal-delivered merchandise into the second and third floors.

3-057

3-058

3-059

3-059. Lock 3 West, Morris Canal, near Lowrance's Landing, Stanhope Vic., New Jersey. From Canal Society of New Jersey, late nineteenth/early twentieth century. P & P, HAER, NJ,21-PHIL,1-38.

3-060. Plane 2 West, Morris Canal, Stanhope, New Jersey (36.8 miles). From Canal Society of New Jersey, late nineteenth/early twentieth century. P & P, HAER, NJ,21-PHIL,1-41.

Plane 2 West had a vertical lift of 70 feet and a gradient of one in ten.

3-061. Morris Canal paralleling the Musconetcong River, Stanhope, New Jersey. From Canal Society of New Jersey, late nineteenth/early twentieth century. P & P, HAER, NJ,21-PHIL,1-40.

3-060

3-061

3-062. Furnaces, Morris Canal, Stanhope, New Jersey. From Canal Society of New Jersey, late nineteenth/early twentieth century. P & P, HAER, NJ,21-PHIL,1-42.

3-063. Morris Canal, near Port Morris, Stanhope Vic., New Jersey. From Canal Society of New Jersey, late nineteenth/early twentieth century. P & P, HAER, NJ,21-PHIL,1-45.

3-064. Looking down Plane 1 West, Morris Canal, near Port Morris, Stanhope Vic., New Jersey (38.1 miles). From Canal Society of New Jersey, late nineteenth/early twentieth century. P & P, HAER, NJ,21-PHIL,1-43.

Plane 1 West had a vertical lift of 58 feet and a gradient of one in ten.

3-062

3-063

3-064

3-065

3-066. Morris Canal and the Delaware, Lackawanna, and Western (DL&W) railroad station (left) at Lake Hopatcong, New Jersey (39.1 miles). From Canal Society of New Jersey, late nineteenth/early twentieth century. P & P, HAER, NJ,21-PHIL,1-48.

Lake Hopatcong was the summit-level reservoir of the Morris Canal, at an elevation of 914 feet above mean high tide at Newark, New Jersey, and 716 feet above Phillipsburg, New Jersey.

3-067. Feeder lock to Lake Hopatcong at the summit of the Morris Canal, Lake Hopatcong, New Jersey (39.1 miles). From Canal Society of New Jersey, late nineteenth/early twentieth century. P & P, HAER, NJ,21-PHIL,1-49.

3-066

3-067

3-065. Morris Canal at Will's Basin, near Lake Hopatcong, New Jersey. From Canal Society of New Jersey, late nineteenth/early twentieth century. P & P, HAER, NJ,21-PHIL,1-47.

3-068. Canal boat traversing the feeder lock to Lake Hopatcong at the summit of the Morris Canal, Lake Hopatcong, New Jersey (39.1 miles). From Canal Society of New Jersey, late nineteenth/early twentieth century. P & P, HAER, NJ,21-PHIL,1-50.

3-069. Stop gate with the feeder lock in the distance, Morris Canal, Lake Hopatcong, New Jersey (39.1 miles). From Canal Society of New Jersey, late nineteenth/early twentieth century. P & P, HAER, NJ,21-PHIL,1-51.

The stop gate could be closed to permit dewatering and repair of the lock and feeder lock beyond.

3-070. Morris Canal, near Lake Hopatcong, New Jersey, ca. 1900. P & P, DPCC, LC-D4-11551.

3-068

3-069

3-070

3-071

3-072

3-073

3-071. Road culvert under the Morris Canal, Ledgewood, New Jersey. From Canal Society of New Jersey, late nineteenth/early twentieth century. P & P, HAER, NJ,21-PHIL,1-53.

3-072. Head of Plane 2 East, Morris Canal, Netcong Vic., New Jersey (41.2 miles). From Canal Society of New Jersey, late nineteenth/early twentieth century. P & P, HAER, NJ,21-PHIL,1-54.

Plane 2 East had a vertical lift of 80 feet and a gradient of one in ten.

3-073. Looking east from the head of Plane 2 East, Morris Canal, Netcong Vic., New Jersey (41.2 miles). From Canal Society of New Jersey, late nineteenth/early twentieth century. P & P, HAER, NJ,21-PHIL,1-55.

The powerhouse and the wooden flume are on the right; the tailrace is in the middle. In the distance is a cradle for canal boats.

3-074. Looking down the tailrace to Plane 2 East, Morris Canal, Netcong Vic., New Jersey (41.2 miles). From Canal Society of New Jersey, late nineteenth/early twentieth century. P & P, HAER, NJ,21-PHIL,1-56.

3-075. Looking up the tailrace of Plane 2 East, Morris Canal, Netcong Vic., New Jersey (41.2 miles). From Canal Society of New Jersey, late nineteenth/early twentieth century. P & P, HAER, NJ,21-PHIL,1-57.

The left-hand water stream, the tailrace, passed through the flume, powerhouse, and turbine to operate the machinery for the inclined plane. The right-hand water stream, the bypass flume or spillway, maintained the level of water on the canal below the plane and carried excess water from the upper level.

3-076. Looking up Plane 2 East, Morris Canal, Netcong Vic., New Jersey (41.2 miles). From Canal Society of New Jersey, late nineteenth/early twentieth century. P & P, HAER, NJ,21-PHIL,1-58.

The rails and lifting cable can be seen on the left; the powerhouse is at the top of the inclined plane.

3-074

3-075

3-076

3-077

3-078. Canal boat in Lock 1 East, Morris Canal, Drakesville, New Jersey (42 miles). From Canal Society of New Jersey, late nineteenth/early twentieth century. P & P, HAER, NJ,21-PHIL,1-61.

3-079. Plane 4 East, Morris Canal, Netcong Vic., New Jersey (45.2 miles). From Canal Society of New Jersey, late nineteenth/early twentieth century. P & P, HAER, NJ,21-PHIL,1-62.

Plane 4 East had a vertical lift of 52 feet and a gradient of one in ten. In this photograph are (left to right) a canal boat in its cradle, the powerhouse, and the flume.

3-077. Approaching Lock 1 East and lockhouse, Morris Canal, Drakesville, New Jersey. From Canal Society of New Jersey, late nineteenth/early twentieth century. P & P, HAER, NJ,21-PHIL,1-60.

3-078

3-079

3-080. Lock 2 East, Morris Canal, Wharton Vic., New Jersey (45.6 miles). From Canal Society of New Jersey, late nineteenth/early twentieth century. P & P, HAER, NJ,21-PHIL,1-65.

3-081. Possibly Lock 2 East, Morris Canal, Wharton Vic., New Jersey. From Canal Society of New Jersey, late nineteenth/early twentieth century. P & P, HAER, NJ,21-PHIL,1-66.

3-082. Lockhouse, Lock 2 East, Morris Canal, Wharton Vic., New Jersey (45.6 miles). From Canal Society of New Jersey, late nineteenth/early twentieth century. P & P, HAER, NJ,21-PHIL,1-67.

3-080

3-081

3-082

3-083

3-083. Plane 5 East, Morris Canal, Dover Vic., New Jersey (47 miles). From Canal Society of New Jersey, late nineteenth/early twentieth century. P & P, HAER, NJ,21-PHIL,1-68.

Plane 5 East had a vertical lift of 68 feet and a gradient of one in ten. The photograph shows workmen removing mud from the bed of the canal.

3-084. Morris Canal, Dover, New Jersey. From Canal Society of New Jersey, late nineteenth/early twentieth century. P & P, HAER, NJ,21-PHIL,1-70.

3-085. Morris Canal, Rockaway Vic., New Jersey. From Canal Society of New Jersey, late nineteenth/early twentieth century. P & P, HAER, NJ,21-PHIL,1-71.

3-084

3-085

3-086. Morris Canal, Rockaway, New Jersey
(52.1 miles). From Canal Society of New
Jersey, late nineteenth/early twentieth century. P & P, HAER, NJ,21-PHIL,1-72.

3-087. Crossing an aqueduct on the Morris Canal, Denville, New Jersey (53.5 miles). From Canal Society of New Jersey, late nineteenth/early twentieth century. P & P, HAER, NJ,21-PHIL,1-73.

3-088. Morris Canal, Denville Vic., New Jersey. From Canal Society of New Jersey, late nineteenth/early twentieth century. P & P, HAER, NJ,21-PHIL,1-74.

3-087

3-088

3-089. Canal basin, Lock 9 East, Morris Canal, Boonton Vic., New Jersey (57.2 miles). From Canal Society of New Jersey, late nineteenth/early twentieth century. P & P, HAER, NJ,21-PHIL,1-75.

3-090. Canal boat at Lock 9 East, Morris Canal, Boonton Vic., New Jersey (57.2 miles). From Canal Society of New Jersey, late nineteenth/early twentieth century. P & P, HAER, NJ,21-PHIL,1-76.

3-089

3-090

3-091

3-092. Powerville Basin and Lock 10 East, Morris Canal, Boonton Vic., New Jersey (57.4 miles). From Canal Society of New Jersey, late nineteenth/early twentieth century. P & P, HAER, NJ,21-PHIL,1-79.

3-092

3-093

3-091. Lock 10 East, Morris Canal, Boonton Vic., New Jersey (57.4 miles). From Canal Society of New Jersey, late nineteenth/early twentieth century. P & P, HAER, NJ,21-PHIL,1-78.

3-092. Powerville Basin and Lock 10 East, Morris Canal, Boonton Vic., New Jersey (57.4 miles). From Canal Society of New Jersey, late nineteenth/early twentieth century. P & P, HAER, NJ,21-PHIL,1-79.

3-093. Lock 11 East, Morris Canal, Boonton Vic., New Jersey (57.6 miles). From Canal Society of New Jersey, late nineteenth/early twentieth century. P & P, HAER, NJ,21-PHIL,1-81.

Located at the end of Powerville Basin, Lock 11 East functioned as a guard lock. Canal boats locked down to the Rockaway River.

3-094

3-094. Morris Canal west of Lock 12 East,
Boonton Vic., New Jersey. From Canal
Society of New Jersey, late nineteenth/early
twentieth century. P & P, HAER, NJ, 21-
PHIL, 1-82.

3-095

3-095. Morris Canal west of Boonton, Boonton Vic., New Jersey. From Canal Society of New Jersey, late nineteenth/early twentieth century. P & P, HAER, NJ,21-PHIL,1-83.

3-096. Summit of Plane 7 East, Morris Canal, Boonton, New Jersey (58.6 miles). From Canal Society of New Jersey, late nineteenth/early twentieth century. P & P, HAER, NJ,21-PHIL,1-84.

3-097. Cradle at the top of Plane 7 East, Morris Canal, Boonton, New Jersey (58.6 miles). From Canal Society of New Jersey, late nineteenth/early twentieth century. P & P, HAER, NJ,21-PHIL,1-86.

The vertical lift of Plane 7 East was 80 feet and the gradient was one in eleven.

3-096

3-097

3-098

3-099

3-100

3-098. Plane tender, Plane 7 East, Morris Canal, Boonton, New Jersey (58.6 miles). From Canal Society of New Jersey, late nineteenth/early twentieth century. P & P, HAER, NJ,21-PHIL,1-87.

3-099. Canal boat and cradle at the bottom of Plane 7 East, Morris Canal, Boonton, New Jersey (58.6 miles), ca. 1890–1901. P & P, DPCC, LC-D4-11523.

3-100. Morris Canal, east of Boonton, Boonton Vic., New Jersey. From Canal Society of New Jersey, late nineteenth/early twentieth century. P & P, HAER, NJ,21-PHIL,1-88.

Lock 13 East is in the background.

3-101. Lock 13 East, Morris Canal, Boonton Vic., New Jersey (59.2 miles). From Canal Society of New Jersey, late nineteenth/early twentieth century. P & P, HAER, NJ,21-PHIL, 1-89.

3-101

3-102

3-103

3-104

3-102. Morris Canal, Boonton Vic., New Jersey. From Canal Society of New Jersey, late nineteenth/early twentieth century. P & P, HAER, NJ,21-PHIL,1-93.

3-103. Morris Canal, east of Boonton, Boonton Vic., New Jersey. From Canal Society of New Jersey, late nineteenth/early twentieth century. P & P, HAER, NJ,21-PHIL,1-94.

3-104. Plane 8 East, Montville, New Jersey (60.4 miles). From Canal Society of New Jersey, late nineteenth/early twentieth century. P & P, HAER, NJ,21-PHIL,1-95.

Plane 8 East had a vertical lift of 76 feet and a gradient of one in eleven.

3-105

3-105. View down Plane 8 East, Montville, New Jersey (60.4 miles). From Canal Society of New Jersey, late nineteenth/early twentieth century. P & P, HAER, NJ,21-PHIL,1-96.

3-106

3-107

3-108

3-106. View down Plane 9 East, Montville, New Jersey (60.6 miles). From Canal Society of New Jersey, late nineteenth/early twentieth century. P & P, HAER, NJ,21-PHIL,1-97.

Plane 9 East had a vertical lift of 74 feet and a gradient of one in eleven.

3-107. View up Plane 9 East, Montville, New Jersey (60.6 miles). From Canal Society of New Jersey, late nineteenth/early twentieth century. P & P, HAER, NJ,21-PHIL,1-98.

The powerhouse is visible to the left of center, in the distance. The house to the left is probably the plane tender's house. The bridge in the foreground is Morris Canal Company Bridge 89, a typical wood trestle bridge used for carrying local traffic over the canal.

3-108. Probably the powerhouse at Plane 9 East, Montville, New Jersey (60.6 miles). From Canal Society of New Jersey, late nineteenth/early twentieth century. P & P, HAER, NJ,21-PHIL,1-162.

The penstock for the turbine is on the left. Excess water was carried off in the spillway (right).

3-109

3-109. Morris Canal, Montville Vic., New
Jersey. From Canal Society of New Jersey,
late nineteenth/early twentieth century.
P & P, HAER, NJ,21-PHIL,1-99.

3-110

3-111

3-112

opposite

3-110. Lock 14 East, Morris Canal, Lincoln Park, New Jersey (66.1 miles). From Canal Society of New Jersey, late nineteenth/early twentieth century. P & P, HAER, NJ,21-PHIL,1-101.

3-111. Morris Canal, Lincoln Park, New Jersey. From Canal Society of New Jersey, late nineteenth/early twentieth century. P & P, HAER, NJ,21-PHIL,1-102.

3-112. Canal boats at the Delaware, Lackawanna, and Western (DL&W) railroad lift bridge on the Pompton feeder canal, Morris Canal, Mountain View Vic., New Jersey, ca. 1890–1901. P & P, DPCC, LC-D4-11553.

this page

3-113. Delaware, Lackawanna, and Western (DL&W) lift bridge, Morris Canal, Mountain View Vic., New Jersey, ca. 1890–1901. P & P, DPCC, LC-D4-11554.

The lift bridge is shown in the up position.

3-114. Morris Canal, Mountain View Vic., New Jersey, ca. 1890–1901. P & P, DPCC, LC-D4-11556.

3-115. Morris Canal east of the Pompton Feeder, Mountain View Vic., New Jersey (67.6 miles). From Canal Society of New Jersey, late nineteenth/early twentieth century. P & P, HAER, NJ,21-PHIL,1-105.

The railroad bridge in the foreground is for the New York and Greenwood Lake Railroad. In the distance is the Pompton River Aqueduct.

3-113

3-114

3-115

3-116

3-116. Pompton River Aqueduct, Morris Canal, Mountain View, New Jersey (72 miles). From Canal Society of New Jersey, late nineteenth/early twentieth century. P & P, HAER, NJ,21-PHIL,1-106.

The aqueduct was 236 feet long and was constructed of wood trestles on nine masonry piers.

3-117. Morris Canal, Little Falls Vic., New Jersey. From Canal Society of New Jersey, late nineteenth/early twentieth century. P & P, HAER, NJ,21-PHIL,1-110.

3-118. Morris Canal, Little Falls Vic., New Jersey. From Canal Society of New Jersey, late nineteenth/early twentieth century. P & P, HAER, NJ,21-PHIL,1-111.

3-117

3-118

3-119

3-119. Morris Canal, probably Paterson area, New Jersey. From Canal Society of New Jersey, late nineteenth/early twentieth century. P & P, HAER, NJ,21-PHIL,1-114.

3-120. Morris Canal, east of Paterson, New Jersey. From Canal Society of New Jersey, late nineteenth/early twentieth century. P & P, HAER, NJ,21-PHIL,1-115.

3-121. Morris Canal, Bloomfield, New Jersey. From Canal Society of New Jersey, late nineteenth/early twentieth century. P & P, HAER, NJ,21-PHIL,1-116.

The head of Plane 11 East can be seen in the distance.

3-120

3-121

3-122

3-123

3-122. Canal boat at the base of Plane 11 East, Morris Canal, Bloomfield, New Jersey (83.6 miles). From Canal Society of New Jersey, late nineteenth/early twentieth century. P & P, HAER, NJ,21-PHIL,1-117.

Plane 11 East had a vertical lift of 54 feet and a gradient of one in twelve.

3-123. Unloading coal, Morris Canal, Bloomfield Vic., New Jersey. From Canal Society of New Jersey, late nineteenth/early twentieth century. P & P, HAER, NJ,21-PHIL,1-109.

3-124. Bridge over Morris Canal, Bloomfield, New Jersey. From Canal Society of New Jersey, late nineteenth/early twentieth century. P & P, HAER, NJ,21-PHIL,1-118.

3-124

3-125. Lock 15 East, Morris Canal, Bloomfield, New Jersey. From Canal Society of New Jersey, late nineteenth/early twentieth century. P & P, HAER, NJ,21-PHIL,1-119.

3-126. Morris Canal, Bloomfield Vic., New Jersey. From Canal Society of New Jersey, late nineteenth/early twentieth century. P & P, HAER, NJ,21-PHIL,1-121.

3-127. Morris Canal, Bloomfield Vic., New Jersey. From Canal Society of New Jersey, late nineteenth/early twentieth century. P & P, HAER, NJ,21-PHIL,1-122.

3-125

3-126

3-127

3-128

3-128. Morris Canal crossing the Second River, Bloomfield Vic., New Jersey. From Canal Society of New Jersey, late nineteenth/early twentieth century. P & P, HAER, NJ,21-PHIL,1-123.

3-129. Morris Canal, east of Bloomfield, Bloomfield Vic., New Jersey. From Canal Society of New Jersey, late nineteenth/early twentieth century. P & P, HAER, NJ,21-PHIL,1-124.

3-130. Morris Canal, west of Plane 12 East, Newark, New Jersey. From Canal Society of New Jersey, late nineteenth/early twentieth century. P & P, HAER, NJ,21-PHIL,1-126.

3-131. Plane 12 East, Morris Canal, Newark, New Jersey. *Engineering* (July 31, 1868). L/C TA1 .E55

3-129

3-130

3-131

3-132. Morris Canal, Newark, New Jersey. From Canal Society of New Jersey, late nineteenth/early twentieth century. P & P, HAER, NJ,21-PHIL,1-127.

3-133. Canal barge, Morris Canal, Newark, New Jersey. From Canal Society of New Jersey, late nineteenth/early twentieth century. P & P, HAER, NJ,21-PHIL,1-128.

The head of Plane 12 East is in the distance, beyond the bridge.

3-134. Head of Plane 12 East, High Street, Newark, New Jersey (89.7 miles). From Canal Society of New Jersey, late nineteenth/ early twentieth century. P & P, HAER, NJ,21-PHIL,1-129.

Plane 12 East, one of the three double-tracked inclined planes, had a vertical lift of 70 feet and a gradient of one in ten. Completed in 1855, it cost $33,890 to build.

3-132

3-133

3-134

3-135

3-135. Cables, rails of inclined plane, flume, and powerhouse, Plane 12 East, Newark, New Jersey (89.7 miles). From Canal Society of New Jersey, late nineteenth/early twentieth century. P & P, HAER, NJ,21-PHIL,1-130.

3-136. Morris Canal passing under Broad Street, Newark, New Jersey. From Canal Society of New Jersey, late nineteenth/early twentieth century. P & P, HAER, NJ,21-PHIL,1-131.

3-137. Eastern end of the tunnel under Newark's Center Market, Newark, New Jersey. From Canal Society of New Jersey, late nineteenth/early twentieth century. P & P, HAER, NJ,21-PHIL,1-144.

The small signs on each end of the building read, "NOTICE: DUMP NO GARBAGE ON CANAL PROPERTY."

3-136

3-137

3-138. Morris Canal near the Ripley & Company Lumber Yard, Newark, New Jersey. From Canal Society of New Jersey, late nineteenth/early twentieth century. P & P, HAER, NJ,21-PHIL,1-132.

3-139. Morris Canal near the Valbesh Smelting and Refining Company, Newark, New Jersey. From Canal Society of New Jersey, late nineteenth/early twentieth century. P & P, HAER, NJ,21-PHIL,1-133.

3-140. Morris Canal paralleling the Passaic River, Newark, New Jersey. From Canal Society of New Jersey, late nineteenth/early twentieth century. P & P, HAER, NJ,21-PHIL,1-134.

3-138

3-139

3-140

3-141

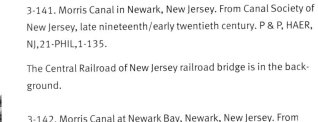

3-141. Morris Canal in Newark, New Jersey. From Canal Society of New Jersey, late nineteenth/early twentieth century. P & P, HAER, NJ,21-PHIL,1-135.

The Central Railroad of New Jersey railroad bridge is in the background.

3-142. Morris Canal at Newark Bay, Newark, New Jersey. From Canal Society of New Jersey, late nineteenth/early twentieth century. P & P, HAER, NJ,21-PHIL,1-136.

3-143. Morris Canal near Avenue D (now Broadway), Bayonne, New Jersey. From Canal Society of New Jersey, late nineteenth/early twentieth century. P & P, HAER, NJ,21-PHIL,1-142.

3-142

3-143

3-144. Morris Canal paralleling the Lehigh
Valley Railroad, Jersey City, New Jersey. From
Canal Society of New Jersey, late nine-
teenth/early twentieth century. P & P, HAER,
NJ,21-PHIL,1-137.

3-145. Morris Canal and the Lehigh Valley
Railroad bridge, Jersey City, New Jersey.
From Canal Society of New Jersey, late nine-
teenth/early twentieth century. P & P, HAER,
NJ,21-PHIL,1-139.

3-146. Morris Canal, Schentzen Park, Jersey
City, New Jersey. From Canal Society of New
Jersey, late nineteenth/early twentieth cen-
tury. P & P, HAER, NJ,21-PHIL,1-140.

3-144

3-145

3-146

3-147. Canal boat between Jersey City and Newark, Morris Canal, New Jersey. From Canal Society of New Jersey, late nineteenth/early twentieth century. P & P, HAER, NJ,21-PHIL,1-141.

3-148. Henderson Street railroad bridge, Morris Canal, Jersey City, New Jersey. From Canal Society of New Jersey, late nineteenth/early twentieth century. P & P, HAER, NJ,21-PHIL,1-143.

3-149. Morris Canal near the Whitlock Cordage Company, Jersey City, New Jersey. From Canal Society of New Jersey, late nineteenth/early twentieth century. P & P, HAER, NJ,21-PHIL,1-145.

3-147

3-148

3-149

3-150. Morris Canal and lift bridge, Jersey City, New Jersey. From Canal Society of New Jersey, late nineteenth/early twentieth century. P & P, HAER, NJ,21-PHIL,1-149.

3-151. Dredge on the Eight Mile Level, Morris Canal, Jersey City, New Jersey. From Canal Society of New Jersey, late nineteenth/early twentieth century. P & P, HAER, NJ,21-PHIL,1-151.

3-152. Morris Canal, Jersey City, New Jersey. From Canal Society of New Jersey, late nineteenth/early twentieth century. P & P, HAER, NJ,21-PHIL,1-152.

3-150

3-151

3-152

3-153

3-154

3-155

3-153. Hudson River Basin, Morris Canal, Jersey City, New Jersey (102.1 miles). From Canal Society of New Jersey, late nineteenth/early twentieth century. P & P, HAER, NJ,21-PHIL,1-155.

3-154. Canal boat near the Hudson River Basin, Morris Canal, Jersey City, New Jersey. From Canal Society of New Jersey, late nineteenth/early twentieth century. P & P, HAER, NJ,21-PHIL, 1-157.

3-155. Hudson River Basin, Morris Canal, Jersey City, New Jersey (102.1 miles). From Canal Society of New Jersey, late nineteenth/early twentieth century. P & P, HAER, NJ,21-PHIL,1-158.

3-156. Hudson River Basin, Morris Canal,
Jersey City, New Jersey (102.1 miles). From
Canal Society of New Jersey, late nine-
teenth/early twentieth century. P & P, HAER,
NJ,21-PHIL,1-159.

CHESAPEAKE & OHIO CANAL

It was George Washington's dream to use the Potomac River valley as a transportation route to the rich new territories of the Ohio valley. Washington promoted this idea before the War of Independence, but it was not until 1785 that the Potomac Canal Company was incorporated to develop river navigation to the Ohio via the Potomac. George Washington was its first president.

The Potomac Canal Company built bypass canals around the principal obstructions, such as Great Falls and Little Falls, but the river was the main avenue for transport (see IN-008, IN-057). This was satisfactory during the high-water months of spring and early summer but inadequate in late summer and autumn.

A successor company, the Chesapeake and Ohio (C&O) Canal Company, was authorized by the Maryland and Virginia legislatures and led by Charles Mercer, a congressman from Virginia who had been a vocal critic of the Potomac Company. The new C&O Canal was to be a stillwater canal alongside the Potomac River. Work on it began on July 4, 1828 (see IN-023). Mercer and his chief engineer, Benjamin Wright, believed that the C&O Canal would be a model for American canals: it was to have a larger prism than the Erie and was to be constructed exclusively of long-lasting, masonry aqueducts and locks. Above all it was to be a national canal, uniting the national capital with the western territories.

The twin engineering successes of the Monocacy Aqueduct (4-064–4-068; see 1-075) and the Paw Paw Tunnel (4-126–4-128; see 2-124) did not lead to commercial success for the company. Not until 1850, many years after the Baltimore and Ohio Railroad had arrived, did the canal reach Cumberland, Maryland, 184 miles from its origin. The C&O made a modest income hauling coal from the fields west of Cumberland, as well as cement, lime, flour, iron, and other local products (see IN-040).

In 1924, after a flood, the C&O ceased operation. Unlike the Morris Canal, most of its facilities were located in rural areas and little activity was undertaken to dismantle structures or fill in the prism. In the 1930s ownership was transferred to the U.S. government and subsequently the canal became a national park.

The C&O Canal begins at the tide lock at the Potomac River in the vicinity of the Watergate apartments in Washington, D.C. Mileage on the canal has traditionally been measured from this lock, mile zero. The mileage is identified for each of the illustrations in this section.

4-001. Chesapeake and Ohio Canal, District of Columbia, Maryland, West Virginia.

Work began on the Chesapeake and Ohio Canal in 1828 at Little Falls, immediately above Georgetown. Initially planned to link the Chesapeake with the Ohio River Valley, the C&O Canal was completed only to Cumberland, Maryland, in 1850. It remained in operation until 1924, primarily to haul coal from the rich coal fields west of Cumberland. The C&O Canal is now a national park and probably the best preserved example of the canal era.

4-001

4-002

4-002. Lock 1, Chesapeake and Ohio Canal, looking west toward Twenty-ninth Street (formerly Greene Street), Georgetown, Washington, D.C. (0.4 miles). Albert S. Burns, photographer, 1935. P & P, HABS, DC,GEO,25-16.

4-003

4-003. Masonry work at the basin, Lock 3, Chesapeake and Ohio Canal, Georgetown, Washington, D.C. (0.5 miles). George Eisenman, photographer, 1967. P & P, HABS, DC,GEO,25-14.

4-004. Lock 3, Chesapeake and Ohio Canal, Georgetown, Washington, D.C. (0.5 miles). George Eisenman, photographer, 1967. P & P, HABS, DC,GEO,25-9.

Lock 3 is located between Thirtieth Street (formerly Washington Street) on the east and Jefferson Street on the west. The Jefferson Street Bridge over the canal is in the background. Also see IN-058; 2-044.

4-004

4-005. Lock 4, Chesapeake and Ohio Canal, Georgetown, Washington, D.C. (0.6 miles). Albert S. Burns, photographer, 1935. P & P, HABS, DC, GEO,25-18.

Lock 4 is located between Jefferson Street on the east and Thirty-first Street (formerly Congress Street) on the west.

4-006. Upper lock gates of Lock 4, Chesapeake and Ohio Canal, Georgetown, Washington, D.C. (0.6 miles). Albert S. Burns, photographer, 1935. P & P, HABS, DC,GEO,25-12.

The buildings behind the towpath are known locally as Tow Path Row.

4-005

4-006

4-007

4-008

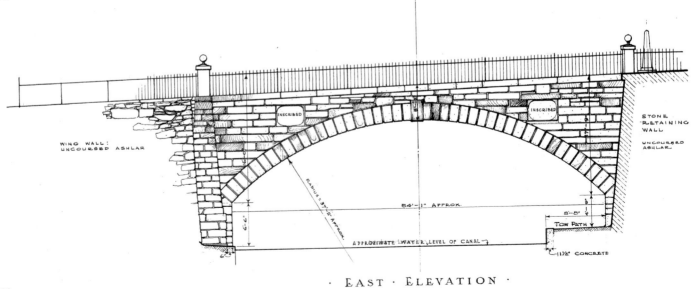

· EAST · ELEVATION ·

4-009

4-007. Chesapeake and Ohio Canal, looking west from Thirty-first Street toward the Wisconsin Avenue (formerly High Street) Bridge, Georgetown, Washington, D.C. (0.6 miles), 1910–20. P & P, DPCC, LC-D4-72863.

The towpath is at the right.

4-008. Chesapeake and Ohio Canal, looking west toward the Wisconsin Avenue Bridge over the dry Chesapeake and Ohio Canal, Georgetown, Washington, D.C. (0.7 miles). From *Pictorial Archives of Early American Architecture*, pre-1924. P & P, HABS, DC,GEO,25-21.

The C&O Canal, shown drained for the winter months. Across its stern, the canal barge reads, "L. M. Hamilton."

4-009. East elevation, Wisconsin Avenue Bridge, Chesapeake and Ohio Canal, Georgetown, Washington, D.C. (0.7 miles). D. McGrew, delineator, 1939. P & P, HABS DC-30, sheet no. 1.

One of five masonry arch bridges constructed by the C&O Canal Company across the canal in Georgetown, the Wisconsin Avenue Bridge is the only one that remains. Shown is the aquia facing stone, from Stafford County, Virginia—the same stone that was used on the White House and the U.S. Capitol. Behind this facade is a barrel arch of irregular masonry blasted from the prism and sold by the canal company to the bridge builder. The arch spans 54 feet. The inscriptions on the bridge record the name of the builder, canal company officers, and engineers. The name of Andrew Jackson is also prominently displayed in the spandrel, although Jackson was an opponent to internal transportation improvements. Also see 2-114.

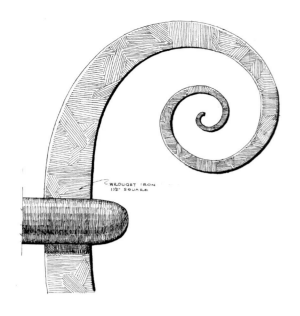

4-010

4-011

4-012

4-013

4-010. Fence detail, Wisconsin Avenue Bridge, Chesapeake and Ohio Canal, Georgetown, Washington, D.C. (0.7 miles). D. McGrew, delineator, 1939. P & P, HABS DC-30, sheet no. 2.

4-011. Looking east along the Chesapeake and Ohio Canal under the Wisconsin Avenue Bridge, Georgetown, Washington, D.C. (0.8 miles). Copy of a photograph in the Library of Congress, pre-1924. P & P, HABS, DC,GEO,25-22.

4-012. Dry laid masonry wall of the Chesapeake and Ohio Canal on the south side of the canal immediately west of the Wisconsin Avenue Bridge, Georgetown, Washington, D.C. (0.8 miles). George Eisenman, photographer, 1967. P & P, HABS, DC,GEO,25-15.

The Georgetown portion of the C&O Canal, from Rock Creek on the east (0.3 miles) to the present-day location of Key Bridge on the west (1.0 miles), was a very large excavation project for the C&O Canal Company. Most of the excavation involved blasting from solid rock, such as that shown here.

4-013. Looking east toward the Wisconsin Avenue Bridge, Chesapeake and Ohio Canal, Georgetown, Washington, D.C. (0.8 miles). Theodor Horydczak, photographer, ca. 1920–50. P & P, LC-H813-1965-003.

4-014

4-015

4-016

this page

4-014. Looking west toward Key Bridge, Chesapeake and Ohio Canal, Georgetown, Washington, D.C. (0.8 miles). Theodor Horydczak, photographer, ca. 1920–50. P & P, LC-H813-1965-002.

4-015. Southeast side of the wing wall of the Georgetown abutment, Potomac Aqueduct across the Potomac River, Alexandria Canal, Georgetown, Washington, D.C. (1.1 miles). George Eisenman, photographer, 1967. P & P, HABS, DC,GEO,1-6.

The C&O Canal runs along the top of the wall shown (top right). The Potomac Aqueduct carried the Alexandria Canal (top left) from Georgetown across the Potomac River. Like most main-line canals, the C&O Canal had feeder canals. The Alexandria Canal was such a feeder, extending 7 miles south from Georgetown to Alexandria, Virginia. To build this canal it was necessary to construct the 1,600-foot-long Potomac Aqueduct. Construction took place from 1835 to 1843, and it was considered one of the engineering wonders of its age. Eight masonry piers and two masonry abutments carried a wood superstructure across the Potomac River. This photograph shows the connection of this canal with the C&O. Wing walls, shown, were used to protect the main masonry structure, the abutment, from being undermined on either side by flood waters. (In plan view, they look like wings of the main structure, hence the name.) During the Civil War, the aqueduct was drained and used as a road bridge for the Union Army (4-18). After the Civil War it continued as a combination road bridge/canal aqueduct. In 1924 it was replaced by the concrete-arch Key Bridge. In 1962, the Corps of Engineers blasted out all piers except Pier 1 to 12 feet below low water line so that local rowing meets could utilize nine full lanes at this location. The remains of Pier 1 can be seen off the Virginia shore. The tracks under the abutment (bottom left) are an abandoned spur of the Baltimore and Ohio Railroad, built after the Potomac Aqueduct was constructed.

4-016. Abutment of the Potomac Aqueduct, Alexandria Canal, Georgetown, Washington, D.C. (1.1 miles). George Eisenman, photographer, 1967. P & P, HABS, DC,GEO,1-5.

opposite

4-017. Potomac Aqueduct, Alexandria Canal, view from across the Potomac River from the Chesapeake and Ohio Canal at Georgetown (foreground) to Arlington, Virginia (1.1 miles). F. Dielman, artist; E. Sachse & Co., lithographers, ca. 1865. P & P, LC-USZC4-1967.

4-018. Looking toward Georgetown, Potomac Aqueduct, Alexandria Canal, Washington, D.C., and Arlington, Virginia (1.1 miles). From a photograph in the Peabody Room, Georgetown Public Library, ca. 1865. P & P, HABS, DC,GEO,1-14.

4·017

4·018

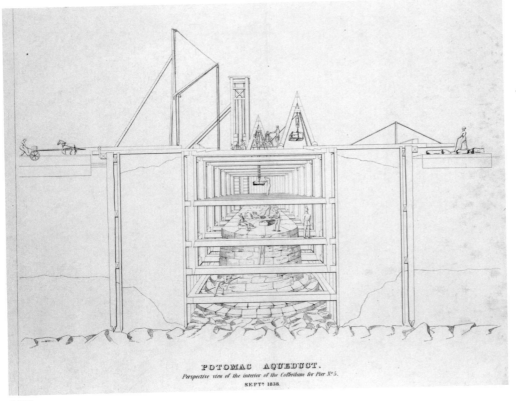

POTOMAC AQUEDUCT.
Perspective view of the interior of the Cofferdam for Pier Nº 5.
SEPTᵣ 1838.

4-019

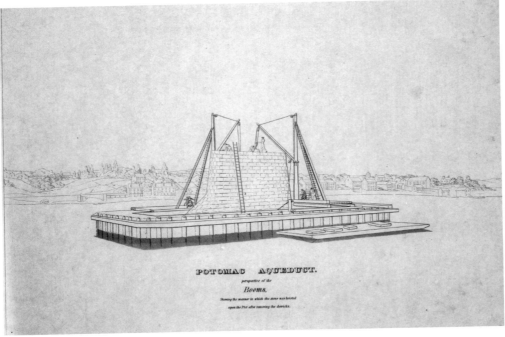

POTOMAC AQUEDUCT.
perspective of the
Booms.
*Showing the manner in which the stone was hoisted
upon the Pier after removing the derricks.*

4-020

4-019. Interior of cofferdam (temporary dams keeping water out of the construction area for pier construction) for Pier 5, Potomac Aqueduct, Alexandria Canal between Georgetown, Washington, D.C., and Arlington, Virginia (1.1 miles). Captain William Turnbull and Lieutenant M. C. Ewing, delineators. From *Drawings Accompanying The Report of Captain Turnbull on the Survey and Construction of The Alexandria Aqueduct Made to the House of Representatives 2d of July, 1838*, Document No. 459, Vol. XI, September 1838. P & P, HABS, DC,GEO,1-24.

The Potomac Aqueduct was one of the first structures built in deep water, defined as 10 feet or more, in the United States. An extraordinary set of drawings was developed by Army engineers Turnbull and Ewing showing how this aqueduct was constructed. These illustrations (4-019–4-020) were disseminated among canal and railroad engineers, and the techniques depicted in building cofferdams and piers were used extensively throughout the country. Cofferdams were constructed by erecting two rows of thick wood supports, which were rammed into the river bottom. Puddling, the clay liner material used to construct canals, was inserted between the supports. Steam-powered pumps then emptied the river water inside the cofferdam.

4-020. Booms hoisting masonry to the top of the pier during the construction of the Potomac Aqueduct, Alexandria Canal, between Georgetown, Washington, D.C., and Arlington, Virginia (1.1 miles). Captain William Turnbull and Lieutenant M. C. Ewing, delineators. From *Drawings Accompanying The Report of Captain Turnbull on the Survey and Construction of The Alexandria Aqueduct Made to the House of Representatives 2d of July, 1838*, Document No. 459, Vol. XI, September 1838. P & P, HABS, DC,GEO,1-23.

4-021. Looking east toward Georgetown and the Potomac Aqueduct (1.2 miles), Chesapeake and Ohio Canal, Georgetown, Washington, D.C. From a drawing in the Washingtoniana Room, Washington, D.C., Public Library, ca. 1888. P & P, HABS, DC,GEO,25-19.

Although still in Washington, D.C., immediately above Georgetown the character of the C&O Canal changed from an urban canal to a rural one. This is still true today.

4-022. Inclined plane, caisson, and plan of the equipment at the head of the plane, Chesapeake and Ohio Canal above Georgetown, Washington, D.C. (2.3 miles). Probably Donald Demers, artist, ca. 1989. U.S. Department of the Interior, *Chesapeake and Ohio Canal: A Guide to Chesapeake and Ohio Canal National Historical Park, Handbook 142* (1989). LC F187 .C47 C47.

In 1875–76 an inclined plane was added to the C&O Canal by the Potomac Lock and Dock Company to avoid the congestion that had developed in Georgetown. Designed by William Hutton, the plane was originally intended to augment the lower five locks (including the tide lock) in Georgetown. Canal boats were hauled up and down a height of 38 feet along a run of 589 feet. Unlike most other inclined planes on American canals, here the boats were hauled in a large tank of water, the caisson, to avoid hogging or distortion of the boat's hull or other weakening caused by removing the boat from the water. The water-powered turbine raising the caisson was a Leffels double-turbine water wheel in a well 29 feet below the surface of the canal and was fed through a 20-inch pipe. The 68-horsepower turbine powering the caisson used counterweights. The water turbine was later replaced by a steam engine. Nothing remains of this inclined plane except a plaque marking the site.

4-021

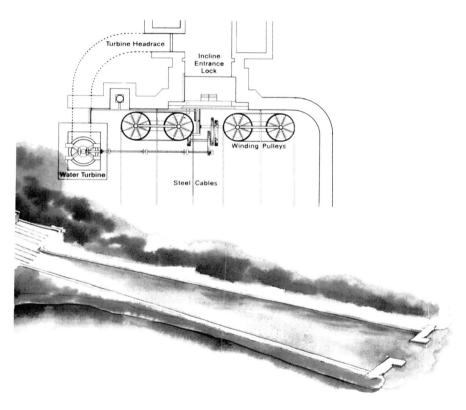

4-022

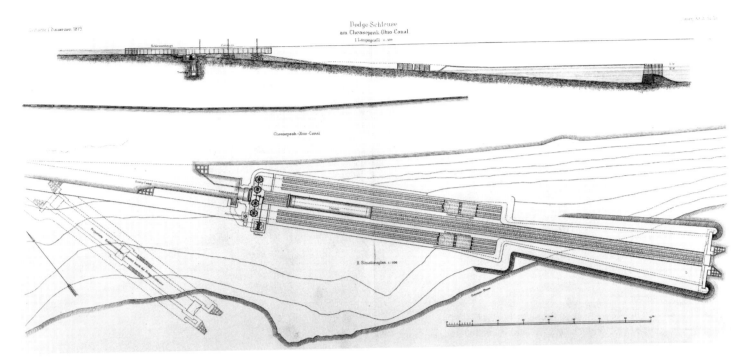

Dodge-Schleuse
am Cheasepeak-Ohio-Canal

4-023

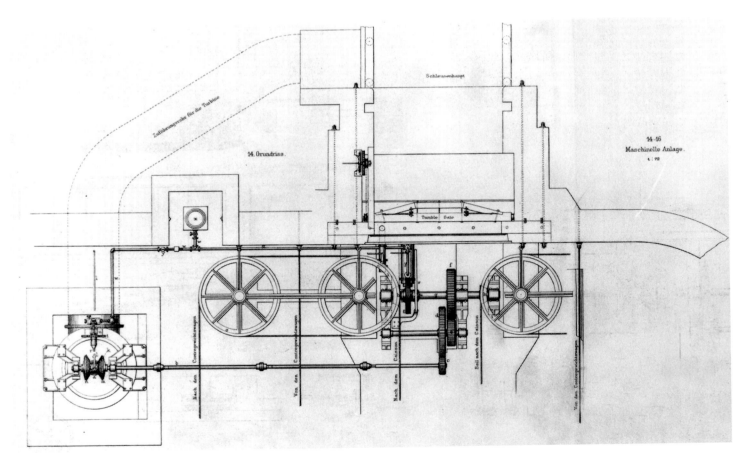

4-024

opposite

4-023. Elevation and plan of inclined plane, Chesapeake and Ohio Canal, above Georgetown, Washington, D.C. (2.3 miles). *Zeitschrift für Bauwesen* (1879). L/C NA 3 .25.

The caisson, without a canal boat, is near the top of its run. The two counterweights are shown near the bottom of their run. Compare with 4-022.

4-024. Plan of upper end of inclined plane, Chesapeake and Ohio Canal, above Georgetown, Washington, D.C. (2.3 miles). *Zeitschrift für Bauwesen* (1879). L/C NA 3 .25.

Shown are the turbine headrace (top left), the top of the turbine (left), the power transmission, three of the winding pulleys, and the steel cables connected to the caisson and counterweights. Compare with 4-022.

this page

4-025. West elevation, Abner Cloud House, Chesapeake and Ohio Canal, Washington, D.C. (3.1 miles). James M. Hamill, delineator, 1964. P & P, HABS DC-99, sheet no. 7.

4-026. North and west elevations, Abner Cloud House, Chesapeake and Ohio Canal, Washington, D.C. (3.1 miles). Russell Jones, photographer, June 1963. P & P, HABS, DC, WASH,167-3.

The Abner Cloud House, a miller's house built ca. 1801, predates the C&O Canal. It was constructed when this area was the terminus of the Little Falls bypass canal of the Potomac Canal Company, built in 1797. The C&O Canal replaced most of the works of the Potomac Canal in this area.

WEST ELEVATION

4-025

4-026

4-027

4-028

4-029

this page

4-027. Chain Bridge, Chesapeake and Ohio Canal, Little Falls Vic., Washington, D.C., (3.6 miles). Augustus Kollner, artist, 1839. P & P, LC-USZ61-1344.

Chain Bridge is the oldest crossing of the Potomac River in the Washington, D.C. area. The first bridge at this location, a wooden covered bridge, was constructed in 1797 and destroyed in 1804. The bridge received its name from the third bridge erected on the site, a 136-foot-long, 15-foot-wide structure suspended from 1¼-inch bars and designed by Judge James E. Finley of Uniontown, Pennsylvania. It was destroyed by floodwaters in 1812. This illustration shows the fourth bridge at this location, also a chain bridge.

4-028. Chain Bridge, Chesapeake and Ohio Canal, Little Falls Vic., Washington, D.C. (3.6 miles). William Morris Smith, photographer, 1865. P & P, LC-B817-7655

The canal is shown in the right foreground.

4-029. Interior of the sixth Chain Bridge at the Chesapeake and Ohio Canal, Little Falls Vic., Washington, D.C. (3.6 miles), ca. 1865. P & P, LC-B817-7656.

The wooden truss bridge shown in 4-028 and 4-029 was the sixth bridge at this site. It was built in the 1850s.

opposite

4-030. West and east elevations of lockhouse, Lock 5, Chesapeake and Ohio Canal, Brookmont Vic., Maryland (5.0 miles). A. Gutterson and D. McGrew, measurers; D. McGrew and Pick, delineators, ca. 1930s. P & P, HABS MD-56-B, sheet no. 2.

4-031. West and north elevations of lockhouse, Lock 6, Chesapeake and Ohio Canal, Brookmont Vic., Maryland (5.4 miles). A. Gutterson and H. Berliner, measurers; Pick, delineator, ca. 1930s. P & P, HABS MD-56-A, sheet no. 3.

4-032. North and west elevations of lockhouse, Lock 7, Chesapeake and Ohio Canal, Glen Echo Vic., Maryland (7.0 miles). D. McGrew, delineator, ca. 1939. P & P, HABS MD-56-C, sheet no. 2.

WEST ELEVATION

EAST ELEVATION

standing seam metal roof

Siding: widths vary 6½ to 7"

no sash

2" Wood Sill

Stone Sill

Concrete

14 courses

9 courses

32' - 4½"

4-030

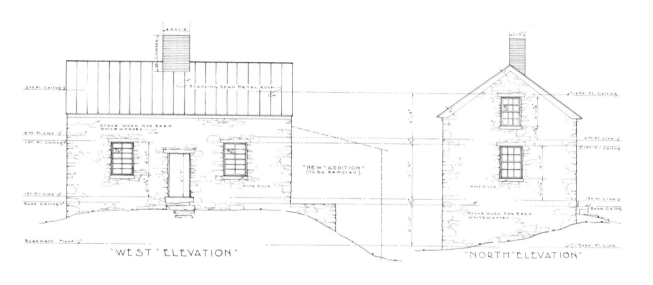

2ND FL. CEILING

2ND FL LINE
1ST FL CEILING

STANDING SEAM METAL ROOF

STONE WORK HAS BEEN WHITEWASHED

"NEW" ADDITION
(TO BE REMOVED)

1ST FL LINE
BASE CEILING

WOOD SILLS

BASEMENT FLOOR

"WEST" ELEVATION

2ND FL. CEILING

2ND FL. LINE
1ST FL CEILING

STONE WORK HAS BEEN WHITEWASHED

WOOD SILLS

1ST FL LINE
BASE CEILING

BASE FL LINE

"NORTH" ELEVATION

4-031

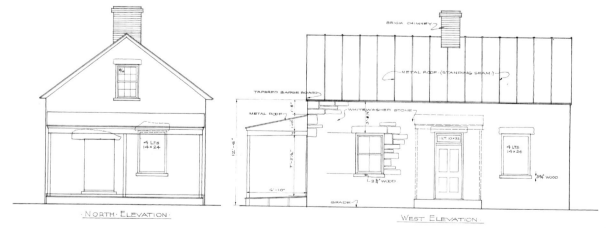

4 LTS
14 × 24

·NORTH·ELEVATION·

BRICK CHIMNEY

METAL ROOF (STANDING SEAM)

TAPERED BARGE BOARD

METAL ROOF

WHITEWASHED STONE

1 LT. 10 × 32

4 LTS
14 × 24

3⅜" WOOD

GRADE

WEST ELEVATION·

4-032

4-033

4-033. Cabin John Aqueduct under construction, Chesapeake and Ohio Canal, Cabin John, Maryland (7.5 miles). June 1859. P & P, LC-USZ62-13085.

At the time of its construction, 1857–63, the Cabin John Aqueduct was one of the largest single-arch bridges in the world, with a span of 220 feet and a rise of 57½ feet. It was built under the supervision of army engineer Montgomery C. Meigs to carry the Washington, D.C., water supply conduit, 9 feet in diameter, and a road bridge over Cabin John Creek. The false centering shown here is how this and all of the C&O Canal aqueducts' arch structures were constructed.

4-034. Cabin John Aqueduct, along the Chesapeake and Ohio Canal, Cabin John, Maryland (7.5 miles), ca. 1900. P & P, DPCC, LC-D401-13030.

4-034

" FRONT " ELEVATION "   " END " ELEVATION "

4-035

4-035. West and north elevations of the lockhouse, Lock 8, Chesapeake and Ohio Canal, Cabin John Vic., Maryland (8.3 miles). D. McClure, measurer; Pick, delineator, ca. 1939. P & P, HABS MD-56-D, sheet no. 2.

4-036. South and west elevations of the lockhouse, Lock 9, Chesapeake and Ohio Canal, Cabin John Vic., Maryland (8.7 miles). A. Gutterson, measurer; Pick, delineator, ca. 1939. P & P, HABS MD-56-E, sheet no. 2.

4-037. South and west elevations of the lockhouse, Lock 10, Chesapeake and Ohio Canal, Cabin John Vic., Maryland (8.8 miles). D. McClure, measurer; White, delineator, ca. 1939. P & P, HABS MD-56-F, sheet no. 1.

" SOUTH " ELEVATION "

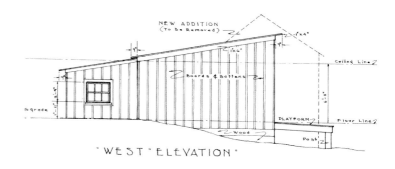

" WEST " ELEVATION "

4-036

SOUTH

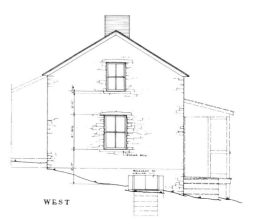

WEST

4-037

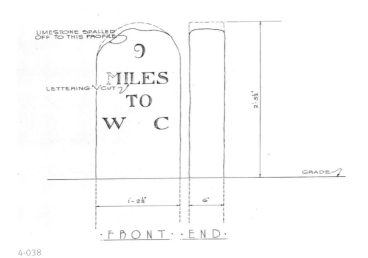

4-038

4-038. Elevation of milestone to Washington City, Glen Echo Vic., Maryland (9.0 miles), ca. 1939. P & P, HABS MD-57-G, sheet no. 5.

4-039. North and west elevations, lockhouse, Lock 11, Chesapeake and Ohio Canal, Cabin John Vic., Maryland (9.3 miles). D. McGrew, delineator, ca. 1939. P & P, HABS MD-56-G, sheet no. 2.

4-040. South and west elevations, lockhouse, Lock 12, Chesapeake and Ohio Canal, Cabin John Vic., Maryland (9.3 miles). D. McGrew, delineator, ca. 1939. P & P, HABS MD-56-H, sheet no. 1.

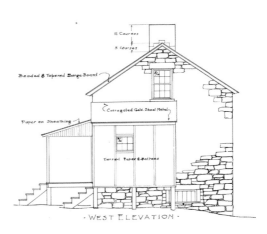

4-039

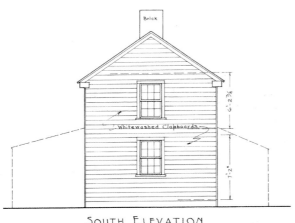

4-040

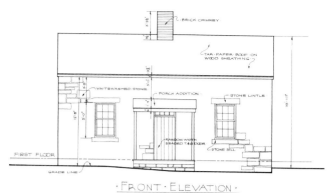

FRONT·ELEVATION·

4-041

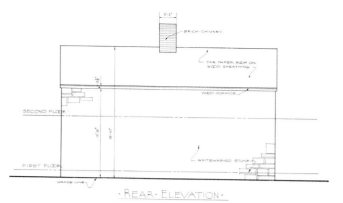

REAR·ELEVATION·

4-041. East and west elevations, lockhouse, Lock 13, Chesapeake and Ohio Canal, Cabin John Vic., Maryland (9.3 miles). D. McClure, delineator, ca. 1939. P & P, HABS MD-56-I, sheet no. 3.

4-042. North and south elevations, lockhouse, Lock 14, Chesapeake and Ohio Canal, Cabin John Vic., Maryland (9.5 miles). D. McClure, delineator, ca. 1939. P & P, HABS MD-56-J, sheet no. 1.

NORTH ELEVATION

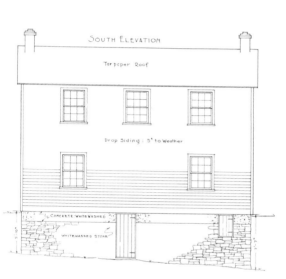

SOUTH ELEVATION

4-042

FRONT·ELEVATION·

RIGHT·SIDE·

4-043

4-043. West and south elevations, lockhouse, Lock 16, Chesapeake and Ohio Canal, Great Falls Vic., Maryland (13.6 miles). D. McClure, delineator, ca. 1939. P & P, HABS MD-56-K, sheet no. 2.

4-044

4-045

4-044. Stop lock, Lock 16, Chesapeake and Ohio Canal, Potomac Vic., Maryland (13.7 miles), ca. 1939. P & P, HABS, MD,16-_____,15-1.

This stop lock, and the 500-foot-long 15-foot-high stone and earth levee associated with it, prevented floodwaters from entering the old river channel, called Widewater, to protect the high banks below. When floods threatened, stout boards would be lowered into the vertical channels in the facing masonry abutments (center). The photograph shows the ruin of the masonry abutment of the stop lock. The stop lock has since been reconstructed by the National Park Service and still serves its original function. Another stop lock, at Dam 4, is shown in 2-017.

4- 045. Lockhouse, Lock 18, Chesapeake and Ohio Canal, Great Falls, Maryland (14.1 miles). Theodor Horydczak, photographer, ca. 1920–50. P & P, LC-H823-0284.

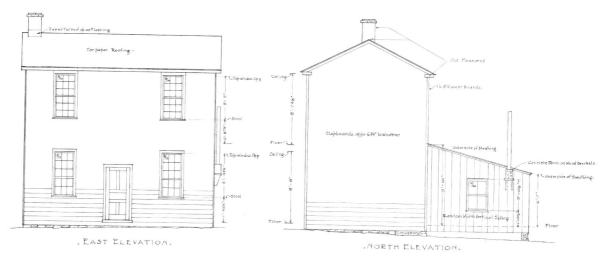

. EAST ELEVATION .

. NORTH ELEVATION .

4-046

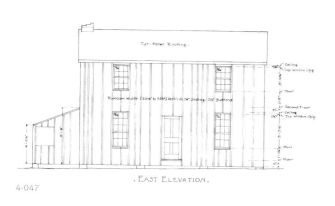

. EAST ELEVATION .

4-047

4-048

4-046. East and north elevations, Frame House 1 Chesapeake and Ohio Canal, Lock 20 Vic., Great Falls, Maryland (14.2 miles). D. McGrew, delineator, ca. 1930s. P & P, HABS MD-56-M, sheet no. 1.

4-047. East elevation of Frame House 2, Chesapeake and Ohio Canal, Lock 20 Vic., Great Falls, Maryland (14.2 miles). D. McGrew, delineator, ca. 1930s. P & P, HABS MD-56-N, sheet no. 1.

4-048. Downstream view of Lock 20 with Great Falls Tavern, Chesapeake and Ohio Canal, Great Falls, Maryland (14.3 miles). Theodor Horydczak, photographer, ca. 1920–50. P & P, LC-H823-0287-001.

Another view of this end of the lock is shown in 2-139. The site plan for Great Falls Tavern opposite Lock 20, is shown in IN-008.

4-049. North and east elevations of the northernmost of the three sections that comprise Great Falls Tavern, Chesapeake and Ohio Canal, Great Falls, Maryland (14.3 miles). John O. Bostrup, photographer, 1936. P & P, HABS, MD,16-_____,20-4.

The north porch (right) and the well house (left) were removed in the 1950s.

4-049

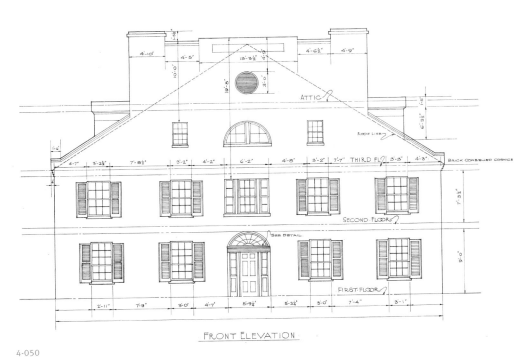

FRONT ELEVATION

4-050

4-050. North, or front, elevation of Great Falls Tavern, Chesapeake and Ohio Canal, Great Falls, Maryland (14.3 miles). D. McClure, delineator, ca. 1939. P & P, HABS MD-56-R, sheet no. 5.

Originally constructed in 1828–29, this was named Crommelin House to honor the Dutch family who bought C&O Canal securities that helped to finance the canal. Over the years it has served as a house, a hotel, and a private club. After World War II the northern wing was damaged by a fire. Instead of demolishing it, in the early 1950s the National Park Service rehabilitated it to serve as a visitor center for the Great Falls portion of the C&O Canal National Historical Park. During the operational period of the canal, this was one of the destinations of packet boats leaving Georgetown. See also IN-018.

· EAST · ELEVATION ·

4-051

4-051. East elevation, Great Falls Tavern, Chesapeake and Ohio Canal, Great Falls, Maryland (14.3 miles). D. McClure, delineator, ca. 1939. P & P, HABS MD-56-R, sheet no. 6.

Great Falls Tavern is composed of three separate buildings. The north portion (right), a two-and-a-half-story structure made of brick with roof dormers, was added to the center section, which was intended as a lockhouse and was built of stone. The southern portion (left), a two-story brick structure, was also an addition.

4-052. Southwest and southeast elevations of lockhouse, Lock 21 (Swain's Lock), Chesapeake and Ohio Canal, Great Falls Vic., Maryland (16.6 miles). A. Gutterson, measurer; Pick, delineator, ca. 1939. P & P, HABS MD-56-P, sheet no. 2.

4-053. North and south elevations of lockhouse, Lock 22 (Pennyfield Lock), Chesapeake and Ohio Canal, Riverside, Maryland (19.6 miles). A. Gutterson, measurer; D. McGrew, delineator, ca. 1939. P & P, HABS MD-56-Q, sheet no. 2.

4-054. South elevation of lockhouse, Lock 24 (Riley's Lock), Chesapeake and Ohio Canal, Seneca, Maryland (22.8 miles), ca. 1936. P & P, HABS, MD,16-____,29A-3.

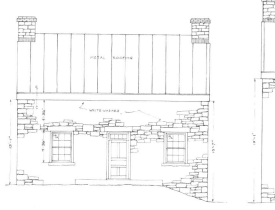

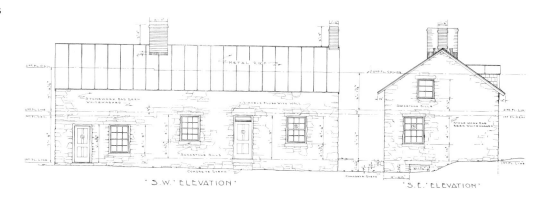

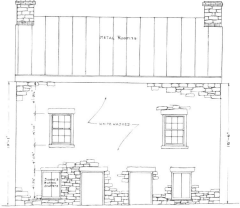

4-052

4-053

4-054

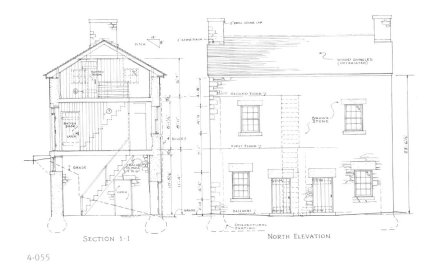

SECTION 1·1   NORTH ELEVATION

4-055

4-056

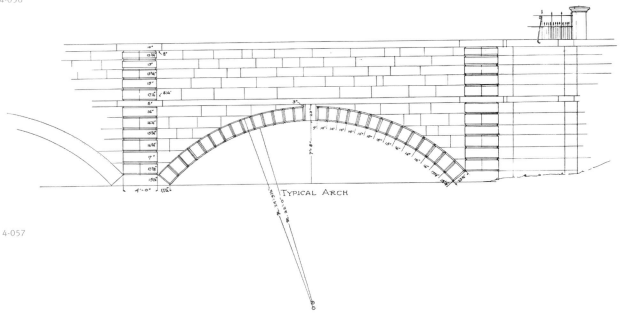

TYPICAL ARCH

4-057

4-055. Section and north elevation of the lockhouse, Lock 24 (Riley's Lock), Chesapeake and Ohio Canal, Seneca, Maryland (22.8 miles). J. G. Roberts, delineator, 1964. P & P, HABS, MD-56-T, sheet no. 2.

4-056. Seneca Aqueduct (Aqueduct 1), Chesapeake and Ohio Canal, Seneca Maryland (22.8 miles). John O. Bostrup, photographer, 1936. P & P, HABS, MD,16-_____,30-1.

First of eleven masonry aqueducts on the main stem of the C&O Canal, Seneca Aqueduct crosses Seneca Creek in three spans, one of which was destroyed by a flood September 11, 1971. The span of each arch is 33 feet; the total length of the aqueduct is 126 feet. This aqueduct and the Monocacy Aqueduct (the second aqueduct) were designed by C&O Canal chief engineer Benjamin Wright. The Seneca Aqueduct was constructed of Seneca sandstone, a distinctive local red stone. During the operational period of the canal, the small town of Seneca that centered on the aqueduct was one of the destinations of packet boats leaving Georgetown.

4-057. Typical arch, Seneca Aqueduct (Aqueduct 1), Chesapeake and Ohio Canal, Seneca, Maryland (22.8 miles). A. Gutterson and D. McGrew, measurers; D. McGrew, delineator, 1939. P & P, HABS MD-57-B, sheet no. 7, detail.

4-058. Broad Run Aqueduct (Broad Run
Trunk), Chesapeake and Ohio Canal,
Martinsburg Vic., Maryland (31.9 miles).
Jack E. Boucher, photographer, 1959–60.
P & P, HABS, MD,16-MARB.V,1-2.

4-059. Plan, Broad Run Aqueduct,
Chesapeake and Ohio Canal, Martinsburg
Vic., Maryland (31.9 miles). William Harris,
delineator, 1961. P & P, HABS MD-741,
sheet no. 2.

Also see 2-073 and 2-074.

4-058

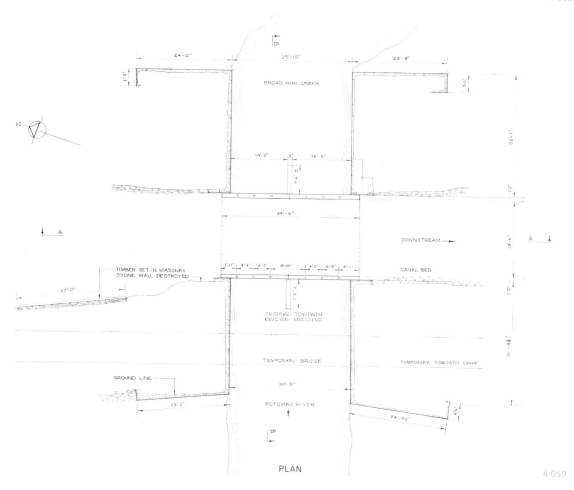

PLAN

4-059

4-060

4-061

4-062

4-060. South elevation of the metal truss bridge, White's Ferry (formerly Conrad's Ferry), Chesapeake and Ohio Canal, Martinsburg Vic., Maryland (35.5 miles). Jet T. Lowe, photographer, 1989. P & P, HAER, MD,16-MARB.V,3-1.

This single-span truss bridge was erected in 1876 to provide vehicular access across the canal to Conrad's Ferry (now called White's Ferry). In the foreground is a typical C&O Canal masonry culvert (Culvert 51). White's Ferry is still operational, although this bridge is no longer used, and is the last operating ferry on the Potomac River.

4-061. Lockhouse and Lock 26 (Woods Lock or Milk Lock), Chesapeake and Ohio Canal, Dickerson Vic., Maryland (39.4 miles). Jack E. Boucher, photographer, 1959. P & P, HABS, MD,16-DICK.V,2-1.

Unlike the masonry lockhouses on the lower part of the canal, this lockhouse is a two-story frame structure on a fieldstone foundation. See 2-062 for the lockhouse at Lock 25.

4-062. Lockhouse, Lock 27, Chesapeake and Ohio Canal, Dickerson Vic., Maryland (41.5 miles). Jack E. Boucher, photographer, 1959. P & P, HABS, MD,16-DICK.V,4-2.

This lockhouse has been subsequently restored by the National Park Service.

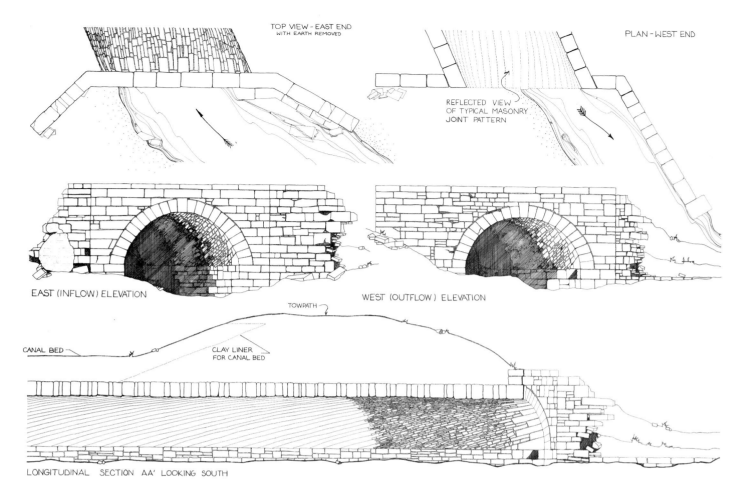

TOP VIEW - EAST END
WITH EARTH REMOVED

PLAN - WEST END

REFLECTED VIEW
OF TYPICAL MASONRY
JOINT PATTERN

EAST (INFLOW) ELEVATION

WEST (OUTFLOW) ELEVATION

TOWPATH

CANAL BED

CLAY LINER
FOR CANAL BED

LONGITUDINAL SECTION AA' LOOKING SOUTH

4-063

4-063. Plans, elevations, and section, Culvert 65, Chesapeake and Ohio Canal, Dickerson Vic., Maryland (39.7 miles). J. R. Frondorff, delineator, 1974. P & P, HAER MD-32, sheet no. 2.

In addition to masonry aqueducts, the C&O Canal Company constructed over two hundred masonry culverts between Georgetown and Cumberland. Some of them, such as Culvert 65 (1832), are impressive in their own right. Culvert 65 has a 12-foot span and is 121 feet long. Most of the culverts are constructed at right angles to the centerline of the canal. Culvert 65, and a handful of others, are skewed—that is, not at right angles to the centerline of the canal.

4-064

4-065

4-064. Monocacy Aqueduct (Aqueduct 2), Chesapeake and Ohio Canal, Dickerson Vic., Maryland (42.2 miles). Jack E. Boucher, photographer, 1959. P & P, HABS, MD,11-_____,37.

The Monocacy Aqueduct is 516 feet long, including abutments—approximately twice the size of the next largest aqueduct on the C&O Canal, the Conococheague Aqueduct at Williamsport. Each of the seven arches of the Monocacy Aqueduct spans 56 feet. It was constructed between 1829 and 1833. The timely completion of this aqueduct was largely instrumental in permitting the C&O Canal Company to meet its charter goal of having opened a hundred miles of the canal within the first five years. It remained in service until 1924, when the canal closed. See 2-087 for a close-up of the wroughtiron fence on the towpath along the aqueduct; see also 1-075.

4-065. Downstream arches, Monocacy Aqueduct (Aqueduct 2), Chesapeake and Ohio Canal, Dickerson Vic., Maryland (42.2 miles). Jack E. Boucher, photographer, 1959. P & P, HABS, MD,11-_____,38.

4-066. Dedication plaque, Monocacy Aqueduct (Aqueduct 2), Chesapeake and Ohio Canal, Dickerson Vic., Maryland (42.2 miles). Jack E. Boucher, photographer, 1959. P & P, HABS, MD,11-_____,316.

Listed on this plaque are the company officers, engineers, and contractors. Omitted is the name of the designer, Benjamin Wright, because he had left his position as chief engineer of the company by the time the plaque was erected.

4-067. Elevation and plan, Monocacy Aqueduct (Aqueduct 2), Chesapeake and Ohio Canal, Dickerson Vic., Maryland (42.2 miles). L. Ewald Jr., delineator, ca. 1936. P & P, HABS MD-19, sheet no. 2.

4-068. Section and elevation, typical arch, Monocacy Aqueduct (Aqueduct 2), Chesapeake and Ohio Canal, Dickerson Vic., Maryland (42.2 miles). L. Ewald Jr., delineator, ca. 1936. P & P, HABS MD-19, sheet no. 1.

4-066

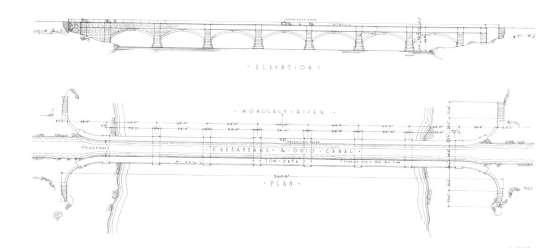

4-067

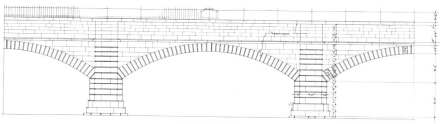

4-068

4-069

4-069. Lockhouse, Lock 28, Chesapeake and Ohio Canal, Point of Rocks Vic., Maryland (48.9 miles). Jack E. Boucher, photographer, 1959. P & P, HABS, MD,11-PORO.V,3-2.

4-070. Lockhouse, Lock 29 (Catoctin Lock), Chesapeake and Ohio Canal, Lander, Maryland (50.9 miles). Jack E. Boucher, photographer, 1959. P & P, HABS, MD,11-LAN,1-1.

4-071. Catoctin Creek Aqueduct (Aqueduct 3), Chesapeake and Ohio Canal, Point of Rocks Vic., Maryland (51.5 miles). Jack E. Boucher, photographer, 1959. P & P, HABS, MD,11-PORO.V,2-2.

This three-span masonry arch aqueduct was nicknamed Crooked Aqueduct for its swaybacked central arch.

4-070

4-071

4-072. Upstream face of Catoctin Creek Aqueduct (Aqueduct 3), Chesapeake and Ohio Canal, Point of Rocks Vic., Maryland (51.5 miles). Jack E. Boucher, photographer, 1959. P & P, HABS, MD,11-PORO.V,2-5.

The cut stone spandrel face was undercut and removed by floods, exposing the rubble fill behind. This seriously weakened the aqueduct, and it collapsed in a flood on October 31, 1973.

4-073. Lockhouse, Lock 31, Chesapeake and Ohio Canal, Weverton Vic., Maryland (58.0 miles). Jack E. Boucher, photographer, 1959. P & P, HABS, MD,22-WEV.V,3-1.

4-074. Interior of lockhouse, Lock 31, Chesapeake and Ohio Canal, Weverton Vic., Maryland (58.0 miles). Jack E. Boucher, photographer, 1959. P & P, HABS, MD,22-WEV.V,3-3.

4-072

4-073

4-074

4-075

4-075. Culvert 93 (Israel Creek Aqueduct), Chesapeake and Ohio Canal, Weverton Vic., Maryland (58.2 miles). Jack E. Boucher, photographer, 1959. P & P, HABS, MD,22-WEV.V,1-2.

The culvert in the background has a span of 20 feet over Israel Creek. The arches in the foreground are from a culvert constructed by the Baltimore and Ohio Railroad.

4-076. View of Harper's Ferry, West Virginia (60.7 miles). Currier and Ives lithograph, ca. 1856. P & P, LC-USZC2-3484.

This pre–Civil War illustration of Harper's Ferry and the confluence of the Potomac (left, center) and Shenandoah (right) Rivers illustrates the narrow stretch of land that was the source of competition between the C&O Canal and the Baltimore and Ohio Railroad. The canal was awarded the narrow strip of land at the base of Maryland Heights while the Baltimore and Ohio Railroad was forced to build a bridge (center) to cross the Potomac River and continue up the opposite side. John Brown and eighteen followers crossed this bridge on the evening of October 16, 1859, to incite a rebellion. He was captured on October 18, 1859, at the right end of the bridge shown and hanged on December 2, 1859.

4-076

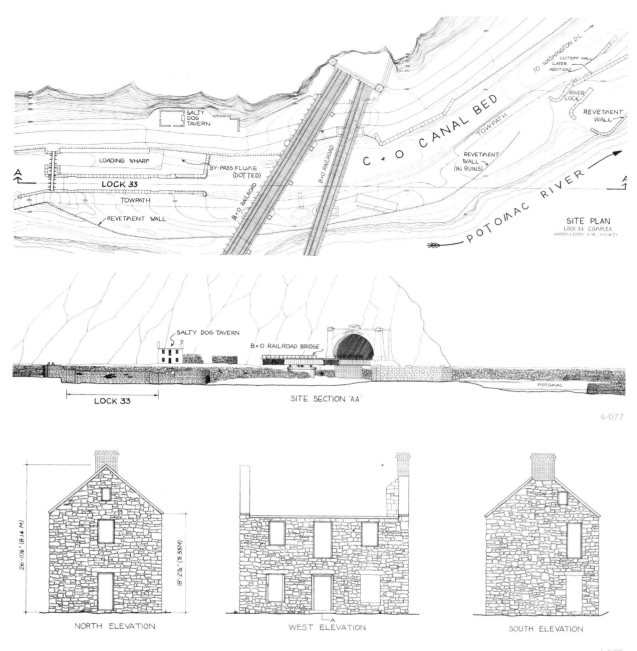

4-077. Site plan and site section of Lock 33 area, Chesapeake and Ohio Canal, Harper's Ferry Vic., Maryland (60.7 miles). J. R. Frondorff, delineator, 1974. P & P, HAER MD-27, sheet no. 2.

The Lock 33 complex is at the base of Maryland Heights, Maryland, immediately across from the mouth of the Shenandoah River at Harper's Ferry. With two rivers converging on a constricted passage through the Catoctin Mountains, it is subject to frequent flooding. The drawings show the remains of the revetment wall built by the canal company to protect Lock 33 from flood damage. Also depicted is the Baltimore and Ohio Railroad tunnel providing access to the Potomac River crossing, the river lock (right) providing entrance into the C&O Canal for boats coming down the Shenandoah River (not shown but below Lock 33) and across the Potomac River, as well as the bypass flume, loading wharf, towpath, and local tavern.

4-078. North, west, and south elevations of the Salty Dog Tavern, Lock 33, Chesapeake and Ohio Canal, Harper's Ferry Vic., Maryland (60.7 miles). Dennis Davis, delineator, 1974. P & P, HAER MD-27-C, sheet no. 1.

4-079. The Salty Dog Tavern, opposite Harper's Ferry, Virginia (now West Virginia). Norrcose, delineator. From William Cullen Bryant (ed.), *Picturesque America, or, The Land We Live In* (1894). LC E168 .P5893.

The Salty Dog Tavern is the two-story structure (middle) in front of Maryland Heights of the Catoctin Mountains (left). A portion of Lock 33 and its lockhouse (right) can be seen. In the distance is the bridge carrying the main line of the Baltimore and Ohio Railroad across the Potomac River.

4-080. Remains of the bypass flume and Lock 33, Chesapeake and Ohio Canal, Harper's Ferry Vic., Maryland (60.7 miles). Jack E. Boucher, photographer, 1958. P & P, HABS, MD,22-HARF.V,3-1.

The Baltimore and Ohio Railroad bridge can be seen in the background and the Salty Dog Tavern at the top (near building).

4-079

4-080

4-081. Lock 34 (Goodheart's Lock), Chesapeake and Ohio Canal, Harper's Ferry Road, Harper's Ferry Vic., Maryland (61.6 miles). Jack E. Boucher, photographer, 1958. P & P, HABS, MD,22-HARF.V,8-1.

See also 2-010.

4-082. Lock 35, Chesapeake and Ohio Canal, Harper's Ferry Vic., Maryland (62.3 miles). Jack E. Boucher, photographer, 1959. P & P, HABS, MD,22-HARF.V,9-2.

Because funds were unavailable for restoration, the National Park Service "buried" this lock in the late 1990s: earth was dumped in the lock chamber to resist the tendency of the two facing lock walls to move toward each other. The technique was used to mothball the structure until restoration—removing and then re-laying stone courses—could be undertaken. The dry dock associated with Lock 35 is shown in 2-020–2-022. A detail of Lock 35's gate hinge is shown in 2-034.

4-083. Feeder lock above Lock 35, Chesapeake and Ohio Canal, Harper's Ferry Vic., Maryland (62.3 miles). Jack E. Boucher, photographer, 1959. P & P, HABS, MD,22-HARF.V,7-1.

The feeder lock provided water to the C&O Canal from the Potomac River to maintain the canal from above Harper's Ferry to below Seneca Creek, a distance of some 40 miles.

4-081

4-082

4-083

4-084

4-085

opposite

4-084. Interior of the feeder lock above Lock 35, Chesapeake and Ohio Canal, Harper's Ferry Vic., Maryland (62.3 miles). Jack E. Boucher, photographer, 1959. P & P, HABS, MD,22-HARF.V,7-4.

4-085. Lockhouse ruins at feeder lock, Chesapeake and Ohio Canal at Dam 3, Harper's Ferry Vic., Maryland (62.3 miles). Jack E. Boucher, photographer, 1959. P & P, HABS, MD,22-HARF.V,12-1.

this page

4-086. Lock 36, Chesapeake and Ohio Canal, Harper's Ferry Vic., Maryland (62.4 miles). Jack E. Boucher, photographer, 1959. P & P, HABS, MD,22-HARF.V,10-2.

4-087. Lockhouse, Lock 36, Chesapeake and Ohio Canal, Harper's Ferry Vic., Maryland (62.4 miles). Jack E. Boucher, photographer, 1959. P & P, HABS, MD,22-WEV.V,4-1.

As the canal company continued the canal up the Potomac River, funds ran low and economies were made. The trim masonry lockhouses of the lower canal gave way to less expensive wooden-frame lockhouses in the upper canal and then to log structures (4-141).

4-088. South and west elevations, lockhouse, Lock 36, Chesapeake and Ohio Canal, Harper's Ferry Vic., Maryland (62.4 miles). R. G. Colville, delineator, ca. 1959. P & P, HABS MD-884, sheet no. 2.

4-086

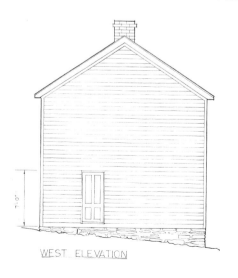
4-087

SOUTH ELEVATION

WEST ELEVATION

4-088

4-089

4-089. Lockhouse, Lock 37, Chesapeake and Ohio Canal, Antietam Vic., Maryland (67.0 miles). Jack E. Boucher, photographer, 1959. P & P, HABS, MD,22-ANTI.V,6-1.

4-090. East and north elevations of the lockhouse, Lock 37, Chesapeake and Ohio Canal, Antietam Vic., Maryland (67.0 miles). William T. Harris, delineator, 1961. P & P, HABS MD-208, sheet no. 5.

4-091. Interior of the lockhouse, Lock 37, Chesapeake and Ohio Canal, Antietam Vic., Maryland (67.0 miles). Jack E. Boucher, photographer, 1959. P & P, HABS, MD,22-ANTI.V,6-4.

EAST ELEVATION

4-090

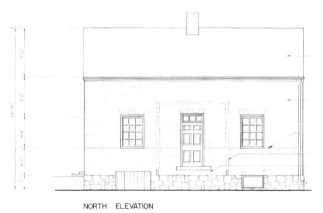

NORTH ELEVATION

4-091

4-092. Antietam Creek Aqueduct (Aqueduct 4), Chesapeake and Ohio Canal, Antietam Vic., Maryland (69.4 miles). Jack E. Boucher, photographer, 1959. P & P, HABS, MD,22-ANTI.V,3-3.

This aqueduct has three arches and is 140 feet long.

4-093. West and east elevations and section, Antietam Creek Aqueduct (Aqueduct 4), Chesapeake and Ohio Canal, Antietam Vic., Maryland (69.4 miles). William Harris, delineator, 1961. P & P, HABS MD-205, sheet no. 3.

4-094. Southwest and northwest elevations of section house, Lock 39, Chesapeake and Ohio Canal, Sharpsburg Vic., Maryland (74.3 miles). William Harris, delineator, 1961. P & P, HABS MD-220, sheet no. 2.

A section house was the residence of the company's section superintendent.

4-092

WEST ELEVATION

EAST ELEVATION

SECTION B-B

4-093

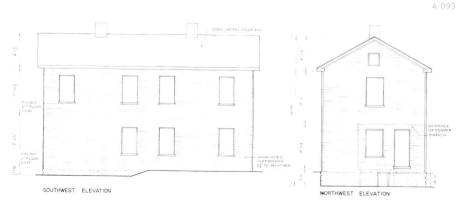

SOUTHWEST ELEVATION

NORTHWEST ELEVATION

4-094

4-095

4-096

4-097

4-095. Lock 44, Chesapeake and Ohio Canal, Williamsport Vic., Maryland (99.3 miles). Jack E. Boucher, photographer, 1959–60. P & P, HABS, MD,22-WILPO.V,4-1.

Lock 44's lock hinge is shown in 2-033.

4-096. Canal boat, Chesapeake and Ohio Canal, Williamsport, Maryland (99.7 miles), ca. 1900–1906. P & P, DPCC, LC-D4-16565.

The bridge in the foreground is the Salisbury Bridge in Williamsport; the Potomac River is in the distance.

4-097. Vertical lift bridge crossing the Chesapeake and Ohio Canal to the Potomac Edison Power Plant, Williamsport, Maryland (99.7 miles). William E. Barrett, photographer, 1970. P & P, HAER, MD,22-WILPO,1-1.

Constructed in 1923, this lift bridge was reportedly used only once before the C&O Canal Company went out of business in 1924. Possibly the smallest bridge of its type in the United States, it is probably also the country's only asymmetrical lift bridge: an extra bay was added to the western end (right) to allow the towpath to pass underneath.

4-098

4-098. Coal loading at the Cushwa Basin,
Chesapeake and Ohio Canal, Williamsport,
Maryland (99.7 miles). William Henry
Jackson, photographer, ca. 1892. P & P,
DPCC, LC-D43-T01-1844.

The Potomac River (upper left) and the
Conococheague Aqueduct are visible immediately beyond the Cushwa Basin (right).

4-099

4-099. Downstream elevation, Conococheague Aqueduct (Aqueduct 5), Chesapeake and Ohio Canal, Williamsport, Maryland (99.8 miles). Jack E. Boucher, photographer, 1959–60. P & P, HABS, MD,22-WILPO.V,2-2.

This is the second largest aqueduct on the C&O Canal. Its three spans are each 62⅔ feet long; the total length including abutments is 196 feet. See also 1-076.

4-100. Plan and southwest elevation, Conococheague Aqueduct (Aqueduct 5), Chesapeake and Ohio Canal at Williamsport, Maryland (99.8 miles). Dana Lockett, delineator, 1997. P & P, HAER MD-123, sheet no. 2.

The upstream spandrel wall of the aqueduct failed on April 20, 1920, when it was hit by Boat Number 73 captained by Frank Myers. Boat and crew were washed into the Conococheague Creek below. The basic cause of the failure is believed to be longitudinal cracks in the arch stones immediately under the upstream wall caused by water pressure in the canal prism; the collision was just the culminating event of the failure. After the spandrel wall collapsed in 1920, the aqueduct was reconstructed using a wooden prism wall. See IN-046–IN-048.

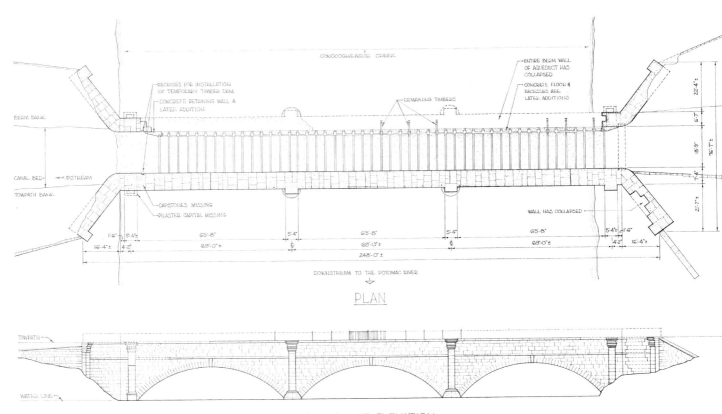

4-100

4-101

4-102

4-101. Charles Mill, Chesapeake and Ohio Canal, Williamsport Vic., Maryland (106.0 miles). Jack E. Boucher, photographer, 1959–60. P & P, HABS, MD,22-WILPO.V,5-1.

4-102. Water wheel of Charles Mill, Chesapeake and Ohio Canal, Williamsport Vic., Maryland (106.0 miles). Jack E. Boucher, photographer, 1959–60. P & P, HABS, MD,22-WILPO.V,5-2.

4-103. West elevation, Charles Mill, Chesapeake and Ohio Canal, Williamsport Vic., Maryland (106.0 miles). Alan McDonald, delineator, 1961. P & P, HABS MD-210, sheet no. 3.

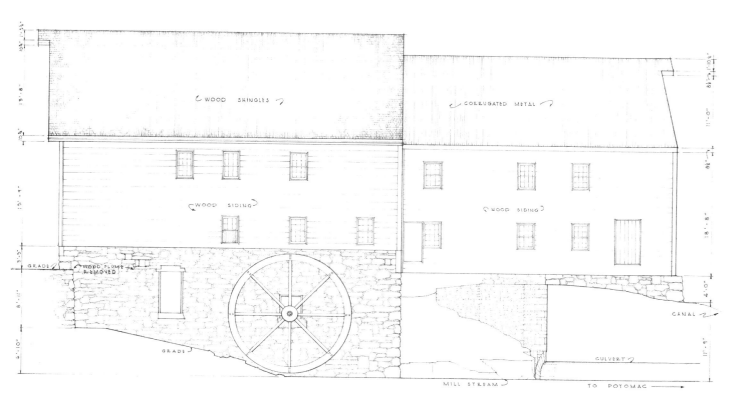

WEST ELEVATION

4-103

4-104

4-105

4-106

4-104. Feeder lock (Inlet Lock 5) at Dam 5, Chesapeake and Ohio Canal, Fort Frederick Vic., Maryland (106.8 miles). Jack E. Boucher, photographer, 1959. P & P, HABS, MD,22-FOFR.V,5-1.

This lock permitted canal boats to enter or exit the C&O Canal from the Potomac River above the dam and also provided water to the canal. Dam 5 is shown in 2-131 and 2-132.

4-105. Lock 46, Chesapeake and Ohio Canal, Fort Frederick Vic., Maryland (107.4 miles). Jack E. Boucher, photographer, 1959–60. P & P, HABS, MD,22-FOFR.V,6-1.

4-106. Lockhouse, Lock 46, Chesapeake and Ohio Canal, Fort Frederick Vic., Maryland (107.4 miles). Jack E. Boucher, photographer, 1959–60. P & P, HABS, MD,22-FOFR.V,12-2.

4-107. Lockhouse, Lock 48, Chesapeake and Ohio Canal, Fort Frederick Vic., Maryland (108.7 miles). Jack E. Boucher, photographer, 1960. P & P, HABS, MD,22-FOFR.V,1-2.

4-108. Southwest and southeast elevations of the lockhouse, Lock 48, Chesapeake and Ohio Canal, Fort Frederick Vic., Maryland (108.7 miles). C. Gustave Wormuth, delineator, 1961. P & P, HABS MD-215, sheet no. 4.

4·107

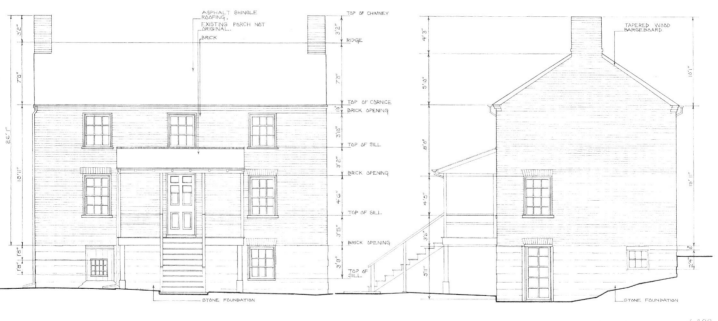

ASPHALT SHINGLE
ROOFING.

EXISTING PORCH NOT
ORIGINAL.

BRICK

TOP OF CHIMNEY

RIDGE

TOP OF CORNICE

BRICK OPENING

TOP OF SILL

BRICK OPENING

TOP OF SILL

BRICK OPENING

TOP OF SILL

STONE FOUNDATION

TAPERED WOOD
BARGEBOARD

STONE FOUNDATION

4·108

4-109

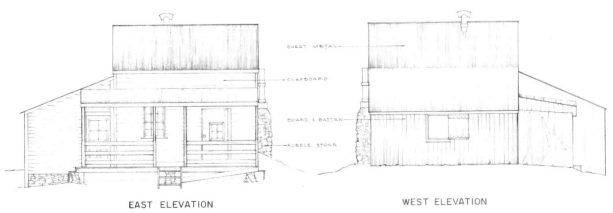

EAST ELEVATION   WEST ELEVATION

4-110

4-109. Lockhouse, Lock 50, Chesapeake and Ohio Canal, Fort Frederick Vic., Maryland (108.9 miles). Jack E. Boucher, photographer, 1960. P & P, HABS, MD,22-FOFR.V,2-1.

4-110. East and west elevations of the lockhouse, Lock 50, Chesapeake and Ohio Canal, Fort Frederick Vic., Maryland (108.9 miles). Michael L. Bobrow, delineator, 1961. P & P, HABS MD-216, sheet no. 3.

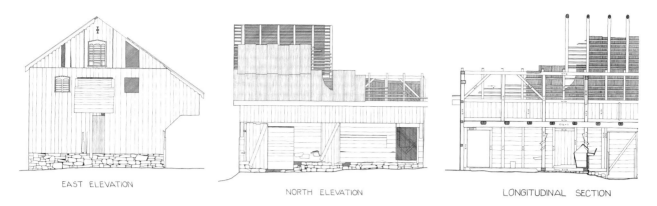

EAST ELEVATION   NORTH ELEVATION   LONGITUDINAL SECTION

4-111

4-111. East and north elevations and longitudinal section of the mule barn, Chesapeake and Ohio Canal, Clear Spring Vic., Maryland (108.9 miles). Denis Davis, delineator, 1974. P & P, HAER MD-28, sheet no. 3.

4-112. Lockhouse, Lock 54, Chesapeake and Ohio Canal, Hancock Vic., Maryland (134.0 miles). Jack E. Boucher, photographer, 1959–60. P & P, HABS, MD,22-HAN.V,7-1.

4-113. Lock 55, Chesapeake and Ohio Canal, Hancock Vic., Maryland (134.1 miles). Jack E. Boucher, photographer, 1959–60. P & P, HABS, MD,22-HAN.V,5-1.

4-112

4-113

4-114

4-114. Culvert 199, Chesapeake and Ohio Canal, Hancock Vic., Maryland (135.0 miles). Jack E. Boucher, photographer, 1959–60. P & P, HABS, MD,22-HAN.V,1-1.

This photograph of Culvert 199, a 6-foot span, illustrates the exposed wooden foundation that was typically constructed under most masonry structures along the canal. Compare with 2-108 and 2-109.

4-115. Masonry detail, Culvert 199, Chesapeake and Ohio Canal, Hancock Vic., Maryland (135.0 miles). Jack E. Boucher, photographer, 1959–60. P & P, HABS, MD,22-HAN.V,1-4.

The masonry failure shown is probably the result of differential settlement as the 170-year-old wooden foundation deteriorates.

4-115

4-116. Masonry detail, Lock 56, Chesapeake and Ohio Canal, Hancock Vic., Maryland (136.2 miles). Jack E. Boucher, photographer, 1959–60. P & P, HABS, MD,22-HAN.V,6-1.

4-117. Interior wall construction detail, lockhouse, Lock 56, Chesapeake and Ohio Canal, Hancock Vic., Maryland (136.2 miles). Jack E. Boucher, photographer, 1959–60. P & P, HABS, MD,22-HAN.V,8-3.

4-118. Coping stone detail, Lock 56, Chesapeake and Ohio Canal, Hancock Vic., Maryland (136.2 miles). Jack E. Boucher, photographer, 1959–60. P & P, HABS, MD,22-HAN.V,6-2.

The grooves along the top of the coping stone, the top layer of masonry, were worn into the stone by the towing ropes of the canal barges.

4-119. Lockhouse, Lock 56, Chesapeake and Ohio Canal, Hancock Vic., Maryland (136.2 miles). Jack E. Boucher, photographer, 1959–60. P & P, HABS, MD,22-HAN.V,8-1.

4-116

4-118

4-117

4-119

4-120

4-121

4-122

4-120. Sideling Hill Creek Aqueduct (Aqueduct 8), Chesapeake and Ohio Canal, Hancock Vic., Maryland (136.6 miles). Jack E. Boucher, photographer, 1960. P & P, HABS, MD,1-HAN.V,1-1.

Constructed in 1848, this aqueduct has a single arch 110 feet long. As can be seen, it is unusual in that it is asymmetrical.

4-121. Towpath and railing detail, Sideling Hill Creek Aqueduct (Aqueduct 8), Chesapeake and Ohio Canal, Hancock Vic., Maryland (136.6 miles). Jack E. Boucher, photographer, 1960. P & P, HABS, MD,1-HAN.V,1-3.

4-122. Busey Cabin, Chesapeake and Ohio Canal, Oldtown Vic., Maryland (151.2 miles). Jack E. Boucher, photographer, 1960. P & P, HABS, MD,1-OLDTO.V,2-2.

The Busey Cabin was used by the company during construction of the Paw Paw Tunnel. It is located approximately 4 miles downstream from the north portal of the tunnel (the downstream portal).

4-123. Notched log construction detail, corner of Busey Cabin, Chesapeake and Ohio Canal, Oldtown Vic., Maryland (151.2 miles). Jack E. Boucher, photographer, 1960. P & P, HABS, MD,1-OLDTO.V,2-3.

4-123

4-124. Carpenter shop at Lock 66, Chesapeake and Ohio Canal, Oldtown Vic., Maryland (154.7 miles). Jack E. Boucher, photographer, 1960. P & P, HABS, 1-OLDTO.V, 3-1.

The carpenter shop was just downstream of the north portal of the Paw Paw Tunnel. A skeleton at the time it was photographed, it subsequently burned.

4-125. Athey's Hollow, the excavated approach to Paw Paw Tunnel, Chesapeake and Ohio Canal, Oldtown Vic., Maryland (155.2 miles). Jack E. Boucher, photographer, 1960. P & P, HABS, MD, 1-OLDTO.V, 4-1.

Athey's Hollow is an 890-foot-long excavation leading to Paw Paw Tunnel. During construction of the tunnel, horse-drawn trams mounted on rails were used to haul the debris from the tunnel down Athey's Hollow.

4-124

4-125

4-126

4-127

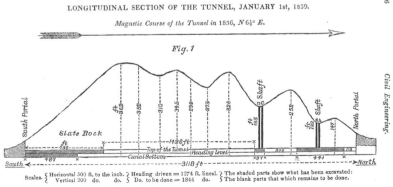

LONGITUDINAL SECTION OF THE TUNNEL, JANUARY 1st, 1839.

Magnetic Course of the Tunnel in 1836, N 6¼° E.

Fig. 1

Civil Engineering.

Scales. { Horizontal 500 ft. to the inch. } Heading driven = 1274 ft. lineal. } The shaded parts show what has been excavated:
{ Vertical 200 do.   do. } Do. to be done = 1844 do. } The blank parts that which remains to be done.

Note.—The whole course of the Tunnel consists of slate rock (in inclined strata sometimes contorted) of a bluish gray colour, containing considerable lime and occasional veins of shell limestone.

4-128

this page

4-126. North portal of Paw Paw Tunnel, Chesapeake and Ohio Canal, Oldtown Vic., Maryland (155.2 miles). Jack E. Boucher, photographer, 1960. P & P, HABS, MD,1-OLDTO.V,4-5.

The Paw Paw Tunnel is 3,118 feet long and was constructed to avoid the double bend of the Potomac River and the extra length of 6 miles by that route. The tunnel was designed and built by Ellwood Morris, assistant engineer, under the direction of chief engineer Charles Fisk. Boring of the tunnel began in 1836. Simultaneous excavation took place from the south portal (upriver), the north portal (downriver), and from workings at the base of two sets of 11-foot-diameter vertical shafts drilled down from the top of the mountain to the line of the tunnel (1-128). The tunnel opened for traffic in 1850. See also 2-124.

4-127. The Paw Paw Tunnel from the inside of the north portal, Chesapeake and Ohio Canal, Oldtown Vic., Maryland (155.2 miles). Jack E. Boucher, photographer, 1960. P & P, HABS, MD,1-OLDTO.V,4-6.

The Paw Paw Tunnel represents several engineering accomplishments. First is the boring of the tunnel itself. Second is the construction of the brick liner within the tunnel, as much as seven courses thick and containing millions of bricks. Third is the excavation through rock of the open cuts at both ends of the tunnel, but particularly at the north end through Athey's Hollow (200 feet at the upstream end and 890 feet at the downstream end). See 4-125.

4-128. Longitudinal section of the Paw Paw Tunnel, Chesapeake and Ohio Canal, Oldtown Vic., Maryland (155.2 miles). Ellwood Morris, engineer. *Journal of the Franklin Institute . . . Devoted to Science and the Mechanic Arts* (1839). LC, T1 .F8.

The vertical access shafts, down which men were lowered and up which excavated materials were drawn, can be seen, marked DC and BA. Compare with William Strickland's drawing of the Thames and Medway Tunnel (2-125).

opposite

4-129. Section house, Chesapeake and Ohio Canal, Oldtown Vic., Maryland (156.2 miles). Jack E. Boucher, photographer, 1960. P & P, HABS, MD,1-OLDTO.V,5-1.

4-130. Rear view of section house, Chesapeake and Ohio Canal, Oldtown Vic., Maryland (156.2 miles). Jack E. Boucher, photographer, 1960. P & P, HABS, MD,1-OLDTO.V,5-3.

4-129

4-130

4-131

4-131. Town Creek Aqueduct (Aqueduct 10), Chesapeake and Ohio Canal, Oldtown Vic., Maryland (162.3 miles). Jack E. Boucher, photographer, 1960. P & P, HABS, 1-OLDTO.V,1-1.

Town Creek Aqueduct has a span of 60 feet. As shown, the left spandrel wall on the upstream face has failed.

4-132. North and south elevations, Town Creek Aqueduct (Aqueduct 10), Chesapeake and Ohio Canal, Oldtown Vic., Maryland (162.3 miles). Dennis Davis, delineator, 1974. P & P, HAER MD-31, sheet no. 1.

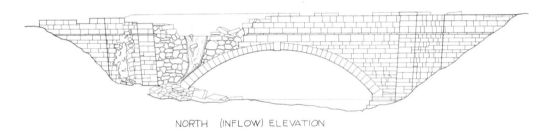

NORTH (INFLOW) ELEVATION

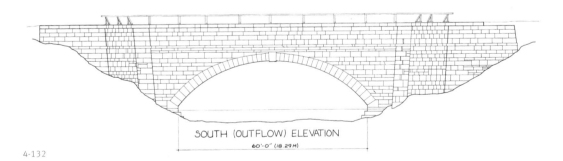

SOUTH (OUTFLOW) ELEVATION

60'-0" (18.29 M)

4-132

4-133. Metal truss bridge at Lock 68, Chesapeake and Ohio Canal, Oldtown, Maryland (164.8 miles). Jet T. Lowe, photographer, 1989. P & P, HAER, MD,1-OLDTO.V,11-1.

This truss was constructed in 1910.

4-134. Lockhouse, Lock 68, Chesapeake and Ohio Canal, Oldtown, Maryland (164.8 miles). Jack E. Boucher, photographer, 1960. P & P, HABS, MD,1-OLDTO.V,6-1.

4-135. Lockhouse, Lock 70, Chesapeake and Ohio Canal, Oldtown, Maryland (166.9 miles). Jack E. Boucher, photographer, 1960. P & P, HABS, MD,1-OLDTO,1-1.

4-133

4-134

4-135

4-136

this page

4-136. Northeast and northwest elevations, lockhouse, Lock 71, Chesapeake and Ohio Canal, Oldtown Vic., Maryland (167.0 miles). Jack E. Boucher, photographer, 1960. P & P, HABS, MD,1-OLDTO.V,8-2.

The sign on the building reads, "Oldtown Sportsmen Club." The smaller sign below says, "Battie Mixon Pond Extends 4.7 m."

4-137. Southwest elevation, lockhouse, Lock 71, Chesapeake and Ohio Canal, Oldtown Vic., Maryland (167.0 miles). Jack E. Boucher, photographer, 1960. P & P, HABS, MD,1-OLDTO.V,8-3.

opposite

4-138. Lock 72 (Ten Mile Lock), Chesapeake and Ohio Canal, Oldtown Vic., Maryland (174.4 miles). Jack E. Boucher, photographer, 1960. P & P, HABS, MD,1-OLDTO.V,9-1.

4-139. Lockhouse, Lock 72, Chesapeake and Ohio Canal, Oldtown Vic., Maryland (174.4 miles). Jack E. Boucher, photographer, 1960. P & P, HABS, MD,1-OLDTO.V, 10-1.

4-138

4-139

4-140

4-140. Lock 75, Chesapeake and Ohio Canal, Cumberland Vic., Maryland (175.6 miles). Jack E. Boucher, photographer, 1960. P & P, HABS, MD,1-CUMB.V,3-1.

This is the last of the locks on the C&O Canal.

4-141. Northeast and northwest elevations of lockhouse, Lock 75, Chesapeake and Ohio Canal, Cumberland Vic., Maryland. John Hanna and Donn Carter, delineators, 1961. P & P, HABS MD-823, sheet no. 4.

This rough log structure, built ca. 1840, is in stark contrast to the cut-stone lockhouses built in the lower reaches of the canal about ten years earlier. As the C&O Canal reached Cumberland, its terminus, its funds were much limited in comparison to the early years and stone gave way to logs.

4-141

NORTHEAST ELEVATION

NORTHWEST ELEVATION

4-142. Evitts Creek Aqueduct (Aqueduct
11), Chesapeake and Ohio Canal,
Cumberland Vic., Maryland (180.7 miles).
Jack E. Boucher, photographer, 1960. P & P,
HABS, MD,1-CUMB.V,2-2.

The last of the eleven masonry arch aqueducts on the main line of the C&O Canal
before the canal terminates in Cumberland,
Maryland, this is also the smallest, at a
span of 70 feet. It was completed ca. 1840.

BIBLIOGRAPHY

BIBLIOGRAPHIES

Zimmerman, Albright G., Ph.D. *A Canal Bibliography With a Primary Emphasis on the United States and Canada.* Easton, Pa.: Canal History and Technology Press, Hugh Moore Historical Park and Museums and Pennsylvania Canal Society, 1991.

ENGINEERING, CONSTRUCTION, AND TECHNOLOGY

Mahan, D. H. *An Elementary Course on Civil Engineering for the Use of Cadets of the United States Military Academy.* New York: John Wiley, 1846.

Millington, John. *Elements of Civil Engineering: Being An Attempt To Consolidate the Principles of the Various Operations of the Civil Engineer into One Point of View. . . .* Richmond, Va.: Smith & Palmer, 1839.

Sganzin, M. A. *An Elementary Course of Civil Engineering. Translated From the French.* Boston: Hilliard, Gray, Little, and Wilkins, 1827.

Stevenson, David. *Sketch of the Civil Engineering of North America. . . .* London: John Weale, 1838.

Strickland, William (ed.). *Reports, Specifications, and Estimates of Public Works in the United States.* London: 1841.

Uhlemann, Hans-Joachim, and Mike Clarke (trans., ed.). *Canal Lifts and Inclines of the World.* Horsham, England: Internet, 2002.

GLOSSARIES

Brees, S. C. *The Illustrated Glossary of Practical Architecture and Civil Engineering: Comprising The Theory and Modern Practice. . . .* London: L. A. Lewis, 1853.

Hahn, Thomas Swiftwater, and Emory L. Kemp. *Canal Terminology of the United States.* Morgantown, W.V.: Institute for the History of Technology and Industrial Archaeology, 1998.

Scott, John S. *A Dictionary of Civil Engineering.* Hammondsworth, England: Penguin Books, 1958.

Tanner, H. S. "Glossary of the Scientific, Mechanical and Other Terms, Employed in Engineering," in *A Description of the Canals and Railroads of the United States. . . .* New York: T. R. Tanner and J. Disturnell, 1840, pp. 235–64.

Woods, Terry K. (compiler). *The Ohio & Erie Canal: A Glossary of Terms*. Kent, Ohio: Kent State Press, 1995.

GENERAL WORKS

Armroyd, George. *A Connected View of the Whole Internal Navigation of the United States. . . .* New York: Burt Franklin, 1971; reprint of 1830 work.

Drago, Harry Sinclair. *Canal Days in America: The History and Romance of Old Towpaths and Waterways*. New York: Clarkson N. Potter, Inc., 1972.

Harlow, Alvin F. *Old Towpaths*. New York: D. Appleton & Company, 1926.

Jacobs, David, and Anthony E. Neville, Robert M. Vogel (consultant). *Bridges, Canals & Tunnels*. New York: American Heritage Publishing Co., Inc., 1968.

MacGill, Caroline E., et al. *History of Transportation in the United States Before 1860*. Forge Village, Mass.: Peter Smith, 1948; reprint of Carnegie Institution of Washington Publication No. 215C.

Shank, William H. *Towpaths to Tugboats: A History of American Canal Engineering*. York, Pa.: American Canal and Transportation Center, 1982.

Shank, William H. (publisher). *The Best from American Canals*. York, Pa.: American Canal and Transportation Center, 1980–1998.

Spangenburg, Ray, and Diane K. Moser. *The Story of America's Canals: Connecting a Continent*. New York: Facts on File, Inc., 1992.

Stapleton, Darwin H. (ed.). *The Engineering Drawings of Benjamin Henry Latrobe*. New Haven: Published for Maryland Historical Society by Yale University Press, 1980.

Strickland, William. *Reports on Canals, Railways, Roads, and Other Subjects Made to the Pennsylvania Society for the Promotion of Internal Improvement*. Philadelphia: H. C. Carey & I. Lea, 1825.

Taylor, George Roberts. *The Transportation Revolution, 1815–1860*. New York: Harper & Row, 1968; reprint of 1951 publication.

U. S. Treasury. *Report of the Secretary of the Treasury on the Subject of Public Roads and Canals. . . .* New York: Augustus M. Kelley, Publishers, 1968; reprint of 1808 work.

Von Gerstner, Franz Anton Ritter. *Die Innern Communicationen der Vereinigten Staaten von Nordamerica (1842–1843)* [Early American Railroads]. Frederick C. Gamst (ed.), David J. Diephouse and John C. Decker (trans.). Stanford, Calif.: Stanford University Press, 1997; reprint of 1842–1843 work.

Walch, George Turner. *Notes on Some of the Chief Navigable Rivers and Canals in the United States During a Tour in 1876.* Madras, India: W. H. Turner, 1877.

Way, Peter. *Common Labor: Workers and the Digging of North American Canals, 1780–1860.* Baltimore, Md.: Johns Hopkins University Press, 1993.

CANALS OF NEW ENGLAND

Anderson, Hayden L.V. *Canals and the Inland Waterways of Maine.* Portland, Maine: Maine Historical Society, 1982.

Clarke, Mary Stetson. *The Old Middlesex Canal.* Easton, Pa.: Center for Canal History and Technology, 1974.

Coburn, Louis Helen. *Canal Projects for the Kennebec, 1825 to 1832.* Self-published, ca. 1935.

Harte, Charles Rufus. *Connecticut's Canals: Reprinted from the 54th Annual Report of the Connecticut Society of Civil Engineers.* Hartford, Conn.: Connecticut Society of Civil Engineers, 1938.

Knight, Ernest H. *A Guide to the Cumberland and Oxford Canal.* Portland, Maine: Cumberland and Oxford Canal Association, 1976; revised 1998.

Milliken, Philip I. *Notes on the Cumberland and Oxford Canal. . . .* Portland, Maine: Bradford Press, 1935.

Roberts, Christopher. *The Middlesex Canal, 1793–1860.* Cambridge, Mass.: Harvard University Press, 1938.

CANALS OF THE MID-ATLANTIC

Cawley, James and Margaret. *Along the Delaware and Raritan Canal.* Cranbury, N.J.: A. S. Barnes and Company, Inc., 1970.

Condon, George E. *Stars in the Waters: The Story of the Erie Canal*. Garden City, N.Y.: Doubleday, 1974.

Hill, Henry Wayland. *Waterways & Canal Construction in New York State*. Buffalo, N.Y.: Buffalo Historical Society, 1908.

Hulbert, Archer Butler. *The Great American Canals: Volume 2, The Erie Canal*. Historic Highways of America. New York: AMS Press 1971; reprinted from the 1902–1905 edition.

Kalata, Barbara N. *A Hundred Miles: New Jersey's Morris Canal*. Morristown, N.J.: Morris County Historical Society, 1983.

Kapsch, Robert J. "The Conewago Canal: Pennsylvania's First Canal," in Lance E. Metz (ed.), *Canal History and Technology Proceedings*, Volume XXIII, March 20, 2004. Easton, Pa.: Canal History and Technology Press, 2004.

Larkin, F. Daniel. *New York State Canals: A Short History*. Fleischmanns, N.Y.: Purple Mountain Press, 1998.

Lee, James. *The Morris Canal, A Photographic History*. Easton, Pa.: Delaware Press, 1973.

LeRoy, Edward. *The Delaware and Hudson Canal: A History*. Honesdale, Pa.: Wayne County Historical Society, 1950.

LeRoy, Edward. *Delaware & Hudson Canal and its Gravity Railroads*. Honesdale, Pa.: Wayne County Historical Society, 1980.

Lord, Phillip, Jr. "The Covered Locks of Wood Creek," in *IA, The Journal of the Society for Industrial Archeology*, vol. 27, no. 1, 2001.

Lowenthal, Larry. *From the Coalfields to the Hudson: A History of the Delaware & Hudson Canal*. Fleischmanns, N.Y.: Purple Mountain Press, 1997.

McCullough, Robert, and Walter Leuba. *The Pennsylvania Main Line Canal*. York, Pa.: American Canal and Transportation Center, 1973.

McFee, Michele. *Limestone Locks and Overgrowth: The Rise and Descent of the Chenango Canal*. Fleischmanns, N.Y.: Purple Mountain Press, 1996.

O'Donnell, Thomas C. *Snubbing Posts: An Informal History of the Black River Canal*. Boonville, N.Y.: Black River Books, 1949.

Schuylkill & Susquehanna Navigation Company and Delaware and Schuylkill Canal

Company. *An historical account of the rise, progress, and present state of the canal navigation in Pennsylvania. . . .* Philadelphia: Zachariah Poulson, 1795.

Shank, William H. *The Amazing Pennsylvania Canals*. York, Pa.: American Canal and Transportation Center, 1981.

Shaw, Ronald E. *Erie Water West: A History of the Erie Canal, 1792–1854*. Lexington, Ky.: University of Kentucky Press, 1966.

Smeltzer, Gerald. *Canals Along the Lower Susquehanna (1796–1900)*. York, Pa.: Historical Society of York County, 1963.

Viet, Richard F. *The Old Canals of New Jersey: A Historical Geography*. Little Falls, N.J.: New Jersey Geographical Press, 1963.

Vogel, Robert M. *Roebling's Delaware & Hudson Canal Aqueducts*, no. 10, Smithsonian Studies in History and Technology. Washington, D.C.: Smithsonian Institution Press, 1971.

Whitford, Noble E. *History of the Canal System of New York*, 2 volumes. Albany, N.Y.: Brandow Printing Company, 1906.

Wyld, Lionel D. *The Erie Canal: A Bibliography*, *Revised Edition*. Cumberland, R.I.: Darcy Associates, Ltd., 1990.

Yoder, C. P. *Delaware Canal Journal: A Definitive History of the Canal and the River Valley Through Which it Flows*. Bethlehem, Pa.: Canal Press Incorporated, 1972.

Zimmerman, Albright G. *Pennsylvania's Delaware Division Canal: Sixty Miles of Euphoria and Frustration*. Easton, Pa.: Canal History and Technology Press, 2002.

CANALS OF THE SOUTH

Bacon-Foster, Corra. *Early Chapters in the Development of the Patomac Route to the West*. New York: Burt Franklin, 1970; reprint of 1912 work.

Brown, Alexander Crosby. *The Patowmack Canal: America's Greatest Eighteenth Century Engineering Achievement*. Alexandria, Va.: Virginia Canals & Navigations Society, ca. 1992; reprint of article from *Virginia Cavalcade*, vol. 12 (1963), pp. 40–47.

Brown, Alexander Crosby. *The Dismal Swamp Canal*. Chesapeake, Va.: Norfolk County Historical Society, 1970.

Brown, Alexander Crosby. *Juniper Waterway: A History of the Albemarle and Chesapeake Canal.* Charlottesville, Va.: Published for the Mariner's Museum, Newport News, Virginia, by University Press of Virginia, 1981.

Dunaway, Wayland Fuller. *History of the James River and Kanawha Company.* N.Y.: AMS Press, 1969; reprint of 1922 work.

Gibson, Langhorne Jr. *Cabell's Canal: The Story of the James River and Kanawha.* Richmond, Va.: Commodore Press, 2000.

Gray, Ralph D. *The National Waterway: A History of the Chesapeake and Delaware Canal, 1769–1965.* Urbana, Ill.: University of Illinois Press, 1967.

Hahn, Thomas Swiftwater and Emory L. Kemp. *The Alexandria Canal: Its History & Preservation.* Morgantown, W.V.: Institute for the History of Technology and Industrial Archaeology, 1992.

Hahn, Thomas F. Swiftwater. *Towpath Guide to the Chesapeake & Ohio Canal: Georgetown Tidelock to Cumberland.* Shepherdstown, W.V.: American Canal and Transportation Center, 1995.

Heine, Cornelius W. "The Washington City Canal," in Holmes, Oliver W. and Cornelius W. Heine, *Records of the Columbia Historical Society of Washington, D.C., 1953–1956.* Washington, D.C.: Columbia Historical Society, 1956.

High, Mike. *The C&O Canal Companion.* Baltimore, Md.: Johns Hopkins University Press, 1997.

Howlett, Lynn Doney. *The Patowmack Canal: From Canal to Constitution.* Lexington, Va.: Virginia Canals & Navigations Society, ca. 1997.

Kapsch, Robert J. "Benjamin Wright and the Design and Construction of the Monocacy Aqueduct," in Lance E. Metz (ed.), *Canal History and Technology Proceedings, Volume XIX, March 18, 2000.* Easton, Pa.: Canal History and Technology Press, 2000.

Kapsch, Robert J. "The Rehabilitation of the Monocacy Aqueduct and Other Historic Structures of the Chesapeake and Ohio Canal National Historical Park," in *International Conference: Preservation of the Engineering Heritage, Gdansk Outlook 2000.* Gdansk, Poland, September 1999.

Kapsch, Robert J. "The Construction of the Potomac Aqueduct (1833–1841): Pier

Construction in Deep Water Conditions," in *Proceedings of the First International Congress on Construction History, Madrid, January 20th-24th 2003*. Madrid: Instituto Juan de Herrera, Escuela Técnica Superior de Arquitectura, 2003.

Kapsch, Robert J. "The Potomac Canal: A Construction History," in *Canal History and Technology Proceedings, Volume XXI*, Lance Metz (ed.), Easton, Pa.: Canal History and Technology Press, 2002.

Kirkwood, James J. *Waterway to the West. . . .* Washington, D.C.: Eastern National Park & Monument Association, 1963.

Kohn, David (compiler and ed.) and Bess Glenn (ed.). *Internal Improvement in South Carolina 1818–1828. . . .* Washington, D.C.: self-published, 1938.

Porcher, Prof. F. A. *The History of the Santee Canal.* Moncks Corner: Berkeley County Tricentennial Committee, 1970; reprint of 1875 work.

Salmon, John S. (compiler). *Board of Public Works Inventory: Records in The Library of Virginia,* second ed. Richmond, Va.: Library of Virginia, 1998.

Sanderlin, Walter S. *The Great National Project*. Baltimore, Md.: Johns Hopkins University Press, 1946.

U. S. National Park Service. *Chesapeake and Ohio Canal: A Guide to Chesapeake and Ohio Canal National Park, Maryland, District of Columbia, and West Virginia.* National Park Service Handbook 142. Washington, D.C.: U. S. Government Printing Office, 1991.

Ward, George Washington, Ph.D. *The Early Development of the Chesapeake and Ohio Canal Project.* Johns Hopkins University Studies in Historical and Political Science, Series XVII, nos. 9-10-11, Herbert B. Adams (ed.). New York: Johnson Reprint Corporation, 1973; reprint of 1899 work.

Weaver, Charles Clinton. *Internal Improvements in North Carolina Previous to 1860*. Baltimore, Md.: Johns Hopkins Press, 1903.

CANALS OF THE MIDWEST

Cozen, Michael P. and Kay J. Carr (eds.). *Illinois and Michigan Canal National Heritage Corridor: A Guide to its History and Sources.* Dekalb, Ill.: Northern Illinois University Press, 1988.

Galbreath, C. B. *Ohio Canals*. Springfield, Ohio: Springfield Publishing Company, 1910.

Howe, Walter A. *A Documentary History of the Illinois and Michigan Canal*. Springfield, Ill.: State of Illinois Department of Public Works and Buildings, 1956.

Huntington, C. C., and C. P. McClelland. *History of the Ohio Canals, Their Construction, Cost, Use, and Partial Abandonment*. Columbus, Ohio: Ohio State Archaeological and Historical Society, 1905.

Putnam, James William. *The Illinois and Michigan Canal: A Study in Economic History*. Chicago Historical Society's Collection, vol. X. Chicago, Ill.: The University of Chicago Press, 1918.

Treverrow, Frank. *Ohio's Canal*. Oberlin, Ohio: self-published, 1973.

Wilcox, Frank. *The Ohio Canals*. Kent, Ohio: Kent State University Press, 1969.

GLOSSARY

ANCHOR AND COLLAR. The device, usually iron, that secures the *quoin post* or heel post of the lock gate to the top of the lock wall and lets it turn so that the lock gate may be opened and closed. The device consists of the *collar*, the metal ring within which the quoin post turns, and the *anchor* (also called anchor irons), metal straps secured in the walls of the lock.

APRON. The floor of the canal immediately below a lock and sometimes above.

AQUEDUCT. A bridge for carrying a canal over an intersecting watercourse or valley.

BALANCE BEAM. A long, heavy beam used to open and close the lock gate.

BATTER. The sloping face of a retaining or other wall.

BAY. The portions of a lock at each extremity of the lock chamber and outside the lock gates. Sometimes called either fore or tail bays.

BERM. A horizontal space about one to two feet wide and located about one foot above the water surface on the side slope of the canal. This space protects the upper part of the interior side slope of the canal. Also called a bench.

BÉTON. A French term used to describe any mixture of mortar with fragments of brick, stone, or gravel. Also called concrete.

BYPASS CANAL. A canal that unites the navigable parts of the river or stream above and below an obstruction, such as a dam or rapids.

COMPOSITE LOCKS. Locks constructed of timber and dry stone.

COUNTERFORT. A pier or buttress that supports a retaining wall or a lock wall.

CRAMP. An iron tie used to secure the stones of a wall together. It is frequently shaped in the form of a "C." Sometimes called a clamp.

CULVERT. A covered channel or pipe for carrying a water course or road under a canal.

CUT. An excavation along the line of a canal.

DAM. A permanent obstacle to the passage of water built across a river for the purpose of impounding water.

DEEP CUT. An excavation of great depth.

DISTRIBUTING RESERVOIR. The tank or reservoir where water is stored and distributed to the canal for use, usually at the summit level of the canal.

DOUBLE LOCKS. Two locks constructed parallel to each other and close together. One lock is used for canal boats ascending and the other for boats descending.

DRY DOCK. A structure designed so that water can be drained, allowing work to be undertaken on the bottom of canal boats.

EMBANKMENT. A mound of earth thrown up to maintain the grade of the canal.

FEEDER. A small canal intended to convey water into the reservoir, to the summit level, or into a particular *reach* of the canal.

FLASHING. A technique of river navigation used to traverse a *sluice* in a dam. Typically, the sluice in the dam is opened and closed by means of a gate revolving on a vertical axis, which permits the boat operator to rapidly descend through the sluice on a flash of water.

FLIGHT OF LOCKS. Several contiguous locks between two levels.

GATE RECESS. The cavity left in the walls of the lock to receive the lock gates when they are in the open position so the inside of the lock does not present an obstruction to a passing boat. Also called a gate chamber.

GUARD LOCK. The lock between an entrance basin and the canal, harbor, or river, which forms a communication between them.

GUDGEON. An upright iron spike fitted into an iron socket at the lower end of the *quoin post* that acts as the pivot upon which the quoin post turns.

HOLLOW QUOIN. The part of the gate recess of the lock wall where the gate turns on its pivot.

HYDRAULIC CEMENT. A natural cement that sets under water. It was used in the nineteenth century for engineering structures such as piers, locks, and docks in wet environments.

INCLINED PLANE. A railroad projecting into the canal designed to carry canal boats over elevations by means of a cradle mounted on wheels, hoisted onto the flat surface, and powered by steam engines, horse power, water-powered turbines, and/or the weight of ascending and descending boats.

INVERTED ARCH. An upside-down arch used when the underlying soil of a structure's foundation requires the weight of the structure to be spread out.

L PLATE. Hardware, usually made of iron, used for reinforcing lock gates. Shaped in the form of an "L."

LEVEL. That portion of a canal between two locks.

LIFT. The difference of level between the surface of the water above and below a lock.

LIFT WALL (of lock). The vertical wall below the upper gate of a lock. Usually the same height as the *lift* of the lock.

LINING. The layer of clay applied along the bottom and up the sloping sides of canals to prevent the water from escaping.

LOCK. A small basin built of wood or masonry (or both) consisting of two parallel walls far enough apart to admit a canal boat and terminated on either end by *lock gates*.

LOCK CHAMBER. The basin portion of the lock, with *lock gates* on either end.

LOCK GATE. The gates on either end of a lock.

LOCKHOUSE. Residence of the lock keeper and his family.

LOCK SILL. The bottom framing against which the gates are shut. Also called the miter sill or mud sill.

MITER SILL. A wood structure shaped like an isoceles triangle at the base of lock gates that provides them support against water pressure.

MORTISE AND TENON. A joint used in wood lock gate construction. The joint is made of a projecting piece, the *tenon*, which fits into a cavity, the *mortise*.

PADDLE GATES. Small gates usually built into the lock gates and arranged to open or shut by turning on a vertical axis in order to drain or fill water from or into a lock.

PILES. Large stakes or beams sharpened at one end and driven into the ground as a foundation for canal locks, aqueduct piers, and bridge piers when necessitated by soft or marshy soil conditions.

PLANKING. Wood lining of the sides and bottom of a canal, canal lock, and *timber crib dams*.

PRISM OF LIFT. The volume of water required to pass a boat up or down a lock.

PROFILE. The outline of a canal as seen in an elevation drawing.

PUDDLE. A mixture of clay and sand that is worked manually to be impervious to water. Used for canal *linings*.

PUDDLING. The process of applying *puddle*.

PUN. A hand tool usually made from a tree trunk and used to compact clay manually to form *puddle*.

QUOIN POST. The vertical posts on each side of the lock gates. Also called a hanging post, heel post, or miter post.

RAILS. Horizontal pieces of wood that are framed into the lock gates.

REACH. The distance between two locks.

RESERVOIR. A large body of water, usually held in reserve to supply the water needed by the canal at the *summit level* and also at lower levels.

ROMAN CEMENT. A nineteenth-century natural hydraulic cement, used in canal construction.

SHEET PILINGS. A row of timbers driven into the ground side by side, used to protect canal foundation walls from the effects of water.

SLACK-WATER NAVIGATION. A method of improving navigation on a river in which a series of dams with locks are built to provide for the passage of boats. Also called lock and dam navigation.

SLUICE. A channel used to convey water. Also, a channel constructed in the riverbed for navigation.

SPOIL BANK. Surplus excavation laid by the side of a canal.

STOP LOCK. A lock designed to prevent water from entering a select reach of the canal, usually by lowering *stop planks.*

STOP PLANKS. Boards used to stop the flow of water through a *lock, waste weir,* or other canal structure.

SUMMIT LEVEL. The highest reach of the canal, usually where the canal crosses a ridge or another elevated topographical feature.

SWING BRIDGE. A type of bridge designed to swing out of position across a canal in order to permit the passage of boats.

TIDE LOCK. A connecting lock located between an entrance basin and a canal, harbor, or river.

TIMBER CRIB DAMS. Dams constructed of logs in rectilinear shapes with large rocks placed on the inside; sometimes sheathed with planking.

T-PLATE. Hardware, usually made of iron, used for reinforcing lock gates and shaped in the form of a "T."

VALVES. Mechanisms for opening or closing small apertures in the lock for the purpose of letting water enter a lock chamber.

WASTE WEIR. A cut constructed through the side of a canal for channeling off any surplus water.

INDEX

Locators that include a section designator followed by a hyphen (e.g., IN-010, 3-090, 4-115) refer to numbered captions. All other locators are page numbers. Individuals who created the original images used in this collection are identified as follows: ph. = photographer; del. = delineator.

ABOUT THE CD-ROM

The CD-ROM includes direct links to four of the most useful online catalogs and sites, which you may choose to consult in locating and downloading images included on it or related items. Searching directions, help, and search examples (by text or keywords, titles, authors or creators, subject or location, and catalog and reproduction numbers, etc.) are provided online, in addition to information on rights and restrictions, how to order reproductions, and how to consult the materials in person.

1. The Prints & Photographs Online Catalog (PPOC) (http://www.loc.gov/rr/print/catalogabt.html) contains about one million catalog records and digital images representing a rich cross-section of graphic documents held by the Prints & Photographs Division and other units of the Library. It includes a majority of the images on this CD-ROM and many related images, such as those in the HABS and HAER collections cited below. At this writing the catalog provides access through group or item records to about 50 percent of the Division's holdings.

SCOPE OF THE PRINTS AND PHOTOGRAPHS ONLINE CATALOG

Although the catalog is added to on a regular basis, it is not a complete listing of the holdings of the Prints & Photographs Division, and does not include all the items on this CD-ROM. It also overlaps with some other Library of Congress search systems. Some of the records in the PPOC are also found in the LC Online Catalog, mentioned below, but the P&P Online Catalog includes additional records, direct display of digital images, and links to rights, ordering, and background information about the collections represented in the catalog. In many cases, only "thumbnail" images (GIF images) will display to those searching outside the Library of Congress because of potential rights considerations, while onsite searchers have access to larger JPEG and TIFF images as well. There are no digital images for some collections, such as the Look Magazine Photograph Collection. In some collections, only a portion of the images have so far been digitized. Because PPOC functions primarily as the local online public access catalog for the Prints & Photographs Reading Room, some instructions and features may not be geared to those accessing the catalog outside of the Library of Congress via the Internet. For further information about the scope of the Prints & Photographs online catalog and how to use it, consult the Prints & Photographs Online Catalog *HELP* document.

WHAT TO DO WHEN DESIRED IMAGES ARE NOT FOUND IN THE CATALOG
For further information about how to search for Prints & Photographs Division holdings not represented in the online catalog or in the lists of selected images, consult the *Reference Services* document on the Prints & Photographs Reading Room home page or contact: Prints & Photographs Reading Room, Library of Congress, 101 Independence Ave., SE, Washington, D.C. 20540-4730 (telephone: 202-707-6394).

2. The American Memory site (http://memory.loc.gov), a gateway to rich primary source materials relating to the history and culture of the United States. The site offers more than 7 million digital items from more than 100 historical collections.

3. The Library of Congress Online Catalog (http://catalog.loc.gov/) contains approximately 12 million records representing books, serials, computer files, manuscripts, cartographic materials, music, sound recordings, and visual materials. It is especially useful for finding items identified as being from the Manuscript Division and the Geography and Map Division of the Library of Congress.

4. Built in America: Historic American Buildings Survey/Historic American Engineering Record, 1933–Present (http://memory.loc.gov/ammem/hhhtml/hhhome.html) describes and links to the catalog of the Historic American Buildings Survey (HABS) and the Historic American Engineering Record (HAER), among the most heavily represented collections on the CD-ROM.

.